Death of the Desert

DIVINATIONS: REREADING LATE ANCIENT RELIGION

Series Editors:
Daniel Boyarin, Virginia Burrus, Derek Krueger

A complete list of books in the series is available from the publisher.

Death of the Desert

Monastic Memory and the Loss
of Egypt's Golden Age

Christine Luckritz Marquis

PENN

UNIVERSITY OF PENNSYLVANIA PRESS

PHILADELPHIA

Published by
University of Pennsylvania Press
Philadelphia, Pennsylvania 19104-4112
www.upenn.edu/pennpress

Printed in the United States of America
on acid-free paper
10 9 8 7 6 5 4 3 2 1

A catalogue record for this book is available
from the Library of Congress.
ISBN 978-0-8122-5362-7

For Tim

Contents

Introduction

> Having liquored up some youths, he [Archbishop Theophilus] fell
> upon the monasteries in the dead of night. . . . First, he ordered
> that their saintly brother Dioscorus, bishop of the mountain,
> be deposed from his throne, literally dragged away by enslaved
> Ethiopians. . . . Next, he raided the mountain, giving the few
> possessions of the monks to his hired youths. . . . He set their cells
> on fire with sticks, burning all the sacred books of Scripture and
> other valued texts.
>
> —Palladius, *Dialogue on the Life of John Chrysostom*
> 7.31–34, 37–38, 41–42

Under the cover of darkness, Archbishop Theophilus and his band of accomplices stormed the desert monastic community at "the mountain" of Nitria. Enslaved individuals violated Bishop Dioscorus's body and the sacrality of his bishop's throne. Meanwhile, the drunken youths hired by Theophilus quickly looted and destroyed monastic property. Soon, the pitch-black sky filled with the light of homes set aflame. Fire devoured Scriptures, other valued texts, and perhaps even took the life of a young boy. The shock of unexpected violence, of abuse and destruction, traumatized the monks. Many left the Egyptian desert in the immediate aftermath. Although they had thought their desert home removed from the world, the monks living in the desert were no longer able to maintain their fragile illusion of separation. The monks were no longer safe, no longer outside the grasp of worldly, ecclesial power. Theophilus's raid rent the monks from their home and shattered the powerful mystique of the desert. The desert as it had been known was dead.

This vignette describing events that occurred in 401 C.E. introduces several of the individuals and adjacent communities central to this book. Theophilus was archbishop of Alexandria from 385 until his death in 412. Initially a student and then a friend of the monks at Nitria, his attack on them marked a sudden and sharp shift in attitude. Prominent among these monks were a group known as the Tall Brothers: Dioscorus, Ammonius, Eusebius, and Euthymius. All four Tall Brothers were ascetics whom others frequently sought for advice and wisdom. Dioscorus, the local bishop, was especially revered. His appointment as bishop to the monks served as a marker of the respect with which the larger monastic community held him. The struggle that ensued pitted worldly, ecclesial power, as represented by Theophilus, against ascetic ideals, as represented by Dioscorus and his fellow Tall Brothers.

Other characters play unnamed but critical roles in the scene above. There are the unknown Nitrian colleagues and supporters of the Tall Brothers. They are depicted in the full version of this story as all rallying around Dioscorus and the other Tall Brothers, hiding three of them from the violence of Theophilus and his band. There are the drunken youths and the enslaved Ethiopians. Both of these groups would have been viewed as unsavory, as the mention of hired young men and enslaved Ethiopians would have evoked tropes concerning violent bandits and uncivilized barbarians, respectively. Finally, there is the author behind the vignette: Palladius, bishop of Helenopolis. Although he paints the scene quite vividly, in the passage from which this excerpt is taken (from his *Dialogue on the Life of John Chrysostom*) he makes clear that he was not himself present. Formerly a member of the northwestern desert's ascetic community, Palladius had left shortly before the events described in order to become bishop of Helenopolis, serving under Theophilus's rival John Chrysostom, archbishop of Constantinople. Palladius relates that his knowledge of Theophilus's violence came from eyewitnesses—presumably, the Tall Brothers and their Nitrian supporters—who fled Egypt the next day, ultimately arriving in Constantinople by way of Palestine.[1]

Previous scholarship has largely glossed over this moment of violence in the Egyptian desert, if it has noted it at all. Consigned to an early chapter in the so-called Origenist controversy, a theological dispute that eventually spanned much of the Christian world, Theophilus's attack has been treated as an anomalous event in Egyptian monasticism's otherwise peaceful Golden Age. In this book, however, I argue that this violent incident ought to hold an important place in historical narrations not only of the Origenist controversy but also of late fourth-century Egyptian monasticism more broadly, and of how it was later remembered. Understanding the significance of Theophilus's attack will require carefully revisiting scholarly reliance on a collection of sayings known as the *Sayings of the Desert Fathers* (hereafter, *Sayings*). Although some scholars have recognized the largely nostalgic cast of the *Sayings*'s depiction of Egyptian monasticism, many still either engage the sayings as relatively transparent historical windows or unintentionally repeat earlier scholarly assertions built on such uncritical readings.[2] But the *Sayings* are not straightforward memories retained and passed down pristinely from monastic generation to monastic generation.[3] Rather, they are reconstructed memorials made by late fifth-century monks in Palestine who gathered and edited the sayings to serve their community's purposes. At best, what was retained across the fifth century were reverberations of a remembered past, one that sought to efface the actual trauma that brought the Golden Age to a close—that is, Theophilus's violence.

This book tells several overlapping stories at once. It moves through chronological layers of the late fourth and early fifth centuries, the late fifth century, and the modern colonial and post-colonial periods. At its base, it attempts to figure out what we can meaningfully say about the history of the late fourth- and early fifth-century Egyptian desert—a time and a place that take on quasi-canonical status in monastic memory and tradition. It is crucial to begin by attending to contemporary voices: Evagrius of Pontus, a transplant to the Egyptian desert but a pupil of some of the most prominent desert abbas and the desert's most prolific extant writer; Palladius of Helenopolis, who wrote not only the *Dialogue* excerpted above but also the better known *Lausiac History*; John Cassian, a previous member of the desert community who went on to found monasteries in Roman Gaul; Rufinus of Aquileia, a visitor and later regular correspondent with the Egyptian brethren; Theophilus of Alexandria himself, whose extant letters remain in translation and help us understand not only his attack on Nitria but also its context and his motives; Jerome, a one-time visitor to the Egyptian desert and later Bethlehem-based ascetic competitor; and the anonymous author of the *History of the Monks of Egypt* (sometimes referred to by its Latin title, *Historia Monachoarum in Aegypto*), the narrated travelogue of some adventurous Palestinian monks. Although scholars have previously deemed the writings of several of these authors to be too one-sided, partial, or hagiographical for reconstruction of the fourth-century Egyptian desert, I foreground them for their contemporaneity: All were written by figures who actually lived among or near the northwestern Egyptian desert monks or who visited them. As with the *Sayings*, the biases of these sources are themselves part of the history to be told, but they do not fully control the writings or the historical uses that can be made of them.

It is not inaccurate to highlight, for example, that Palladius is negatively biased in his presentation of Theophilus's attack or that Cassian's focus is more on appropriation of Egyptian monastic culture for his Gaulic monasteries than on presenting it on its own terms.[4] However, I contend that historians can account for the agendas of these authors, situating their descriptions in context rather than erasing them from histories of fourth-century Egyptian monasticism. Both Palladius and Cassian had Evagrius as an abba during their tenure in Egypt. Thus, when they share thoughts on monastic life that resonate with Evagrius despite their later agendas, we would do well to note this congruence. That Rufinus and his counterpart Melania the Elder sent Evagrius to the Egyptian abbas in the first place highlights the tight network of many of our sources. As Elizabeth Clark argued several decades ago, the social networks of these fourth-century figures were rich, complex, and often entangled through both alignment and confrontation.[5] Theophilus and, to a lesser extent, Jerome offer important evidence of individuals who once allied themselves with the northwestern Egyptian monks but who later found themselves in deadly opposition to the abbas. I do not disagree that this list of authors fails to offer us a complete or fully accurate picture of this era of Egyptian monasticism. But if we accept that the text of the *Sayings* does not offer a direct window into the late fourth- and early fifth-century Egyptian desert, then we must wrestle fully with the witnesses we do have. As I show throughout this book, doing so reveals the politics that permeated not only the lives and careers of monastics and bishops but also the desert itself and its later legacy.

That later legacy constitutes the second and third layers of my historical reconstruction. I explore how particular portrayals of the earlier era came to be, alternately, either amplified or erased by other authors across the fifth century, especially in the depictions found in the *Sayings*. Given that the pithy format and legendary nature of the *Sayings* calls for careful contextualization, I attempt to align them with known fourth-century witnesses in order to understand both what the later *Sayings* tradition retained and how it altered or expanded these traditions for new purposes in Gaza. By attending to the dynamics of the late fifth-century, post-Origenist world, I show how later authors suppressed Theophilus's violent role in monastic loss and instead played on popular rhetorical schemas concerning the inherent violence among barbarians, focusing on the propensity of desert attacks from barbarian raiders, to account for damage wrought in the desert. Finally, to explain how this late fifth-century revision came to be uncritically accepted by modern historians, I unpack and address the historiographical reasons for the replacement of fourth-century monastic voices and Theophilus's violence with the *Sayings* and tales of barbarian attacks. This last layer is far more recent, inviting us to grapple with the racialized rhetoric of a colonialist and post-colonialist scholarly world that made such a continued misremembering possible.

Ultimately, this book demonstrates that the sources for the Origenist controversy and the *Sayings* must be considered alongside one another in order to more accurately trace the history of monasticism in both late fourth- to early fifth-century Egypt and late fifth-century Palestine. The violent attack of Theophilus with which we began serves as a pivotal link between these two important areas of late ancient scholarship. Moreover, violence is a critical thread that weaves through the three historical eras this book covers. Indeed, I argue that violence was inherent in the Egyptian monastic project from its outset. The desert as it was imagined did not exist without ascetic violence—violence in struggle with the demons, especially through prayer and psalmody, and divinely sanctioned violence against self and others when needed. This violent orientation of ascetics coupled with rhetorical portrayals of barbarians as inherently violent made it imaginable for late fifth-century collators of the *Sayings* to memorialize their predecessors as being even more violent than they portrayed themselves and to displace Theophilus's attack with stories of ravaging barbarians. Later, and in turn, modern colonialist violence that authorized domination of other peoples and their lands produced modern scholars who could easily accept narratives about barbarian attacks as congruent with contemporary experiences of the uncivilized Other. Although my main focus is on following the dialogue between ideological and real violence in the fourth and early fifth centuries, it is not hard to imagine that the later periods I consider more briefly could yield further examples of this dialogic relation. Among late fourth- to early fifth-century Christians, a dynamic relationship between ideologies of the violent ascetic and actual performances of violent activities culminated in a traumatic desecration of the desert. What I have dubbed the "death of the desert" was the death of an ideal as much as anything. It was not the result of an ecological disaster. Nor was it brought about by so-called barbarian raids. It did not even represent a total abandonment of the desert by monks. Rather, the phrase is meant to describe the loss felt by late ancient Christians, lay and monk alike, across the fifth century after the possibility and power that had been projected onto the Egyptian desert and its ascetic inhabitants was shattered by Archbishop Theophilus's raid on the monks.

Origenist Controversy

Palladius's story above is extracted from a much longer text, his *Dialogue on the Life of John Chrysostom*, written less than a decade after Theophilus's raid, a year or two after Chrysostom had died in exile in 407, and in the immediate aftermath of the Origenist controversy. The controversy over Origen's works, written more than a century and a half before, arose because their increasing popularity over the latter half of the fourth century, in a post-Nicene world, had implications both for late ancient Christian theology and for ascetic praxis. Epiphanius, bishop of Cyprus, had already linked Origen and another heretic, Arius, in the 370s. In his linking of heretical movements, Epiphanius asserted that Origen's ill-formed ideas about the Godhead had begotten Arius's heretical view of the Son. Because such a genealogical chain of tainted theological ideas could be traced back to Origen's texts, Epiphanius asserted that anyone who engaged Origen's works or built upon them were Origenist heretics. Thus, a large swath of Christian bishops and ascetics faced accusations of heresy.

While Theophilus initially sought to arbitrate between Epiphanius and John of Jerusalem, whom Epiphanius targeted as an Origenist, Theophilus soon himself began deploying the language of Origenism as heresy in his accusations against John Chrysostom, the Tall Brothers, and their fellow refugee ascetics. Theophilus could successfully smear the Egyptian monks as Origenists because of the crucial role that Origen's teachings had come to play in ascetic views of human embodiment and materiality.[6] The argument circled around how humanity was to understand its creation in the image of God. Interpretations of the transformability of bodies and the role and form of matter in the individual's return to the divine were crucial to the monastic practices that unfolded in the desert and to the meaning of the desert itself. Most individuals involved inflected their views concerning matter and embodiment through their opinions on how or whether to import Origen's teachings on the descent and eventual return of the soul. The writings of Evagrius of Pontus, whom I mentioned above and who spent the latter part of his life in the northwestern desert as an ascetic, represent the elaborations of Origen's views most often under scrutiny. As will be discussed in Chapters 1 and 2, Evagrius's expansion of Origen's system affected how monks understood demonic comportment and activity as well as what it meant to be a monk striving to pray and psalm like the angels. That is, Origen's thought permeated every aspect of asceticism for those who accepted Origen. Moreover, the developing ecclesial hierarchy often perceived the powerful movement of asceticism as a potential competitor to be defeated or at least tamed.[7] A nexus of these many issues was acutely present both in Alexandria and in the ascetic communities of the northwestern Egyptian desert. In this way, the struggle around Origen was not only a theological battle but also one that pitted ecclesial authority against monastic empowerment—precisely the battle lines drawn by Theophilus's raid.

Palladius's rendition of events is one of four roughly contemporary sources for telling the history of the Origenist controversy. Palladius sought to rehabilitate the damned memory of Chrysostom as well as to salvage the reputations of Chrysostom's compatriots—including Palladius himself—from the noxious title of "Origenist." To do so, Palladius narrated not just the raid of the Egyptian desert but also the larger ecclesial struggle between Theophilus and John Chrysostom. It is in this deeply oppositional context that we should place Palladius's particular recounting of Theophilus's entrance into the desert. His version is not merely or even primarily a factual retelling of the events that unfolded between the Tall Brothers and Theophilus. Instead, his story is meant to persuade a larger audience of Theophilus's unjust behavior and of the so-called Origenists' orthodoxy and unjustified mistreatment.[8]

By the time of Palladius's *Dialogue*, Theophilus had already publicly proclaimed his version of events. From the moment he entered the desert in 401, Theophilus attempted to control the narrative of his actions through letter writing. Among the most important letters for understanding his position are those addressed to the bishops of Palestine and Cyprus, to Pope Anastasius I seeking Roman support, to Jerome as his translator for a wider Latin-speaking audience, and to the monks living in the desert, including one especially addressed to the community of Scetis near Nitria, and even one to the Origenist brothers themselves. In his letters to his Palestinian and Cypriote ecclesial counterparts, Theophilus asserted that it was the Tall Brothers and their community who had been hostile and violent toward him and his numerous supporters.[9] Repeatedly throughout the letter, Theophilus links their aggressive behavior to their wayward, "Origenist" beliefs. Thus, he articulates a version of events that portrays violent ascetic behavior and heretical ascetic views as part of a seamless whole. Such a vision of monks as violent was possible because violence was already baked into the ascetic project. As I argue in Chapters 1–3 of this book, the desert was imaged as the battlefield of ascetics and the ascetics themselves as angelic-like conduits of divine violence. Thus, Theophilus could easily warp the broader late ancient image of monastic

violence from one of righteous zeal to one of heretical danger. Similar vitriolic critiques of the Tall Brothers and their fellow brethren filled the letters
to Anastasius I and Jerome.[10] Theophilus's actions, however, were not well-
received by the monks, as is hinted at in his letter to the Scetian brethren in
which he implies that he had little choice but to correct their heretical ways.[11]
By contrast, Theophilus's letter to the Origenist brothers is far less concilia-
tory.[12] In it, he exhorts them to repent, especially as Anastasius I and his fellow western bishops have likewise condemned the brothers. Across his letters,
Theophilus paints the monks as wayward, Origen-mad brethren whom he has
reluctantly had to chastise and then expel from the Church as its protector.

Beyond the prominent writings of Palladius and Theophilus, two other
texts mention the fight between Theophilus and the Nitrian brethren: an
anonymous eulogy for John Chrysostom and the *Dialogues* of Sulpicius Severus.
The *Funeral Oration*, composed in the immediate wake of Chrysostom's death
in exile in 407, is the work of someone in his circle of followers. Traditionally,
the piece had been attributed to a certain Martyrius, who cannot be the author
as he had already died. For this reason, the author of the *Oration* is often
referred to as Ps.-Martyrius. The most plausible candidates for authorship
are either Philip of Side or Cosmas the deacon, but there remains no scholarly consensus.[13] Thus, while the nomenclature of Ps.-Martyrius is inexact, I
follow it in this book. Despite the lack of precise knowledge of the author's
identity, there can be no question that the text emerged from John's community of supporters. The *Funerary Oration* clearly is meant to serve panegyric
purposes in the absence of a proper funeral for Chrysostom. Given its purpose
of praising Chrysostom and exonerating him from accusations of Origenism,
it is perhaps surprising that Theophilus's attack on the Nitrian monks receives
mention at all. While precisely what occurred in the desert is not discussed,
the charges that were brought against Theophilus are. In Ps.-Martyrius's larger
caricature of Theophilus as the Devil's servant, Theophilus's abuse of the holy
men functions as proof of his unholy nature.

Perhaps the briefest and most circumspect of any of the witnesses is that
of Sulpicius Severus. A Latin ascetic who lived in Gaul and, as a devotee,
had also authored the *Life of Martin*, Sulpicius Severus wrote his *Dialogues*
partially as an attempt at competitive one-upmanship with the Egyptian
monastic community. Situated in his own local struggles in Gaul concerning
appropriate ascetic severity, he tells the story of a certain Postumianus who
had recently visited Egypt and returned to relay stories of their lives. Written
between 403 and 406, Sulpicius Severus's *Dialogues* witnesses, however briefly,

to the optics of the ensuing Origenist controversy. Through Postumianus, he describes the "strife" that had broken out between bishops and monks in Egypt.[14] Postumianus was purportedly invited to stay with Theophilus while in Egypt, an invitation he demurely declined. When explaining to his Gaulic counterparts why he refused Theophilus's invitation, he expresses his discomfort at keeping company with one who had so mistreated fellow brethren. Thus, Sulpicius Severus allows a glimpse into how Theophilus's actions vis-à-vis the Nitrian brethren were perceived by western monks.

As my description of each source indicates, every witness to the attack on the Nitrian brethren narrates the events within a larger political agenda. Lacking a version from the Tall Brothers or any Nitrian monk of Theophilus's entrance into the desert, only these depictions remain. In order to best image what happened between Theophilus and the monks, I weigh these competing narrations against one another in Chapter 5. Taken together, we glimpse the fraught relations among many of the Egyptian bishops and monks as well as the ramifications the image of monks as violent had for late ancient Christians throughout the Roman Empire, especially as regarded the power and meaning of the image of the Egyptian desert. Later fifth-century memorializations of this moment, and of earlier Egyptian ascetics more generally, would amplify several aspects of an earlier period: Images of holy monastic violence and the desert as the locus of such violence became more vivid and intense in later reimaginings of the lost fourth-century past, especially as found in the famous apothegmatic collection *Sayings of the Desert Fathers*.

Sayings of the Desert Fathers

To refer to the *Sayings* is not to point to a singular text but rather to a rich and complex tradition. The *Sayings* are collections of short stories, sometimes even just single sentences. The narratives themselves attribute content primarily (though not exclusively) to ascetics of fourth-century Egypt. This pretext helps explain how the *Sayings* have held a place of prominence in historiography of the origins of fourth-century monasticism in Egypt. At their origins, most apothegms plausibly circulated as oral knowledge rather than as written records, though at least one small grouping of sayings was already written down in the late fourth century.[15] Pithy wisdom of the desert mothers and fathers was eventually collected and textualized in multiple formats (e.g., alphabetical, anonymous, and systematic) and in a wide variety of languages

(Greek, Coptic, Latin, Syriac, Ethiopic, and Arabic, to name just a few). This textual evidence indicates the popularity this tradition quickly gained and still has in many Christian circles.

The fact that most scholarship now situates the earliest *Sayings* collations in the late fifth or early sixth century at a Palestinian monastic center, well after the conclusion of the first Origenist controversy,[16] has been used to bolster the scholarly consensus that the *Sayings* are anti-Origenist in nature. Although I concur with the Palestinian contextualization of the *Sayings*, describing the *Sayings* as simply anti-Origenist is problematic. Instead, this book argues that the *Sayings* offer a muted critique of both sides in the Origenist controversy. The juxtaposition of the nuanced voices attributed to Evagrius of Pontus and the Tall Brother Dioscorus within the *Sayings*, however, alongside those of Theophilus and Epiphanius of Cyprus, is indeed notable in apothegmatic collections. A particular saying attributed to Abba Lot is often pointed to as explicitly asserting an anti-Origenist position. Even James Goehring, who has been a prominent voice in asserting monastic ability to live in the midst of theological diversity, reads the saying as anti-Origenist.[17] While such an interpretation is possible, it is by no means the only one.

The saying is a brief story of an ill, elder monk who came to live with Lot.[18] When this old abba begins quoting Origen to visitors, Lot becomes anxious. Unsure of how to handle this disturbing situation, Lot visits Abba Arsenius to seek advice. Arsenius suggests not kicking out the old man but rather asking him either to be silent regarding Origen or to leave. Understandably, the saying has been slotted into the stark divides that emerged between advocates of Origen and their opponents. But nowhere does the saying actually critique Origen's teachings. The tale does not explicitly depict the old abba as errant for quoting Origen. His behavior nonetheless causes distress. Such upset around discussing Origen's writings only makes sense after the first Origenist controversy. And although the story might record a situation that occurred right after Theophilus's attack on Nitria, the saying does not appear in the older Greek or Syriac traditions or in the extant Sahidic Coptic tradition. More plausible is that the story was invented later, a context that might indicate anti-Origenism. Or it might express in a coded way continued anxiety around the appearance or politics of monks engaging Origen's works at all rather than a harsh condemnation of the content of so-called Origenist interpretation.

Whom Lot seeks advice from—Abba Arsenius—is also important for interpreting the passage. The later tradition depicts Arsenius as coming from a powerful background and having deep connections to the imperial family, having been a teacher of the emperors Arcadius and Honorius during their youth.[19] And while the *Sayings* includes a few stories attributed specifically to Theophilus (more on those in a moment), Theophilus is also prominent as a figure appearing in *Sayings* stories concerning Arsenius. The archbishop visits, desires to visit, or desires to send a visitor to Arsenius on these occasions.[20] Every instance narrates Arsenius's disinterest or even outright hostility to such visits. In one saying in particular, Theophilus decides not to visit Arsenius because of the answer he receives.[21] That is, Theophilus submits to Arsenius's wishes rather than assert his ecclesial authority. Likewise, in a saying attributed to Theophilus on his deathbed, he proclaims Arsenius as wiser for having always held God's final judgment in his mind.[22] If we accept as reliable Arsenius's previous prominent role in the early lives of Arcadius and Honorius, displeasing him may have been something Theophilus had to negotiate with more care. Although Theophilus may have genuinely respected Arsenius, it is equally plausible that Arsenius, as a representative of imperial influence, indicated in his person the tenuous power the archbishop wielded over the desert monks.

The potential problem with such a reading of Arsenius's role vis-à-vis Theophilus is that the saying's absence in several of the oldest collections throws its historical reliability into question. It seems certain that an abba named Arsenius (often referred to as "the Great") dwelt in the Egyptian desert in the late fourth to early fifth centuries. Jerome mentions him in a letter to the virgin Eustochium, describing prominent Egyptian ascetics that his protégé Paula had met in person.[23] In a similar fashion, Palladius refers to an "Arsisius the Great" that both lived at Nitria and met with the great amma Melania the Elder during her travels in Egypt.[24] Given the confusion of names that could occur in the late ancient world, we might well imagine this Arsisius the Great as synonymous with Arsenius the Great, the name perhaps becoming muddled by a later scribe. Such a suggestion becomes more plausible when we note that both Arsenius and Arsisius are mentioned in proximity to a certain Serapion as well as to the Macarii (more on whom later). Given that Jerome and Palladius were active in the first Origenist controversy on opposing sides and had each briefly lived in the Egyptian desert before Theophilus's incursion, we may trust that there was a historical Arsenius.

Any elaboration on his life or role in the desert, however, must rely on later sources. So, Sozomen, writing in the mid-fifth century, mentions an Arsisius linked to the Tall Brothers.[25] And the later fifth-century *Life of Peter the Iberian* mentions an Arsenius as an exemplum to emulate, alongside the Cappadocian fathers and John Chrysostom.[26] Some extant letters, preserved in Georgian, have tentatively been attributed to him.[27] And a monastery bearing his name at Troa (modern-day Tura) is the site of the discovery of the Tura papyri, including many fragments from the writings of Origen.[28] Taken as a whole, the later evidence, if anything, indicates that Arsenius was quite likely tied to the Tall Brothers or even himself implicated in the reading of Origen. In any case, whatever historical Arsenius we can tentatively trace was not an anti-Origenist. So even if the exchanges between Arsenius and Theophilus in the *Sayings* are later imaginings, we would be on surer footing as interpreting the author of Lot's saying as using Arsenius as a representative of a hesitant Origen sympathizer, not as a hostile opponent.

After the fallout between Theophilus and the Tall Brothers, we can plausibly imagine that Theophilus continued to assert his ecclesial authority through threats of Origenist accusations. The later addition of a saying about the old abba living with Abba Lot indicates that the desert was remembered as continuing to host lingering Origenists (including perhaps even Abba Arsenius). If such monks were still present, Theophilus undoubtedly knew of them and sought to keep them under control. If we read the representation of Arsenius's tense relationship with Theophilus (and, in turn, Lot's seeking of Arsenius's advice) in this context, the saying of Abba Lot becomes less an anti-Origenist sentiment and more a reminder of the lingering fear Origenist accusations evoked. The saying, added by later fifth-century monks, retrojects their anxiety back into the plausible context of the immediate aftermath of Theophilus's attack. The fear of being accused of Origenism would have remained a powerful trope for the later generations of monks who were descended from those who had fled from Theophilus to Palestine. As will be noted in Chapter 5, strong critiques of Theophilus would no longer have been palatable when the *Sayings* were finally gathered, allowing only coded references like the anxiety expressed by Abba Lot. Thus, Theophilus and Arsenius would have remained useful figures for symbolizing the tense relations between bishops and monks.

Likewise, the presence of narratives attributed to Theophilus in the *Sayings* indicates his rather mixed legacy among the monks. As the saying from his deathbed noted above indicates, Theophilus tends to be imagined in the *Sayings* as submissive to the abbas rather than the other way around. Another saying, which will be discussed in Chapter 3, depicts Theophilus as having fed veal to the otherwise vegetarian abbas in his company. The meal is depicted as, at the very least, a careless error by Theophilus that required correction from an abba present.[29] Another saying has him seeking out the wisdom of an abba at Nitria (the community he would later assault), imaging him as a student seeking this older abba's wisdom.[30] And on a visit to Scetis, he is answered with only silence by Abba Pambo.[31] The longest of his sayings is a discourse on the separation of body from soul at death and the ensuing legal trial he foresees the soul experiencing.[32] In it, he questions the value of worldly glory, wealth, and nobility among other things. Given the accusations leveled against Theophilus by his opponents about his own greedy behavior, it feels a bit ironic that such questions are laid on his lips.

Even if the *Sayings* is not best described as anti-Origenist, there is no doubt that the *Sayings* tradition had to deal cautiously with the legacy of another of its characters, Evagrius of Pontus. Evagrius, originally a prominent figure in the church as a protégé of the Cappadocian fathers, had taken up the ascetic life to escape his attraction to a powerful woman, ending up under the tutelage of Rufinus of Aquileia. It was Rufinus and his female counterpart, Melania the Elder, who would send Evagrius to Egypt's northwestern deserts, his home until his death in 399. And, as noted above, it was Evagrius who was the mouthpiece, if not creator, of the more elaborate Origenist theology that Theophilus sought to eradicate from the desert shortly after Evagrius's death. Akin to Theophilus's legacy, Evagrius's longest saying invites recollection of one's impending death and the potential for positive or negative appraisals of one's life by the Divine.[33] Other sayings focus less controversially on practices such as indifference to the world and undistracted prayer, which will be considered more closely in Chapter 2.[34] However, one passage describes Evagrius as being humbled for presumptuous speaking among the other abbas. In it, he is reminded that he could have been a great bishop, but in his new home he is yet a stranger.[35] In this way, Evagrius too is remembered in this recollection as needing correction. A similar story of being humbled sits in the Greek tradition under the name of Euprepius but is attributed to Evagrius in the Coptic tradition.[36] Thus, even the Coptic collection, the one perhaps most inclined to erase Evagrius after the Origenist controversy, does not do so but rather retains a story of his being humbled despite his deep erudition. These various examples do not highlight a strong anti-Origenist tendency in the *Sayings* but instead point to attempts by multiple versions of the tradition to retain voices from both sides while cautioning against entanglement in the legacy of the controversy. As we shall see in Chapter 5, this urge in the *Sayings* matches well other attempts across the fifth century to smooth over the volatile disagreements that arose around 400 C.E.

As noted above, this book avoids traditional scholarly readings of the *Sayings* as anti-Origenist. Such a misreading of this source material has at times perpetuated scholarly reconstructions of the fourth-century monks through the *Sayings*, even as scholars acknowledged its historical unreliability for the fourth century. To wrestle with this scholarly legacy, apothegms from the *Sayings* are present in every chapter of this book. But my reading of the *Sayings* throughout highlights how they are rememberings of a monastic past for a new monastic moment a century later. As I show, the sayings amplify images of the monastic project and the desert itself as violent even as they simultaneously depict the monks as avoiding conflict regarding the theologies and politics surrounding the figure of Origen. This latter aversion became coupled with barbarian tropes that allowed late fifth-century monks to gesture toward a violent rupture in the desert while shifting blame from Theophilus to barbarian raiders.

As a practical matter, I will limit myself to those *Sayings* collections found in Greek, Coptic, and Syriac. Undoubtedly, a richer, more nuanced picture might emerge by expanding to other linguistic variations, but I have drawn these parameters because they allow enough breadth to trace the developments of the early collections. The best-known Greek edition of Cotelier serves as my basis for the alphabetical collection, but I note whenever a saying is not likewise present in what is known as the oldest Greek thread. I also make recourse to Nau's anonymous Greek *Sayings*, as versions of them were appended to alphabetical collections from an early stage. The Coptic tradition contains some overlap with the Greek, but it also comprises otherwise unknown apothegms, and thus offers us a window into alternative Egyptian threads that continued to be valued. And for Syriac, I have used a manuscript from the first half of the sixth century, as it represents some of the earliest extant manuscript translations that were made.[37] Collectively, these stories represent the range of the emerging collections that came to be known as the *Sayings*. Throughout, I refer to the tradition as *Sayings*, asking the reader to keep in mind that when I do gesture to a particular textual lineage (e.g., Greek, Alphabetical) I am never referring to some long-lost singular original text but rather to one thread in a rich and varied textual tradition. Notation of a given saying will include in parentheses first the language of origin and then any structuring (e.g., alphabetical, anonymous, or systematic). Further information, such as the abba to whom a saying is attributed or numeration will follow the parentheses.

Violence, Memory, and Desert Asceticism

As the preceding discussion indicates, to understand and contextualize fully Theophilus's attack requires wrestling more broadly with what constitutes violence and how we are to comprehend it. Theophilus's violence—the burning and beating of the Nitrian community—may appear to be a straightforward example of violence, but his actions were located within a far larger matrix that requires us to reckon also with Roman and local law, political and ecclesial power, symbolic violence, communal boundaries, and racialized tropes. Beyond Theophilus's attack, this book examines several other acts of violence: those that occurred between demons and monks, in which demons manipulated monastic memories and monks lashed demons with psalmody and prayer; the performances of memory sanctions, which warped rather than erased both internal memories and external objects and spaces; the imagined violence projected onto "barbarian" Others as well as monks; and the racialized violence of colonialist dehumanization.

Before I delve into these particular cases of violence, a few words about how I theorize violence are in order. Throughout the book, I navigate between several registers of violence, tending both to physical and to spoken or written activities that ancients or moderns might describe as violent.[38] I consider acts of physical harm and acts of harm done through words together, even if they are distinguishable, for it seems clear that each type of harm informed and potentially invited expansion of the other. And, as we shall see, such violence might be directed toward others or toward oneself. The relationship between violence against self and violence against others likewise might serve as a feedback loop for heightening violence.

When I use the language of violence in this book, I point to something broader than the narrow use of ancient terms. There are places where the language of violence is used and, when that is the case, I note it. But I also include in my discussion a larger swath of activities, both those that might and those that might not have been termed by ascetics as violence proper. While I attempt to trace with care each type of violence along the way, I also highlight how certain types of violence made possible other types. Part of what makes violence hard to theorize is that there is slippage not only between ancient and modern meanings but also between various modalities we often wish to hold as separate. Above all, I understand violence as situated in the dynamic relations between parties, be they between Theophilus and the Tall Brothers as representatives of larger legal claims within the Christian communities; between monks and demons, monsters, and barbarians; or between monks, on the one hand, and angels and God, on the other. Such a dynamic theorizing of violence clarifies how self-violence in ascetic formation ultimately led to violent engagements alongside and against ecclesial authority.

In the late ancient imagination, violence permeated the cosmos. God, angels, humans, and demons all were understood as violent actors. What mattered was whether given individuals and their acts were to be understood as legitimate violence. In Chapters 2 and 3, I use the language of "divinely sanctioned violence" to describe the violent activity of God, angels, and monks in the world. To call such violence divinely sanctioned points to late ancient claims that God and God's angels were always justified in their actions by necessity of their divinity. This view is a particularly (though not exclusively) Christian understanding of God as parental figure rightly punishing a disobedient humanity. Such actions were occasionally performed by God, but more often than not were mediated by God's angels doing the dirty work. Given that monks sought to mimic the angels, it is unsurprising that monks occasionally claimed that their own violent actions were likewise divinely sanctioned. Building on David Brakke's reading of monks as constructed in and through their relations with demons, I highlight the violence inherent in such a linkage.[39] If the demons who constantly attacked the monks were violent, then the monks were their violent counterparts, striking back through psalmody and prayer understood as violent. Because demonic and monastic comportment were both constructed as violent, the desert over which they wrestled in turn was imaged as a locus of violence. The monk and his chosen home, the desert, were both centrally understood through the lens of legitimate or divinely sanctioned violence.

Beyond appeal to the divine, a violent act might be deemed legitimate or not in relation to local and imperial legal systems. Roman Egypt, in particular, had a reputation in late antiquity for being a locus of violence. Later in this section I consider the ethnic and racialized aspects of such a characterization, but for the moment let us focus on characterizations of violence in Egypt gleaned from papyri containing legal petitions. As Roger Bagnall has noted, scholars have used the same evidence to support opposing conclusions: Violence was rare, or violence was commonplace in Egyptian daily life.[40] Part of what complicates understanding violence through the lens of legality is the malleable nature of what constituted violence. For instance, imperial and local laws often stood in tension, and citizens might appeal to either. Moreover, it can be challenging to know the extent to which laws were actually enforced at either level. Ari Bryen rightly asserts that perception of violence as such was constantly negotiated between opposing parties.[41] In Chapter 5, when I analyze violent moments during the Origenist controversy, it becomes clear that each party makes the case that the violence done *against* it is the "real" violence and that that party's own behavior is merely a necessary defensive response. Although Theophilus first leaned on his relations with a local governmental official for support of his entrance into the desert, the Nitrian brethren would in turn exploit their social links to Emperor Arcadius's court in Constantinople for legal protection. Recognizing that violence in the late ancient world was constantly negotiated in and through legal terms renders more meaningful the forensic rhetoric that Theophilus and Palladius each used to defend his side.

Appeals to divine and legal supports overlapped in the work of the Church. The question of who could legitimately enact divine violence to protect communal boundaries and who could legitimately enact legally sanctioned violence rested in the person of a bishop or an archbishop. Repeatedly throughout his career, Theophilus justified acts of violence by making recourse to both worldly legal systems and divine decree. Two such moments appear in this book: his actions around the raid on the Nitrian brethren and his attack on the temple to Serapis in Alexandria. As discussed in Chapter 5, Theophilus's epistolary appeals to the legal system appear both in the local government's sanctioning of his assault on the brethren and in the jurisdictional issues he raises against John Chrysostom's interference in matters of his see. Those letters simultaneously claim his divinely ordained right to discipline the brothers as defender of orthodoxy against their Origenist heresy. Thus, analysis of Theophilus's violence against the Nitrian brothers must be situated simultaneously within legal and ecclesial frameworks in order to better understand how Theophilus exploited each on its own and in relation to the other.

In Chapter 3, I explore another, better-known violent act of Theophilus—his sack of the Serapeum of Alexandria. While Theophilus certainly made appeals to both divine and legal legitimacy, this case falls into grayer areas. For one, his appeal to divine justice relied on the support of monastic brethren, some of whom were from the northwestern desert he would later attack. That is, his claim to God's support rested not only on his position as archbishop of Alexandria but also on the holiness of the monks he recruited. As for his actions in relation to the law, his own behavior and that of his crowd of supporters at the Serapeum are better understood as extralegal actions, moments of violence that were only sanctioned posthumously by the local or imperial government. Given these complexities, I instead suggest that Theophilus's actions and those of the monks are better understood through late ancient practices of memory sanctions.

Memory sanctions refer to violent actions that alter previous memories or memorializations. Traditionally, modern scholarship has referred to such erasure or defacement of objects as *damnatio memoriae*. The problem with such language is that it gives the illusion that there was a clear local or imperial law for such actions, when in fact there were as many laws that might discourage such behaviors as there were laws that might be applied to support them. But the Latin neologism *damnatio memoriae* does highlight the violent underpinnings of such alterations: The goal was to damn permanently the memory of a past official or the memorialization of a deity. In this way, memory sanctions intimately connect memory practices and violence. As I discuss in Chapter 3, memory sanctions concern the violent reorienting of memories, the layering of new meanings atop old ones. So, in the case of Theophilus, his attack on the Serapeum did not erase previous worship of Serapis—nor was that its intention. Rather, he and his supporters desecrated memorializations of Serapis in the name of Christianity as a means of displaying Christ's power and, by extension, Theophilus's.

Attending to the pervasiveness of memory sanctions in late ancient life also renders sensible the monastic project regarding one's past life. Further in Chapter 3, I consider not only outward monastic involvement in the Serapeum's destruction but also inner monastic engagement of memory sanctions against one's own memories. Just as with statuary, the violence done to one's memories aims not at erasure but rather at reorientation through the violent reframing both of one's past actions and of one's future judgment in the afterlife. This inward violence was coupled with erasure of outward markers of status. Thus, the uncomfortably coarse, worn tunic and cloak of a monk expressed externally the inward sanctioning of memories of his past life. In this way, the violence of memory sanctions pervaded monastic life: Monks participated in violent reorientations of the world, such as sacking the Serapeum; sat in their cells remembering their past sins through fear of future divine retribution; and outwardly abused their bodies and sartorially expressed this self-reorientation and abuse.

The coarse appearance of a desert monk invited confusion between the holy man and other violent inhabitants of the desert: "barbarians." Barbarians were those who fell outside Roman imperial control and thus were imaged as violent outsiders. As I argue in Chapter 4, Roman rhetorical imaginings of the violent barbarian often obscure actual knowledge about these non-Roman peoples. The ethnic logics that Romans deployed meant that they depicted as violent not only foreigners but also Egyptians, as both were located on a periphery of the empire. Seeking to counter such stereotypes, Egyptians themselves sought to other those with whom they lived in close proximity as the truly problematic ones. The result was a racializing of barbarian neighbors that marked them as dangerous, even as monks themselves were sometimes confused with said neighbors.

Barbarian influx, while not a common occurrence according to extant evidence, served a powerful role as an imagined ever-present risk of violence. The monastic desert itself became doubly imbued with violence, by the presence both of demons (whom the monks fought) and of barbarians (from whom the monks sought to distinguish themselves). Desert space was constructed as an arena in which struggles for divine, paradisiacal embodiment on earth played out. But charging the space and its various inhabitants with violence meant that its power competed with that of the civilized "world" of the Church, as represented by Archbishop Theophilus. Thus, when Theophilus entered the desert to enact a violent raid on the Nitrian brethren, violence in the desert was not the surprise; shocking, instead, was the very identity of the violent attackers.

The trauma of an archbishop attacking holy men reverberated across the fifth century even as monks were called in to fight alongside or against other bishops during tumultuous Church councils. By the time the *Sayings* recorded its own memorializations of violence in the desert, the violence of the inhabitants (monk, demon, barbarian) had been amplified even as Theophilus's violence was obscured. That a textualized memorialization of a lost Golden Age required its own memory sanctions in order to be considered legitimate squares with the ways in which violence bubbled up in debates around orthodoxy and the role of monks within the Church. In turn, a certain nostalgia for a lost early era of Christianity allowed modern scholars to imagine the stories of the *Sayings* as historically accurate rather than as nostalgic rememberings of a past. That past was imagined as more violent, and colonialist scholars were only too willing to wed that image of violence to barbarian rhetoric, seeing in the occasional reference to barbarians their own uncivilized Berbers. Thus, ways of remembering and forgetting, simultaneously evoking and erasing violence, have continued to trick modern scholars into accepting a later imagined past as a historical truth.

Outline of the Book

As I have already indicated, this book addresses three historical periods and their relationship to one another: the so-called Golden Age of Egyptian monasticism circa 400, its revisionist memorialization a century or so later, and its modern scholarly rendering. Movement between these historical layers and their respective source materials necessarily results in some structural complexities. The first three chapters are concerned primarily with what we can reconstruct about fourth-century monastic praxes and imaginings vis-à-vis violence and memory. Chapters 4 and 5, by contrast, move among all three eras as necessary. Chapter 4 recontextualizes evidence gathered in the early twentieth century in order to debunk the commonly accepted narrative regarding a barbarian raid as the cause of the end of the Golden Age of monasticism. In turn, Chapter 5 offers a more historically sound replacement for understanding how violence permanently altered monastic community in Egypt.

The goal across the whole book is to offer a new, more textured view of the landscape of fourth-century Egyptian monasticism, while addressing why and how this era has often been misunderstood. A key piece in that corrective is a resituating of the *Sayings* in order to unsettle the dominance that its version of the Golden Age has held for so long. Chapters 1–3 all end with passages from the *Sayings* in order to highlight clearly both resonances and perceptible deviations between known fourth-century sources and the *Sayings's* late fifth-century imaginings of this earlier era. Subsequently, in Chapter 4, the misdating of the *Sayings* helps explain how the story of a "barbarian" raid came to be rehearsed unproblematically for almost one hundred years of scholarship. Finally, in Chapter 5, I place the *Sayings* in their proper historical context and suggest that their silence about Theophilus's attack was built into their later reimaginings in the light of political and ecclesial realities surrounding Theophilus's legacy. Thus, the book as a whole presents a fresh reading not only of fourth-century Egyptian monasticism but also of how to best engage the *Sayings* in relation to this period.

This book begins by closely scrutinizing what we know about the northwestern desert through texts and archaeological remains. I first explore linguistic and rhetorical construals of the desert before turning to the critical role demons as inhabitants of the desert played to desert portrayals. Along the way, I note the central place of self-violence in ascetic construction vis-à-vis demonic opponents. Theological questions around human and demonic embodiment, both its possibilities and its limitations, loom large in understanding the interactions between monks and demons in the desert. I also highlight how the desert itself was already constructed, and then reconstructed, as an "other" space in tension with the world. Engaging archaeological evidence from the desert and rhetorically rich imaginings of the desert found in late ancient texts, I articulate how both types of evidence can reverberate off one another in the process of scholarly reconstruction. Taken together, material evidence and literary portrayals depict the desert as ever elusive, a repeatedly marked locale that continuously slipped away. I conclude Chapter 1 by pointing to how elevation of the desert to levels of paradisiacal possibility was amplified by later fifth-century authors, including several apothegms preserved in the *Sayings*. Once the desert was perceived as "dead," it was available for more fanciful memorializations.

Having established the powerful presence of the desert itself, Chapter 2 turns to the role of prayer in daily ascetic life. Acknowledging the complex meanings inherent in prayer (and psalmody as a type of prayer), I focus on the violent images monastic writers used to explain and imagine prayer. Ascetic writers described prayer, in both its baser and its higher renderings, as a weapon for fighting demons. And the mimesis of angels that ascetics sought to embody through prayer likewise carried with it a host of violent imagery, as ascetics became divinized conduits for divinely ordained violence. The chapter concludes that such understandings of prayer and ascetic embodiment centered violence on ascetic formation. Such intense identification between angels and the holiest of monks translated in the later memorializations of the *Sayings* to a conflation of the two, as violent imagery of fiery angelic-like monks rhetorically magnified the idea of the "true" monk as violent.

Chapter 3 deepens this exploration of ascetic formation by considering how ascetics stretched the cultural logics of memory sanctions to encourage damning of one's past life. By considering possible ascetic involvement in actual *damnatio memoriae* at the Serapeum in Alexandria, it becomes clear that ascetics would have been both well aware of the cultural logics of memory sanctions and willing participants in violence. Extending the idea that partial erasure of an object served as performed punishment, ascetics attempted to create a palimpsest self. I especially note Evagrius as encouraging fellow monks to excise unhelpful passions from past memories, or to reinscribe past memories as sins that risked demonic temptation. Among the figures Evagrius praises is Abba John the Little, who also looms large in the *Sayings*. By tending to the ways memorializations shifted from the fourth to the late fifth century, I argue that the later elevation of certain forms of forgetting lionizes these earlier attempts at sanctioning one's own memories.

Given the violence inherent in the desert project, in its demonic inhabitants, and in the ascetics who themselves appropriated it, Chapter 4 explores how rhetoric invoking "barbarian" peoples was used to characterize certain groups as innately violent across the fourth and into the fifth centuries. The chapter analyzes these characterizations in order to reconsider the plausibility of a "barbarian" raid on the ascetic community at Scetis. Since the early twentieth century, this narrative has been cited to explain the downfall of asceticism in Egypt's northwestern desert despite lacking convincing evidence supporting its occurrence. The chapter concludes by suggesting that we are better served by examining an actual and significant moment of violence in the desert—Theophilus's incursion into Nitria. I argue that previous scholarship has overemphasized the barbarian raid narrative and that the far more traumatic violence for the monastic community and the desert's legacy was Theophilus's own violent encroachment.

Chapter 5 begins by revisiting competing narrations of Theophilus's raid on the Nitrian monastic community. Theophilus's attempt to assert his ecclesial authority over the desert and its ascetic inhabitants destroyed for many the powerful image of the desert as otherworldly utopia, bringing a Golden Age of asceticism to an abrupt close. The chapter imagines the aftermath of the loss of the desert as Other to the world. Knowing that many of the monks who fled Egypt landed in Palestine, later generations of ascetics (the intellectual descendants of these exiles) helped expand the monastic school of Gaza across the fifth century. These individuals played a crucial role in the process of collating and adapting the *Sayings*. The chapter suggests that both content and structure of the *Sayings* indicates that the collection was constructed by the Gazan monks as a memorialization that sanctioned certain memories in order to reimagine a lost past within the context of a new monastic community. Given the loss of the desert after the Origenist controversy, the book concludes that the *Sayings*'s nostalgia for northwestern desert monasticism a century earlier resulted in the remembering of the lost power-filled desert as a textualized, portable memory.

Throughout, the book examines how memory-acts (both constructive and sanctioning), as well as real places and imagined spaces, were refracted through actual and rhetorically constructed violence, especially "barbarian" rhetoric. Although the book focuses on a particular period in monastic history from fourth- to fifth-century Egypt to late fifth-century Gaza, it also more broadly participates in scholarly conversations about how violence shapes memories and spaces even in our own time. Attending to how violence, including racialized rhetoric, informs how memory praxes construct spaces offers a better understanding of the relationship between Egyptian monasticism, the "death" of its desert, and the creation of the *Sayings*. But such attention also invites us to reconsider the nexus of violence, race, memory (including nostalgia for an imagined past), and place in our own past and present. When explicitly addressed, the intersection and interplay of these pieces highlight how violence is enacted against othered peoples through manipulations of memory, racialized language, and struggles over contested locales.

Chapter 1

Imagining and Inhabiting the Desert

> Shall we allow this man to stay in this place, the desert to become a
> port, a place of rest for everyone in danger, and especially to become
> a city like heaven for those who hope for eternal life? If we allow
> him to remain here, multitudes will gather around him and the des-
> ert will not be under our power. But, what's more, they will chase
> us away through the lash of their prayers.
>
> —*Life of Macarius the Egyptian* 18

As the demons feared, Macarius's bodily presence in the desert signaled the
desert's transformation into a space of paradisiacal possibility. The repetition
of "allow" and "become" mark an impending power struggle between demons
and monks in the fourth century as imagined a century or so later. The language of permission underscores that the demons were native inhabitants
who understood themselves to be the owners of desert regions. But sole pro-
prietorship would soon be revoked, the phrase "to become" pointing forward
to the occupation of the desert by new, ascetic inhabitants. The transition
would not occur merely through ascetic presence but would further require
the violent act of lashing the demons with prayer. Such appropriation of the
desert promised a new space, the desert as a safe haven from worldly dangers,
a utopian heavenly city.

Here, in the *Life of Macarius the Egyptian*, we have a creative riff on the
well-known scene from the fourth-century *Life of Antony*, in which demons
confront Antony, crying, "Leave what belongs to us! What do you want with
the desert?"[1] The arrival of Antony's mortal body, like Macarius's, produces
in the demons anxiety about their desert ownership. Both passages depict
the desert as the rich background upon which Egyptian monasticism sought

to transpose itself. In both the fourth-century portrayal of Antony and the later fifth-century imitation concerning Macarius, the desert is not described as it actually exists but rather as it is richly imagined in order to further each author's rhetorical agenda. The desert and its associated power *belonged* to the demons. By definition, it was habitable *not* for human bodies but only for cold, fleshless demonic ones. Framed in this way, ascetic inroads into the desert strive to claim ownership of a space constructed as Other and to reenvision the possibilities of human embodiment. As we shall see, late ancient Christians imagined the act of entering the desert as informing and transforming constructions of bodily and terrestrial spaces; the fleshy human body endeavored to become spiritual, potentially returning to its pre-Fall Adamic nature, as a way of simultaneously changing the desert into a heaven-like city.

Examining the desert's crucial role in the creation and elaboration of Egyptian asceticism, as well as in later imaginative retellings of monasticism's origins,[2] reveals a historical moment ripe for displaying the complicated, intricate meanings ascribed to desert space by late ancient people in both the fourth and fifth centuries, albeit for different purposes. The desert that Egyptian ascetics inhabited was a space conceived of as imbued with incredible power, but it was also a place marked by harsh conditions and demons. The desert meant great possibility and great risk. This chapter explores the settlement patterns that transformed the desert into a city, a process that relied on displacing native dwellers (demons) and replacing them with virtuous, heaven-worthy inhabitants (monks). To begin, the chapter offers a broad understanding of the desert's significance and cultural accretions. Given ancient valuation of the desert as a place of power, I consider how late ancient ascetics envisioned demons, the desert's primary inhabitants. Knowledge of demons, however, was not regarded as sufficient for success in claiming the desert. Thus, I turn also to exploring how ascetics as desert colonizers coupled such demon-related information with self-fashionings of their own bodies and of their roles in cosmic warfare. Then, returning focus to the desert, I examine resonances between literary portrayals and archaeological remains, arguing that late ancient Christians, including ascetics, had a particularly rich and complex vision of the desert that infused the space with paradisiacal, heavenly longing. This chapter ends by reconsidering how different groups envisioned the relationship between ascetic bodies and desert space—specifically, the (in)ability of both to be transformed. This intersection of desert and body emerges through my close reading of multiple versions of a single ascetic story. Thus, the chapter begins and ends by attending to how later monastic literature, those materials written after the perceived end of the Egyptian ascetic Golden Age, refracted the meaning of desert inhabitation.

Envisioning the Desert

When the demons complain that Macarius and those who follow him will alter their "desert places," they use a Coptic word for desert that was fairly rare: a nominalization of the verb *shwf*, meaning to be deserted, laid waste, or destroyed.[3] Ancient readers and hearers would have recognized the connotations associated with using this particular word to refer to the desert, the image of a desolate, ruinous place emerging in their imaginations. At the very least, the rarity of the word would have attracted attention. Three other Coptic words were far more often deployed in late ancient literature to refer to the desert: *t.erēmos* (a direct borrowing of the Greek word for desert), *p.jaeie* (a term roughly synonymous with *t.erēmos*), and *p.toou* (a translation of the Greek *oros*, "mountain"). The choice to use a less common word to describe the desert Macarius entered thus performed larger rhetorical work. *Nai.shafeu* evoked the desolate place that Macarius's body (and those of his disciples) would fill. The term invites the audience to understand these destroyed places as available to demonic presence because of their ruined nature, as locales that were not yet transformed by ascetic inhabitation but that would be soon.

The dichotomy between the pre- and post-monastic desert becomes clearer when one considers how the other, more common words for desert (both in Coptic and Greek) were deployed. As noted above, while Coptic had three alternate terms, two of these were derived from Greek usage: *erēmos* and *oros*. While *erēmos* translates more precisely to our modern notion of a vast, flat expanse of sandy desert, *oros*, which is usually rendered "mountain," came also to carry the valence of desert spaces. In fact, *oros* (especially in papyrological evidence) was a multivalent term. Sometimes synonymous with *erēmos*, referring to a large desert plateau or oasis, *oros* might also describe the nearby deserted areas where the land became hilly or led to overhanging cliffs or might even imply any space outside an inhabited town or village where irrigation (and therefore inhabitation) ceased. Most pertinent for our purposes, *oros* also was capable of suggesting a religious locale, namely, the home of monks, the location of either a monastery or a group of monasteries.[4] So, the monastic community at Nitria that fought with Theophilus (discussed in the Introduction) was described with the term "mountain." And, as Dag Endsjø has convincingly shown, at least from Athanasius's *Life of Antony* (that is, from the fourth century on), we should imagine that the desert evoked ideas associated with the term *eschatia* (that is, the "wilderness") as well, even if the word itself rarely appeared in desert literature.[5] In later fifth-century reimaginings, even when a single term such as *erēmos* was used, the desert itself might be even further charted. For example, in the *Sayings of the Desert Fathers*, Macarius's desert home is referred to as the "great desert," a place that stood in contrast to the "other desert" where fellow brethren lived.[6] In this way, the desert became more textured, more deeply explored in later recollections.

As careful as such delineations between various monastic desert places were, imaginings of the desert were most productive when they construed a space formulated as the world's Other. The desert was a space always constructed in relation to the *polis*—the inhabitable, civilized world. The desert was imagined as a special space precisely because as Other it did not (indeed, it could not be expected to) obey the laws of the world. It was a place where expectations were reversed; harsh conditions meant one could not count on access to food, water, shelter from the intense beating of the sun's rays, or the harsh winds that whipped sand to and fro. It was its unfamiliarity, the otherness of the desert, that imbued it with power, making it desirable, if formidable, real estate. Devoid of civilized, human presence, the desert served as the repository for things unfamiliar and dangerous: demons, dead bodies, brigands, "barbarians," and monstrous creatures. While we will discuss these other inhabitants in Chapter 4, for now let us focus on the desert's most infamous natives: demons. For long before Christianity's arrival in Egypt, the desert was home to a variety of Greco-Roman deities as well as lesser spirits.[7] Locating nonhuman creatures, especially divine or ethereal-bodied beings, in desert space underscored its definition as Other, as not worldly.

It is tempting to succumb completely to the neat dichotomy between "desert" and "world," to the exoticizing of the Other such portrayals offer. But to do so risks effacing the rich complexity of desert space. Pre-Christian temples were constructed near sites of perceived power. So, for example, many temples were located near the Nile, near other bodies of water, or near natural resources, places vital to the survival and prosperity of the population.[8] Interpretation of the northwestern desert as a powerful space was rooted in the presence of both oases and valuable resources such as alum and natron (the substance from which "Nitria" takes its name). Building a temple to a given deity monumentalized a community's attempt at harnessing and manipulating this power, even as it was forced to reckon with the fact that such power was located in a space traditionally understood as *not* habitable for humans but only for nonhuman demons. By the Christian era, the desert was fixed in the Egyptian imagination as the location of Greco-Roman gods and demons, and, therefore, power. Furthermore, as the popularity of the *Life of Antony* developed in late antiquity indicates, Egypt exported more than grain to the larger Roman Empire: It also proffered an image of its desert as a significant locus of power.

Desert-Dwelling Demons

Despite the long-standing respect among Greco-Roman peoples for demons (including philosophical interest in them),[9] these spirits gained a peculiar prominence in the newly Christianized world.[10] As demons became deeply implicated in the "Roman cultural imagination" of evil, all spirits began to be demonized, even the "traditionally revered, protective and procreative" gods.[11] The perceived infiltration of evil into Roman lands demanded a response. As David Frankfurter has noted, demonological lists emerged as tools to gain control of and power over a vast disarray of evils. In this way, demonologies served as meaning-making tools that helped Christians cope with the real and imagined dangers that surrounded them. They were especially powerful weapons for ascetics who themselves sought to infiltrate demonic territory. As the phrase "demonological lists" suggests, such efforts to organize the dangerously disordered were often achieved through writing. The textualizing of knowledge about demons served as a physical manifestation of the order that ascetics sought.

Such lists also point to how, in this dangerous new desert world, demons came to serve a crucial role as the opponents of ascetics.[12] David Brakke has argued that demons played an essential role in ascetic identity formation, exploring how the *monachos* ("single one") was "imagined, embodied, legitimated, and reconceived" through his conflicts and engagements with demons.[13] Demons were believed to embody that which ascetics sought to deny in their own persons. In fact, the construction of demons as ascetics' Others relied on a fairly developed understanding of the origins of demons and of their somatic comportment.

A full discussion of the history of the gods and demons who were located in the Egyptian desert and elsewhere in the Greco-Roman world is beyond the scope of this book, but a few words of explanation about how these spirits became Christian demons are needed to understand the foundation on which ascetics built their appropriated desert. Among the most influential figures early in this process was Justin Martyr. As Annette Yoshiko Reed has shown, Justin wed Enochic traditions about fallen angels and their offspring, particularly as found in the *Book of the Watchers* (a text preserved for us in 1 Enoch 1–36), to the Greco-Roman pantheon.[14] Through intertextual readings of the *Book of the Watchers*, Genesis 6, and Psalm 95, Justin slotted Greco-Roman deities and lesser demons into the narrative of the *Book of the Watchers* as its fallen angels and their hybrid angelic-human offspring who illicitly instructed humanity. As Reed notes, "Justin helped to integrate the motif of illicit angelic instructions into Christian demonology."[15] Even as the popularity of the *Book of the Watchers* waned or was contested in many locales, Justin's equation of pagan deities with demons left a lasting legacy for later Christians.

The *Book of the Watchers* became particularly popular among Egyptian Christians, and it was only Origen's wariness of the *Book of the Watchers* as a Christian resource that dampened enthusiasm for the book (though not successfully in all quarters).[16] As discussed in the Introduction, Origen deeply influenced many ascetics in the Egyptian desert, a situation that would cause rupture among the monks themselves, not to mention between them and the ecclesial hierarchy in Alexandria. Thus, understanding Origen's views of demons helps clarify ascetic engagement with demons a century and a half later. In the course of refuting Celsus's critiques of Christianity as demonic-based magic, Origen became aware of how Greco-Roman detractors might turn the *Book of the Watchers* to their own interpretive advantage.[17] But even without Celsus as an impetus, Origen's cosmogony tended to retroject fallen angels/demons[18] closer to the moment of creation than in intertextual readings of the *Book of the Watchers* and Genesis 6. Whereas the *Book of the Watchers* places the fall of these angels after the creation of humanity, Origen saw the cooling of souls (including those of demons) previously adhering to the Godhead as an act that helped initiate the unfolding of creation.[19] Like those who favored the *Book of the Watchers* before him, Origen understood the Devil and his army of demons as angels, albeit ones that had cooled in their ardor for God and fallen away. Reading Ezekiel 28:11–19 alongside Isaiah 14:12–17,[20] Origen assured his readers that demons were fallen angels. As he notes, the ability to sin *had* to be an option for all.[21] That angels chose not to sin was what led to their status as angels. Conversely, demons and the Devil himself were angels who sinned, freely distancing themselves from the divine, an act that resulted in the cooling of their bodily comportment.

To claim that the Devil and his demons were by nature sinful would be to impute to God the creation of evil, an idea by which Origen was confident his audience would be repulsed. While those after Origen agreed with his view of demons as angels who freely chose to disobey and therefore fall away from God, Origen's view that the Devil and his demons could conceivably return to God one day was not as palatable an explanation for all. An alternate view of demons apparently was developing in tandem with expansions of Origen's systems; this view asserted that demons were irredeemable.[22] Yet it seems that as long as no one forced a discussion of demons and salvation, ascetics with differing understandings lived peaceably together.[23] Such coexistence is plausible, as all seemed to agree that demons were jealous of human embodiment. In fact, before the arguments of the first Origenist controversy, there was a growing corpus of knowledge regarding demons that was particularly reliant on Origen, as evidenced in Evagrius's writings.

As part of his larger cosmological project, Origen offered a nuanced explanation for demonic jealousy of human bodies. As he explained, demons loved bodies, coveting the opportunity to be enfleshed. For this reason, demons greedily enjoyed libations and odors, imagining that they might actually ingest them.[24] Likewise, the chance to influence human bodies was how sorcerers compelled demons to perform.[25] Unfortunately, because of the sensitive nature of humans, the more frequent situation was demonic possession, with the demon fully controlling the human body.[26] For Origen, demonic desire was pitted against human autonomy, producing many of the struggles of this world.[27] Citing both the *Shepherd of Hermas* and the *First Epistle of Barnabas*, Origen argued that two angels, one who incited good thoughts and the other who incited evil ones, accompanied every person.[28] Underlying this idea was the presumption that angels and fallen angels attached to humanity, desiring to direct human bodies. This interdependent situation arose because, as Ellen Muehlberger notes, angelic, human, and demonic embodiment were always constructed in relation to one another.[29] Weaving together Platonic, Stoic, and Christian thought, Origen's cosmogony offered an account of such bodily diversity. In his system, all bodies—angelic, human, demonic—were acquired after their respective souls cooled in their ardor for God.[30] Thus, falling away from God to varying degrees resulted in embodiment; each body served simultaneously to limit and to instruct its soul, turning it back toward its proper focus, God. While not all cooled souls required or earned enfleshment, all received a body of sorts. For Origen, bodilessness was an aspect of the Trinity alone.[31]

It was, in particular, his view of the demonic body as malleable, and the resulting human struggles with demons, that Origen bequeathed to future generations of ascetics like Antony, Macarius, and Evagrius. Demons, having most intensely cooled in their love of God, earned chilly, non-fleshy bodies.[32] Envious desire for a fleshy human body heightened demons' animosity toward ascetics. Demons took advantage of their somatic comportment, deploying their bodies as useful tools in the haunting and deception of ascetics. Their somatic malleability enabled them to manifest themselves in a variety of forms, allowing them to tailor their appearance to an ascetic's (erotic) longings or deepest fears, while the lightness of their bodies enabled them to travel more rapidly across the desert than could humans.[33]

Seizing the Desert: Ascetic Aggressors

Whereas Greco-Romans both feared and respected the variety of demons residing in the desert, Christian ascetics who stepped into the barren wilderness did so with a decidedly negative view of these spirits.[34] Following Jesus's model, ascetics viewed these native inhabitants as demonic opponents to be overthrown and cast from the desert. Christian ascetics entered the desert in the hopes of controlling it. Forcing demons out by wounding them with the violent lashes of prayer, ascetics sought to seize the desert, a process that they hoped would transform their own bodies and the desert itself. Evagrius articulated well this conquering impulse and the violent process through which it would be achieved, saying, "It is necessary to know these things [that is, how to tell if someone has attained impassibility] for our zeal and power, so that we may know if we have traversed the Jordan and are near the city of palms or if we still reside in the desert and are beaten by foreigners."[35] In this passage, Evagrius makes explicit the power that ascetics sought to gain by populating the desert. Evagrius's reference to the "City of Palms," an epithet given to Jericho in Deuteronomy 34:3, would have evoked in his audience memory of God's promise to Moses, God's gift of the Promised Land. Using the imagery of fording the Jordan River, Evagrius paints a vivid image of ascetic success: The desert was no longer the desert, filled with "foreigners" (that is, the demons who beat them), but instead was approaching transformation into the "City of Palms," into the Promised Land. The hoped-for result was the complete recreation of the desert into a space of paradisiacal promise.

Given the impulse behind ascetic invasion of the desert, it is perhaps less surprising that the demons were not especially eager to welcome the ascetics into their space. For demons to "allow" ascetics to relocate themselves to the desert would result in them being lashed by prayers and displaced. Thus, the antagonism between demons and ascetics was framed as a daily battle between opposing forces. This framing emerges already in fourth-century descriptions of Antony's inroads into the desert as a violent struggle; demons attacked Antony's chaste body, while Antony countered with prayers.[36]

The image and interpretation of the chaste ascetic body, especially the image of Antony's idealized body, was once again indebted to Origen. For Origen, the virginal body allowed its soul to manifest physically something of its original, paradisiacal state.[37] In this way, the human body was also understood as malleable. Given Origen's high appraisal of the chaste body, it is unsurprising that his views appealed to the ascetics taking over the Egyptian desert. Ideally, the ascetic body was disciplined through strictly regimented food consumption, sleep deprivation, work, prayer practices, and poverty performed in the harsh conditions of a desert landscape. As early as Abba Antony, we read of the renovation of the body through such control mechanisms. In his letters, Antony explained to fellow ascetics that the body was subject to three types of movements: those natural to the body, those produced through excessive consumption of food and drink (causing one's blood to warm), and those incited by demons. Knowledge of these different bodily motivations was meant to assist an ascetic in ordering and orienting his body properly. Antony's rigid lifestyle transformed his body into a better body, one closer to his soul's original state.[38]

Building on such traditions, Evagrius, so influential in the desert in the last decades of the fourth century, likewise articulated a physiognomy in which the body needed to return to its natural state.[39] Once more, tightly regulated bodily practices (food, prayer, sleep, etc.) were recommended, but what Evagrius also eloquently emphasized was the passions inherent in the body. One of his clearest expressions of how to control the body is found in his *Talking Back*.[40] In it, he articulates a demonological list of eight types of demons in ascending order of danger: gluttony, fornication, love of money, sadness, anger, *acedia* (the noonday demon, provoking dissatisfaction and/ or laziness), vainglory, and pride. Knowledge of how these demons might manipulate ascetic bodies, and, in particular, their thoughts, memories, and passions, underwrote each of his descriptions. Evagrius asserted that embodied Scripture could serve as an antidote to such situations.

Performing Evagrius's demonology allowed an ascetic to reorient his focus on rightly engaging natural passions. Only through carefully observing bodily movements and the thoughts associated with them could an ascetic hope to dominate his passions. Thus, for example, anger was not an improper emotion as long as it was directed toward its proper recipients, that is, the demons.[41] A similar concern for anger is retained in the later *Sayings*: "A certain one from the old men approached Abba Achilles and beheld him spitting blood from his mouth. And he asked Abba Achilles, 'What is this, father?' And the old man (Abba Achilles) said, 'Because a word of a brother had distressed me and I struggled not to tell him, I asked God to take it from me and the word became as blood in my mouth and I spat it and I had rest and I forgot the distress.'"[42] Here the danger of retaining the memory of a brother's words, and thereby a grudge that might in turn wound his brother, led Abba Achilles to seek God's intercession. Abba Achilles's cautionary approach was rewarded: God answered, transforming the word (and his memory of it) into a bodily fluid, blood, that might be ejected from the body (via spitting), manifesting somatically Abba Achilles's rejection of harboring the word.

That Abba Achilles's bodily fluid was blood also highlights how thoroughly self-violence was imagined to constitute ascetic identity by later monastic generations. Abba Achilles's prayer to God was answered by a divine wound that produced blood in Achilles's mouth. Ascetic praxis was envisioned as entailing physical difficulties, and adherents of Egyptian desert asceticism, in particular, were especially revered for their strenuous self-deprivation.[43] Having renounced the world, these individuals relocated themselves outside the inhabited sphere. Ascetics were imagined as intentionally subjecting themselves to a dual brutality—that of the desert (the stark temperatures, extreme heat during the day and extreme cold at night)[44] and that of self-imposed pains resulting from limited consumption of food or drink, extended periods without sleep, and prayers such as Abba Achilles's. Such self-inflicted punishments indicate that an expectation of violence to self was remembered as inherent in constructions of the ascetic body. In fact, the gatherers of the *Sayings* imagined the role of violence to self as standing at the heart of ascetic identity for the earlier generation. So, the young monk Abba Zacharias could claim that "he is a monk who does violence to himself in everything."[45] Likewise, Amma Theodora described a monk as one who does violence to him- or herself.[46]

Elsewhere in the apothegmatic tradition, two stories expand on this memorialization of self-violence as central to ascetic identity. The first concerns Abba John the Little, an ascetic who lived in Scetis. The story relates how John eventually managed to help an extremely forgetful brother. The saying concludes, "Thus was the daily labor of those of Scetis, to offer zeal to those battling, even having violence done to themselves in order to gain for each other the good."[47] Here, violence is defined as practices performed zealously on one another's behalf. Another relevant saying narrates that once while Abba Macarius the Egyptian (whose body the demons fretted about in the tale at the start of this chapter) was visiting Nitria, the brethren there requested a word from Macarius. Macarius's reply to his fellow ascetics was that he was *not* a monk himself but had only ever *seen* monks. He goes on to tell of a trip he took into the deeper desert:

> And I saw in the midst of these animals two naked men. . . . They said, "We are from a monastery and we came to an agreement and we came here, lo, forty years ago. One of us an Egyptian and the other a Libyan . . . then I asked them, "How can I become a monk?" They said to me, "If one does not separate from all those of the world, one cannot become a monk." I said to them, "I am weak and not able to do like you." So they said to me, "If you are not able to do like us, sit in your cell and cry for your sins." And I asked them, "When the winter comes, do you not freeze? And when the sun's heat comes, do your bodies not burn?" They said, "God made for us this arrangement. We neither freeze in winter, nor in the summer are we burned."[48]

Macarius concluded that because he could not maintain their severe way of life, he was not a monk but only had seen monks. Once again, self-violence, here exposure to the elements, was asserted by later generations as a prerequisite to legitimate self-identification as a monk. According to Macarius's definition, most of those living in the desert (in this case, at Nitria and Scetis) were *not* actually monks, including himself. Clearly though, communal understandings of monkhood were ambiguous, as the saying makes clear, for Abba Macarius *was* considered by most to be a monk and one worth listening to, despite his need for clothes. The story situates somatic ideals vis-à-vis harsh desert conditions as crucial to ascetic identity. In this way, it underscores how some Egyptian ascetics understood their embodiment and how later ascetic heirs amplified this earlier framing: Such impossible somatic feats were possible *because* they were performed in the Other space of the desert.

Reenvisioning the Desert

Problems arose, as the story of Abba Macarius's encounter with monks living deep in the desert makes clear, because the desert functioned *simultaneously* as the place where monks lived, the space they wandered into, and the region where most were not able to survive. The desert was *both* where one's cell was and where one's cell was not. Although an ascetic may have moved out to the desert, he still did not dwell in the desert-desert, the "real" desert. Even as ascetics overtook portions of the desert, the desert they sought slipped from their grasp, receding further into the sands and away from the world.

The desert in the above Macarian apothegm points to how rhetorically constructed the image of the desert would become by the end of the fifth century. Yet Macarius's shifting desert correlated to an actual physical locale: the northwestern desert of Egypt. This area included the region west of modern-day Cairo and south of Alexandria, a stretch that encompassed the famous settlements of Scetis, Nitria, Kellia, and Pherme. To better understand the desert into which Macarius and other ascetics incorporated themselves, not only examination of general depictions of the desert but also portrayals of these particular sites is needed.

Egyptian ascetics initially inhabited the two sites of Scetis and Nitria. Scetis[49] (located in the modern-day region of Wadi al-Natrun, that is, "oasis of natron") in late antiquity consisted of four monastic communities: the monasteries of Macarius, John the Little, Bishoi, and Baramus. Named for their founders, these communities housed revered abbas, including both Macarius the Egyptian and John the Little, of whom stories have already been mentioned. While very little is known about the four sites before the late sixth century,[50] they were in existence by the late fourth century, as John Cassian mentions them in his discussions on prayer.[51] Cassian's reference to the four communities is in fact incidental to his discussion, as he focuses his attention on Abba Paphnutius as the only priest who would allow Theophilus's troublesome *Festal Letter* to be read, sparking a debate about whether humanity retained God's image. Cassian's witness confirms that the four communities existed by the time the first Origenist controversy broke out. Prominent abbas associated with Scetis include Macarius of Egypt, Macarius of Alexandria, Isidore the Priest, Arsenius, and John the Little.

Nitria, approximately forty kilometers southeast of Alexandria, is located in the vicinity of the present-day village al-Barnudj in the Delta region.[52] According to tradition, the ascetic community at Nitria was established in the early fourth century by a certain Abba Amoun.[53] Inspired by Amoun's example, more ascetics quickly populated the neighboring desert. Palladius claims that he witnessed around two thousand monks at Nitria, living either alone or with one or two others, in the last years of the fourth century.[54] Although an exaggerated figure, it does convey the visual density a monk or visitor experienced while standing in the community's midst. Eminent abbas associated with Nitria include Macarius of Alexandria, Evagrius, Isidore, Pambo, and Ammonius.

Both Scetis and Nitria were known in antiquity as important sources of natron (Nitria being named for its proximity to natron and Scetis's modern appellation, Wadi al-Natrun, likewise, pointing to the presence of natron). As mentioned earlier, natural resource–laden places were believed to be especially imbued with power. Thus, we should note that Scetis and Nitria were intentionally chosen as ascetic locales *because* the presence of natron had previously marked these places as power-rich. When we consider that natron, a salt, was most frequently excavated for use in Egyptian burials, the purposefulness of ascetic location intensifies.[55] Recall that the desert was imagined as a space uninhabitable for humans, that is, as a space of death. Both Scetis and Nitria as ascetic sites sought to appropriate a space affiliated not only with power but also with the dead. Thus, ascetics who laid claim to these areas were implicated in a complex project. Their entering natron-rich Scetis and Nitria symbolized their internal claims of dying to the world and their hopes of transformation into inhabitants of paradise or heaven. But to die to the world and transform the desert, they had to wrest the power associated with natron from its demonic inhabitants.

As Palladius's description of thousands of monks at Nitria indicates, such ascetic sites quickly became popular. Moreover, his portrayal represents the very thing that the demons feared in the Macarian story that began this chapter: Multitudes *had* filled the desert. But it was not only demons who were troubled by the density of human bodies. As Palladius describes it, during the nine years he lived there, Kellia was an ascetic locale of its own, with its own churches and priests, the famous Abba Macarius of Alexandria among them.[56] The later *Sayings* tradition would attribute Kellia's founding to Abba Amoun, who was no longer able to find sufficient solitude at overpopulated Nitria.[57] Because too many individuals had come to Nitria to live the ascetic life, the most austere and seasoned monks fled further into the desert for quiet. Kellia (sixty kilometers south of Alexandria and forty kilometers west of the western branch of the Nile River),[58] situated as it was in such close proximity to Nitria, may then have been an overflow space for Nitria. Certainly, by the end of the fifth century, Kellia was remembered as such. Pherme, too, seems to have been an offshoot community, though of which community, Scetis or Nitria, is less clear. Pherme is only mentioned by Palladius once as the home of a certain Paul and five hundred other monks.[59] While Palladius describes Pherme as bordering Scetis,[60] modern archaeological excavations have unearthed ruins of Pherme as part of topographical studies of Kellia.[61]

Ambiguity about Pherme's community of origin underscores how fluid (or perhaps sometimes even absent) boundaries were between various ascetic clusters. While John Cassian, an ascetic resident of the region for many years, recognized Kellia as situated between Scetis and Nitria, the author of the Greek *History of the Monks of Egypt*, a visitor to these communities, made no mention at all of Kellia despite relating stories about monks who lived there.[62] This absence of references to Kellia points to how indistinguishable Nitria and Kellia could be to outside visitors. The multiplicity of cells that might be attributed to a single abba, likewise, indicates how fluid movement was both within the northwestern desert and beyond. Palladius's portrayal of Abba Macarius of Alexandria is particularly instructive in this regard. In his description, Palladius mentions that Abba Macarius of Alexandria had four cells: one at Nitria, one at Kellia, one at Scetis, and one in Libya.[63] Palladius's summary of Abba Macarius of Alexandria's property holdings indicates that ascetics who had lived in the community (like Palladius) were perhaps more aware of distinctions among the ascetic settlements of Nitria, Kellia, and Scetis (and indeed the Libyan desert further to the west), and that some ascetics moved back and forth from one settlement to another. The interconnected, overlapping relationship of these ascetic regions is heightened in later stories of abbas frequently visiting one another despite injunctions to stay in one's cell. So, for example, Abba Ammoes and Abba Bitimius are depicted in the *Sayings* as traveling from Kellia to Scetis in order to visit Abba Achilles.[64] And, in the Macarian apothegm above, Abba Macarius the Egyptian has made the trip from Scetis in order to visit the brethren at Nitria.[65]

Imagining the gradual building of cells belonging to Abba Macarius of Alexandria also points to the slipperiness of the desert noted above. *This* Abba Macarius lived in Alexandria before entering the desert. While no tradition associates him primarily with Nitria, it is reasonable to assume that this was the first community in which he situated himself, as it is located in closest proximity to Alexandria. After this initial emplacement, he would have moved deeper into the desert, gaining his cells at Kellia and Scetis, until he finally was able to establish himself beyond the "innermost part of the great Desert" in Libya.[66] While this narrative helps make sense of his accretion of landholdings, we should not imagine that Abba Macarius of Alexandria's only movements were westward. Various traditions continue to associate him with Scetis (both the Greek *History of the Monks of Egypt* and Rufinus's later translation) and with Kellia as its priest (Palladius). While the sources may not reflect the actual travels and career of Macarius, the piecemeal garnering of Macarius of Alexandria's cells does highlight the gradual shift further into the desert that not only was imagined in literature but also is shown by later archaeological evidence.

Analysis of the architectural development of one section of Kellia, Qusur al-Izeila, over the course of roughly two hundred years (500–700 C.E.) corroborates the literary image of an ever-shifting ascetic community. While slightly later than the chronological boundaries of this study, evidence from Qusur al-Izeila allows us to imagine the ways in which the northwestern desert may have developed during an earlier period. Around 500 C.E., the site, located in a depression on the north face of a ridge, consisted of only nine buildings, each approximately one hundred twenty meters away from the next. Over the next seventy-five years, the inhabited spaces shifted. There were twenty-six occupied buildings, eight of the previous structures having been abandoned, and the distance between buildings having now been reduced to only ninety meters. Within twenty-five more years, forty more buildings had been added and their degree of separation had once more shrunk (thirty to forty meters). About 625 C.E., Qusur al-Izeila consisted of around one hundred and fifteen structures, with most newer additions being made on the site's southern end, deeper into the desert ridge. The gradual shift most likely occurred because the central portion of the community was so densely populated that no more building in that section seemed possible. But such extensive growth also led to the restoration of older, previously abandoned buildings. At the height of its occupation (around 660 C.E.), Qusur al-Izeila had gained only an additional ten structures, most being constructed on the community's periphery and at a slightly higher elevation. Over the course of the early eighth century, the site seems to have been gradually abandoned, though no exact date can be discerned given the limited extent of excavations.[67]

Qusur al-Izeila's building history indicates a growth pattern that helps us imagine how, near the end of the fourth century, someone like Abba Macarius of Alexandria came to own four cells, each one deeper into the desert than the last. We might imagine that, first, a site was established by a handful of ascetics who placed their cells at some distance from one another. Over time, the site gathered popularity, attracting more and more newcomers eager to live there as well. As the number of inhabitants expanded, the density of buildings likewise grew. Eventually, a climactic moment was reached at which no further building could occur at a given site and additions were forced to establish themselves higher up the ridge, further into the desert, in rougher terrain. Archaeological evidence does not tell us of the level of devotion to asceticism further outlying inhabitants may have had. So, perhaps more established abbas, like Abba Macarius of Alexandria, took it upon themselves to move deeper into the harsh terrain, at least for certain periods. Such a course of development was certainly imagined in the late fifth century, as witnessed in literary portrayals of figures like Abba Amoun who, located in Nitria, suddenly found himself living uncomfortably close to his brethren and thus moved deeper into the desert in search of solitude and more space.

Elusive Utopia

Beyond the practicalities of spatial constraints, the movement of ascetic bodies deeper into the desert had a corollary ideological component. These shifts were also the result of continued attempts and failures to transform the desert into "a heaven-like city" and its ascetic inhabitants into angelic-like beings. The continual slipping away of the "true" desert was reflected in the elusiveness of a paradise on earth. Traditionally, the asceticism of the desert-dwelling abbas has been understood as rooted in God's promise of the desert qua paradise.[68] The paradisiacal possibility of living peaceably with animals, without care for food or shelter, is represented in the above apothegm about Abba Macarius of Egypt meeting two "true" monks in the deep desert. Those two monks embodied the ascetic desire to regain an Adamic pre-Fall body, naked yet impermeable to the elements. But it was not only their bodies that had been altered; it was also the deep desert they inhabited. The desert itself was now a lush island with a watering hole for these monks and their bestial neighbors. The situation offered Abba Macarius the opportunity to experience both the desert and his own body as transformable. But Abba Macarius's response to the incident reflects how elusive such a paradise came to be viewed by later generations; he was not able to give up the world entirely and thus was condemned to the next best thing, weeping in his cell. As Anton Voytenko has noted in his analysis of the *Life of St. Onnophrius* (a life likely composed sometime across the fifth century), there was a motif that competed with the image of the desert turned paradise: "the theme of the escaping and disappearing Paradise, the place which one can touch but not hold on to, where it is possible to enter but impossible to remain."[69] It was just such an almost instantaneously lost paradise that Abba Macarius of Egypt found.

The problem of the possibility of paradise was compounded by how paradise's relationship to heaven was envisioned. Were ascetics to become angels, to return to Adam's pre-Fall state, or both? And, more pressing, was such transformation of materiality, the human body and its terrestrial surroundings, achievable and, if so, desirable? We glimpse traces of ascetic attempts to address these complex issues in the multiple extant versions recounting *an* Abba Macarius (whether "of Alexandria" or "of Egypt" varies across versions) visiting the garden of Jannes and Jambres.[70] These competing memories of a Macarius in the northwestern desert help illustrate the complexity of late ancient views across the fourth and fifth centuries regarding paradise, its relationship to heaven, and the (im)possibility for malleability both of the desert and of the ascetic body. There are five witnesses to such a visit to the garden of Jannes and Jambres: the story from the *Sayings* about two naked men and Abba Macarius discussed above (late fifth century), a reference by Evagrius in his *Talking Back* (late fourth century), a passage by the Palestinian author of the *History of the Monks of Egypt* (written in Greek; late fourth century), the same passage from the *History of the Monks of Egypt* translated into Latin by Rufinus (turn to fifth century), and a version by Palladius in his *Lausiac History* (early fifth century).[71] The narrative from the *Sayings* and the Greek version of the *History of the Monks of Egypt* similarly associate the story with Macarius of Egypt (living at Scetis), while Evagrius, Rufinus, and Palladius attributed the story to Macarius of Alexandria (Rufinus locating him at Scetis, but Palladius primarily identifying him with the community at Kellia).[72] As Samuel Rubenson has rightly noted, the common narrative underlying these variations indicates the fluid nature of the textual tradition. Which Macarius the story was tied to is ultimately less important to discern than the purposes to which the story was put.[73]

All five versions narrate some iteration of an Abba Macarius desiring to see or incidentally encountering a garden established by the long-dead pharaonic magicians Jannes and Jambres. Earlier Egyptian generations had developed a tradition that the two magicians, servants of one of the pharaohs, had gone into the desert to rebuild paradise. The two earliest witnesses are Evagrius, in *Talking Back*, and the author of the Greek *History of the Monks of Egypt*; both texts were written in the last decade of the fourth century. Evagrius makes only fleeting reference to the garden visit, serving primarily as an example of how his own teacher modeled the fight against the demon with a sword.[74] And yet the setting of Macarius of Alexandria's encounter outside the garden of Jannes and Jambres was important enough for Evagrius to include it. Evagrius seems to hint at how fantastical and dangerous Macarius's visit was, for he encountered an especially violent demon near the entrance to the garden. In order to thwart said demon, Macarius skillfully deploys a verse from Scripture—1 Kings 17:45. Through his articulation, Macarius embodies Scripture, such that the sword, spear, and shield of the demon are now pitted against the more powerful Lord's name. We can perhaps surmise a bit more about Evagrius's brief reference, for he situates this story in his discussion of the demons of sadness. Evagrius frames the opportunity to encounter such a vision as dangerous as it risks succumbing to sadness. Evagrius's claims elsewhere that sadness stands in opposition to a monk's ability to experience pure prayer (which, as we will see in the next chapter, was itself an ascetic's greatest weapon against the demons) highlight the inherent danger Evagrius and his audience would have understood.[75] That is, Evagrius depicts attempting to visit Jannes and Jambres, as did Macarius, or even encountering the sword-wielding demon at all as an event that could disarm an ascetic against demonic attackers, putting him in grave danger.

The Greek *History of the Monks of Egypt*, written around 395 C.E. by a Palestianian visitor, likewise narrates a visit to the garden of Jannes and Jambres, though this time the figure making the journey is Abba Macarius of Egypt.[76] The story here is much more intricate and extended than that of the Evagrian witness. Wandering in search of the garden for three weeks until he had run out of food and was failing, Macarius is suddenly transported to the garden by an angel. While demons guarding the entrance initially blockade him, through prayer Abba Macarius is allowed to enter. (Prayer defeated the demon, just as in Evagrius's version.) Inside this paradise (the Greek word here is *paradeisos*, meaning "paradise" or "garden" more generally), Macarius finds three large springs gushing forth, trees bearing "every type of fruit under heaven," and two holy men. When the holy men see him, they "rejoiced exceedingly," and proceed to wash his feet and feed him luscious fruits. Conversing about the luxury of the garden, they deem that "it is good for all monks to be this way."[77] Despite this assertion, the holy men disagree with Macarius about the feasibility of actually returning to the garden with other monks. They warn Macarius, "The desert is great, and vast and numerous are the demons throughout the desert, leading astray and destroying monks, so that so many others wishing to come have been destroyed."[78] Undeterred, Abba Macarius heads home, carrying fruits as proof of the paradise's existence. But when he arrives, the fathers do not wish to join him, fearing that, enjoying the earthly garden, they might forfeit future pleasures when they finally enter God's presence. The risk of exchanging earthly delight for heavenly reward was too high, and even Abba Macarius decides not to return.

Throughout the story, the anonymous author of the *History of the Monks of Egypt* consistently uses the Greek word *paradeisos* to describe the garden. The term *paradeisos* is repeated on three other occasions in the *History of the Monks of Egypt* as a whole, and only in one instance, where it appears in the plural to describe the walled confines of the monastery of Isidore, does it clearly mean an everyday garden.[79] Elsewhere, in the singular (as is the case here), *paradeisos* ambivalently means "garden" while simultaneously seeming to refer to a place unusual to the Egyptian landscape, perhaps even the Garden of Eden. This dual referentiality is explicit, for the author tells us that the brothers *intentionally* built their *paradeisos* as a "copy of the true Paradise."[80] And a pretty successful copy it was, as Macarius encounters a thriving, lush garden several centuries after its original creation. But the author also hints that the garden was only a physical manifestation of *a* paradise, one distinct from the heavens that monks would experience at the end of their earthly life.

Elsewhere in the *History of the Monks of Egypt*, the author relates two brief vignettes about Abba Patermuthius that clarify the distinctions he holds between paradise and heaven. In the first story, Abba Patermuthius describes how he was "taken up in a vision into the heavens and saw all the good things that await true monks."[81] Here the heavens are a space accessible only through mystical vision and only to "true monks." By contrast, the latter narrative finds Patermuthius visiting paradise "in the flesh."[82] Like Macarius's garden, this paradise is lush, full of fruit, and inhabited by holy men. Patermuthius, too, brings back a piece of fruit, a fig, as evidence of his visit. While the fate of Macarius's fruit remains unknown, Patermuthius's fig apparently goes uneaten, remaining perfectly ripe and performing healings by its mere scent. So it would seem that our anonymous author knew of a tradition where paradise was a place of materiality that stood in contrast to heaven, a nonterrestrial space. Paradise was a place that could be experienced by enfleshed ascetic bodies, while heaven was only possible to visit through disembodied vision.

While Patermuthius's paradise seems to be a good place, even if not on par with the heavens, Macarius's paradise (and, in particular, his desire to bring other brethren to inhabit it) provoked some anxiety among the fathers. These other brothers neither disbelieve Macarius nor condemn him for his visit. Rather, they argue that they do not need such earthly experiences, as their rewards before God in heaven will be far greater. While Macarius initially believes reproduction of a paradisiacal place on earth was both plausible and desirable, the author's view (represented by Macarius's brethren) is clear: A material paradise, while possible, was neither the goal of nor reward for asceticism. Taken together, these stories from the Greek *History of the Monks of Egypt* express the ambivalence felt among ascetics about whether an earthly paradise in the desert was to be sought out, enjoyed, or perhaps even created at all.

Translating the *History of the Monks of Egypt* into Latin a few years later (probably sometime between 401 and 405 C.E.), Rufinus, himself a former visitor to the desert abbas, corrects the attribution of the Jannes and Jambres narrative: It was not Macarius of Egypt but rather Macarius of Alexandria who had made the journey into the deep desert. As Rufinus explains, Abba Macarius of Alexandria loved the desert "above all others, so that he explored the further and inaccessible desert places."[83] (This love of the desert helps account for his ownership of four different cells.) Rufinus, though abbreviating the story, goes on to largely replicate the version found in the original Greek. He briefly describes the garden as lush, full of good fruits, and inhabited by two brothers. The narrative then quickly turns to Macarius of Alexandria's desire to bring other brothers to the garden. As in the original, the two brothers living there warn him that the desert is full of demons whom most brethren would be unable to bear. Nonetheless, Abba Macarius of Alexandria heads home to try. In Rufinus's translation, when Macarius arrives, his stories excite several of the young monks to return with him. Troubled by this development, the older fathers are only able to dissuade a return voyage by contrasting the pleasures of this earthly garden with those hoped for "in the future age," that is, heaven. Rufinus ends the story abruptly with the younger brethren being convinced to stay. Thus, Rufinus's translation downplays the incident by shortening its telling, while largely retaining the moral of the original Greek. Such an earthly paradise was possible but not desirable. Rather, the proper focus of ascetic attention was on heavenly rewards. Perhaps the most interesting adjustment Rufinus made was his addition of Macarius's initial success in enticing young monks to follow him into the deep desert. This shift in the story subtly pits youthful monks against older fathers, the former escaping great folly only through the wise guidance of the latter. In this way, Rufinus's version amplifies ambivalence not only about the possibility and value of an earthly paradise but also about Macarius of Alexandria's intentions and wisdom, grouping Macarius with the foolish young men and not the wise elders.

Palladius's narration of Abba Macarius of Alexandria's visit to Jannes's and Jambres's garden, written around 420 C.E., seems to be an explicit response to the earlier, more generous readings found in the Greek *History of the Monks of Egypt* and Rufinus's translation. While the *History of the Monks of Egypt* and Rufinus questioned the value of an earthly paradise in the desert, they offered their response as a gentle corrective. By contrast, Palladius utterly and harshly forsakes any type of earthly paradise. Palladius uses not *paradeisos*, but rather *kēpotaphion*, meaning garden-tomb, to describe the place. The image of a garden-tomb evokes the death and desolation that Palladius associates with this portion of the desert. He enhances this unfavorable portrayal throughout his Macarian narrative, emphasizing that Jannes and Jambres are pharaonic magicians, a negatively connoted profession under an ungodly ruler. Further, while in the *History of the Monks of Egypt* an angel assists in Macarius's arrival at the garden, Palladius implies that the garden is not a place that the Divine would wish Macarius to reach. In Palladius, the garden is no longer the home of holy men but rather of demons. And it is these demons whom Abba Macarius converses with, even striking a deal with them to enter. Whereas other versions depict Macarius as enacting prayer to enter, here there is no prayer. By having Macarius seek admittance through conversation with demons rather than through prayerful appeal to God, Palladius underscores that it is *not* God but Macarius's own curiosity that has led him to the garden. Perhaps most telling is Palladius's portrayal of the garden's interior. A place lacking any lushness, it contains only rusting metal, desiccated pomegranates, and, of course, demons. Thus, Jannes's and Jambres's garden physically manifests its temporality, its materiality—it has succumbed to decay and ruin.

Palladius's desire to downplay the importance of this garden visit is also evidenced in the structuring of his narrative. Only half of his story actually takes place on the way to or in the garden. The entire second half is devoted solely to the miraculous events that occur when Macarius of Alexandria attempts to return home. Lost for twenty days, he runs out of supplies and is comforted by a maiden carrying water. Some days later, a she-buffalo adopts Macarius, amazingly rejecting her own calf in order to suckle Macarius all the way back to his cell. This strange second portion to Palladius's Macarian visit deploys literary conventions that used animal-ascetic relationships as examples of the possibility of a "peaceable kingdom" in which wild animals and humanity might happily coexist.[84] In considering the ascetic desire to regain paradise, Tim Vivian argues that the myriad examples of wild beasts and ascetics living alongside one another and, on occasion, assisting one another (as our she-buffalo does Macarius) points toward the possibility of or at least the desire for the restoration of paradise. Playing on this expectation, Palladius shapes the latter half of the Macarian garden narrative to serve as a contrast to the *supposed* paradise of Jannes and Jambres. Palladius shifts the reader's attention away from the material, temporal paradise on earth, doomed to perish, and redirects it toward the promise of an immaterial, eternal paradise evidenced in the miracle of a she-buffalo assisting in Macarius's survival. Palladius's rendering of Abba Macarius of Alexandria's visit to the garden stands in stark distinction to earlier portrayals, emphatically asserting that there is no earthly paradise to seek in the desert.

Palladius's alternate interpretation makes sense of his choice to avoid using the term *paradeisos* to describe Jannes's and Jambres's garden, for Palladius elsewhere elides paradise and heaven. Paradise is a set-apart space of significance, one that does not have a material component. This elision of concepts emerges across several stories in his *Lausiac History*.[85] So, for example, Palladius describes the experience of hearing divine psalmody sung from each monk's cell as allowing one to "imagine one is high above in Paradise."[86] That is, the desert can be *like* paradise without being divinized space. Similarly, he has Abba Isidore contrast the earthly, "irrational" food he must now eat (such as the fruits Abba Macarius brought back to his brethren in the *History of the Monks of Egypt*'s version) with his comestible-less future existence "in a Paradise of pleasure."[87] Elsewhere, he asserts that paradise is the place of "saved souls,"[88] where one stands before God.[89] Most explicitly, in a saying conveyed by Abba Cronius, Abba Antony is said to have prayed to see "the place of the just and the sinners."[90] In answer to his request, Antony witnesses a black giant with "hands stretching out to Heaven."[91] A voice explains the strange image to Antony, saying that the souls who slip by the giant fly into paradise and are saved. In this instance, Palladius explicitly uses paradise and heaven interchangeably to refer to the same place.[92] The cumulative force of Palladius's *Lausiac History* asserts paradise/heaven as a positively valenced, immaterial place distinct from all that is earthly. That the desert could not be paradise had been confirmed two decades earlier by Theophilus's assault.

And yet, alongside Palladius's negative portrayal, a tradition that was more ambivalent about this garden would persist in the late fifth-century *Sayings*. The apothegm of Macarius of Egypt's discovery of two naked holy men deep in the desert resonates productively with these other Macarian visits to a paradisiacal garden. As we saw above, Macarius the Egyptian would be remembered as regaling his brothers with stories of the two naked, paradisiacal monks—the true monks—he had found in the deep desert. Most scholars see this saying as yet another version of Macarius's visit to the garden of Jannes and Jambres, although reference to the magicians is absent. There remained a thread in the ascetic tradition that said visits to such an earthly place had once been possible. The question that remained, though, circled around whether such a visit was profitable. As with all the other versions of this story, the moral remains that such a lifestyle, while perhaps the ideal sought after, is impossible for even the holiest among the abbas, as signified by Macarius's own inability to join the two "true" monks. Macarius, as revered as he was, was still not a true monk, for he could not live as these two did but could only anticipate his future transformation. The paradisiacal desert that Macarius glimpsed had disappeared.

These versions of a Macarian visit to Jannes's and Jambres's garden taken together betray the multiple and often competing expectations regarding terrestrial and somatic malleability that were associated with desert asceticism across the fourth and fifth centuries. Each version ultimately deemed the garden *not* a place for ascetics but in different ways and for different reasons. For Evagrius, the locus was more a site of danger than a place of possibility. The original Greek *History of the Monks of Egypt* and Rufinus's translation both attest to a tension about the plausibility of an earthly paradise. While the fathers eventually convinced Macarius that he should not return, nor should other brethren go, the narratives do not deny outright the possibility of such an earthly paradise. Both versions depict the garden as lush and alive, its vivaciousness and luxury being what makes it a compelling ascetic retreat. Perhaps most important, it is a place in which holy men can and *do* live. But while the men living in Jannes's and Jambres's garden might have been holy men, they were not to be emulated. Rather, their choice to inhabit the garden was framed as placing their future rewards before God at risk. In both versions, the story seems, in fact, to be addressing and attempting to correct those who *do* desire terrestrial and somatic transformation in this life. Its authors concede that there might be lush gardens deep in the desert and that holy men might live there, but the existence of such things does not mean such locales house properly oriented asceticism. The author of the *History of the Monks of Egypt* and Rufinus are quite clear that succumbing to such an earthly orientation could mean ascetic failure.

In sharp contrast to the *History of the Monks of Egypt*'s and Rufinus's softer corrections, Palladius, writing several decades later, would no longer concede that any earthly paradise was possible, let alone desirable. For Palladius, the garden of Jannes and Jambres (and we can imagine all such similar places) can only represent the inherent decay to which all earthly things, both terrestrial and somatic, succumb. The garden, no longer tempting, merely stands as the example par excellence of ruin, only habitable for demons. The desert is dead. His moral, firmer than his predecessors', is to place one's hope on heavenly and not earthly things. Given that there clearly was an alternate position that argued for an earthly paradise and somatic stability at resurrection, Palladius's harsher pronouncement only makes sense when one situates his retelling within his continued post-Origenist controversy struggles. Opponents such as Jerome, Epiphanius of Salamis, and probably also Theophilus of Alexandria had articulated paradise as a real, physical place, entailing resurrection of a body that remained physical and even gendered.[93] Moreover, they had successfully achieved condemnation of some of Palladius's mentors and peers for articulating an alternate salvific vision. While Rufinus and the Palestinian monks from his monastery who likely stand behind the authorship of the *History of the Monks of Egypt* wrote in a moment when gentle correction of such overly materialistic views of the desert and the body were still possible, as we will see in later chapters, such was not the case by the time of Palladius's writing. As the example from the *Sayings* indicates, idealizing somatic and terrestrial transformation remained palatable for some of the later generations only if it was framed as no longer unattainable.

Conclusion

A later recension of Palladius's *Lausiac History* expands on the narrative of Abba Macarius's garden visit. While its author/editor used multiple words, including *paradeisos*, to refer to the garden, the place remains one of ruin, not of paradisiacal possibility. Here, Abba Macarius's explicit purpose for approaching and entering the garden is not to see the place; rather, it is rooted in his desire to encounter demons, which he knew he would find in abundance there. The version includes lengthier demonic complaints against Macarius's presence and the division of space. The demons whine,

> "What do you want, Macarius, tempter among monks? Why did you come to us? We did not harm any of the monks, did we? *Over there* you have what belongs to you and your kind, the desert, from which you chased our kin. We want nothing to do with you. Why do you enter our places? As an anchorite, be satisfied with the desert. This place, its builders allotted to us. You cannot stay here. Why are you seeking to enter where no living human has entered since our brothers, who built this, were buried by us?" And the many demons were agitated and wailed. He said to them, "Let me enter only and observe, then I will leave."[94]

Their extensive protests attest to how desert inhabitation during the so-called Golden Age of asceticism was reimagined by later Christians. For at least the brief time during which Abba Macarius of Alexandria lived, the desert could be portrayed as overtaken by ascetics and the demons as utterly defeated. The desert, now belonging to Macarius and his brethren, was *over there*. It had been ceded to them by fleeing demons. But as the demons' demand ("as an anchorite, be satisfied with the desert") makes clear, there was always a further desert periphery to explore. Even if Macarius of Alexandria had been willing to leave the rotten garden to demonic ownership, his entrance and observation still symbolized the dominance he and his brethren had achieved over the desert; they could enter even those places that had not been touched by a "living human" since their foundation.

This chapter began with a later imagining of Macarius of Egypt's settling in Scetis, the demons expressing angst about his presence, the prayer lashings it promised, and the demons' inevitable eviction. The longer retelling of Abba Macarius of Alexandria's encounter with demons at the garden of Jannes and Jambres indicates that demonic fears regarding ascetic entrance into the desert were well-founded. These two stories about the Macarii both witness to later imaginings of the Golden Age of asceticism in the desert. This distinct historical moment was envisioned as beginning with the demons articulating their fears: They would be wounded by ascetic prayers, they would be violently displaced from their home, and *their* desert would be transformed into a "heaven-like city." Several years later, another Macarius could be found standing outside a dilapidated funerary garden located deep in the desert, his presence there symbolizing ascetic appropriation of the desert as complete. No longer did the demons attempt to hurt the monks. They only wished to avoid them and live in the last bastion of desert available to them, Jannes's and Jambres's decrepit faux paradise. These later visions of a ruined desert would have resonated powerfully in the aftermath of the first Origenist controversy. As we shall see in Chapter 5, Theophilus's violent incursion into Nitria led some to view the entire desert's promise as permanently ruined. Every version of the Macarius garden story gathered after Theophilus's attack on the Nitrian monks at the close of the fourth century reflects ambivalence not only about the possibility of a paradisiacal desert but also about the dangers of engaging the Jannes and Jambres tradition at all. For, in his *Sixteenth Festal Letter*, Theophilus would assert that Origen, and presumably all those who used his writings, were "supporters" of Jannes and Jambres against Moses.[95] But violence permeated the ascetic desert long before Theophilus's arrival as imaged in the battles between monks and demons. Even if the epigraph to this chapter is a later reimagining, as we shall see in the next chapter prayer (and psalmody) were imagined as an ascetic weapon in the unending war for the desert already in the fourth century.

Chapter 2

Psalmody and Prayer as Ascetic Weapons

> As for the one who has been recently admitted to the radiant
> assembly of the monks . . . when he has left his cell in the late
> evening hours, let him not cry out with fear and leap back in fright,
> as if demons were running after him; rather, with knees bent in the
> spot where he takes fright, let him make a prayer . . . and when you
> get up, encourage and exhort your heart with the psalm verse.
> —Evagrius, *To Eulogios* 23

In his treatise to a novice monk named Eulogios, Evagrius offers the preceding advice about how to handle the fear of demons that can overcome a monk standing in the desert.[1] The new monk is portrayed as having recently joined a community, the members of which are notably depicted as "radiant." In stark contrast to these luminescent monks, the novice suddenly finds himself standing in darkness. The monk, not yet a pillar of light, is quickly consumed by fear. Evagrius asserts that the appropriate response is immediate prayer, followed by psalmody. The particular psalm he recommends is Psalm 90:5–6 [Ps. 91:5–6]: "You shall not fear the terror that comes by night, nor the arrow that flies by day, nor a thing that moves in the darkness, nor a chance event, or the noonday demon."[2] Strengthened through prayer and armed with this psalm, the recent convert was steeled against any dangers, especially those of the demons.

Here, the new monk is the one found to be filled with fear, worrying that demons chase him and are about to do him harm. By contrast, the quotation from the *Life of Macarius the Egyptian* that began the last chapter expressed the opposite situation: The demons feared the monks. In particular, the demons were afraid of the prayer flagellations that the monks would dole out, exclaiming, "They will chase us away through the lash of their prayers."[3] The demons know that the onslaught of monastic prayer would harm them, casting them from their desert home. Evagrius's advice supports the expectation that psalmody and prayer would repel demonic danger. In this way, psalmody and prayer were envisioned as weapons to be used for divinely sanctioned violence. Juxtaposed, the two passages reflect the battle ascetics and demons waged in the desert. As discussed in Chapter 1, the battle was, among other things, one for control of the power and possibility of the desert.

This chapter explores how the monastic tradition deployed psalmody and prayer as weapons against the demons. I begin by considering where and how monks prayed, especially attending to the role of the cross in relation to prayer. Having set the stage, the next section unpacks the multiple understandings of prayer and psalmody available to ascetics. Given the prominence of angels as models to imitate during prayer and psalmody, I turn to considering angelic bodies and their relationship to monastic bodies. I conclude with a closer examination of the angel-human nexus at prayer, attending to the presence of fire imagery in such portrayals. Liturgical activities, while primarily meant as a mode of achieving closer proximity to or intimacy with the divine, were simultaneously imagined as divinely sanctioned tools of violence that could be used against the demons.

Orienting Ascetic Prayer

Chapter 1 established the desert as the locus in which ascetic-demonic struggles were imagined and lived. As Abba Macarius of Egypt attested, while there were a few individuals capable of living naked to the elements in the desert, most of those who found themselves in the desert required a bit more protection from the sun, wind, and wild beasts. By the time Evagrius wrote advice for his novice monk, the desert was already being filled with ascetic bodies in need of monastic cells. A monk's cell served as some protection from the elements and wild animals that inhabited the desert (scorpions, snakes, hyenas, and the like). But the cell did more than preserve a monk from the everyday realities of the desert; it also served as the means by which an ascetic's entire being might be reoriented toward the divine and away from the demonic. The cell was simultaneously a place of solace and struggle, functioning as the space in which monks focused their energies toward the divine and away from their past lives and related demonic temptations.

Very little is known about the architecture of these earliest cells. The few examples that have been dated prior to the sixth century are very simple in construction. The interior offered a small living space, often with a niche in the eastern wall. The niche allowed a monk to orient himself toward the divine during prayer practices.[4] As more bodies populated the desert and greater access to materials emerged, cell structure in the northwestern desert became more complex, yet orientation toward the east remained central to building practices.

Recently, Darlene Brooks Hedstrom has argued that, given the heavy population of regions like Kellia, an ascetic's cell served as the only place where a monk might achieve the solitude required for engaging God in an otherwise "noisy" desert. She asserts that the cell became an ascetic practitioner's main sacred space.[5] The view that cells (or at least parts of them) were meant to be special, set-aside spaces is confirmed by the directional layout of the entire site of Kellia. As topographical studies of Kellia show, over the course of development almost all cells were built roughly oriented around an east-northeast axis.[6] Thus, not only were psalmody and prayer performed with an eastward orientation within the cell, but also the *entire* structure of the cell faced the east. The choice of an eastern orientation symbolized numerous affiliations with the east: the rising of the sun, the direction of Jerusalem, and a broader inclination to locate paradise and/or heaven in the east. A later apothegm highlights how such prayer orientation was remembered: "It was also said of him [Abba Arsenius] that on Saturday evenings, preparing for the glory of Sunday, he would turn his back on the sun and stretch out his hands in prayer towards the heavens until once again the sun shone on his face. Then he would sit down."[7] While a full discussion of the valence of these affiliations is not possible here, it is worth noting that such an understanding of monastic orientation is in keeping with the monastic desire to transform the desert into a paradisiacal or heavenly space as laid out in Chapter 1.

Prayer and Apotropaic Crosses

Certainly by the era of the more complex sixth-century cells, an oratory or room devoted to prayer tended to be present in monastic habitations. While it is hard to know how common such rooms were in early structures, even when oratories are extant, the presence of similar niches in the eastern walls of other rooms indicate that prayer could and likely did occur in numerous places throughout a cell.[8] The earliest evidence for oratories in cells in the northwestern desert (at Kellia) consists of a main decorative program of crosses in and near prayer niches as well as near doorways.[9] A later oratory often might have multiple crosses depicted throughout the room, but the most ornate examples were always on the eastern wall, into which the niche was carved.[10]

That ascetics troubled to paint crosses in their living structures points toward what these crosses meant for ascetic prayer. Elizabeth Bolman in her study of the crosses has seen multivalent symbolism in their presence, including evocation of Christ's death and the tree of life in paradise.[11] The vegetative imagery surrounding many of the later dated crosses (noted by Bolman) resembles Evagrius's earlier reference to a "cross of life" while describing the experience of escaping the demons of avarice.[12] To overcome some of the demons was to inch closer to the fruits of paradise. Moreover, cross imagery carried more than just resonances with paradise or Christ's death, as Evagrius's description of the analabos, a piece of ascetic attire, indicates: "The *analabos*, which is the form of a cross folded over their shoulders, is a symbol of faith in Christ that upholds the meek (cf. Psalm 146:6 [Ps. 147:6]) and always restrains what hinders them and provides them with an activity without obstacles."[13] Here, Evagrius's description of the symbolism of the analabos as serving to "restrain what hinders them" hints at the apotropaic functions crosses served for early Christian ascetics.

This apotropaic reading of the cross is echoed by remembrances about Amma Syncletica, who urges her fellow ascetics to endure against the enemy by holding to the cross as rightly guiding the ascetic's course.[14] Both in this later case and in the earlier Evagrian explanation of the analabos, the cross serves as a means of protection against demonic onslaught. Evagrius also asserts that "meditation on the cross" helps an ascetic persevere against the demon of acedia.[15] The cross serves as a focalizing tool, and the painted crosses at Kellia referred to above may well have been used for just such purposes. Here, "meditation" should be understood as synonymous with prayer given Evagrius's notion of "pure prayer" (to which we will return). Thus, the protective capacity of the cross should likely always be understood as coupled with prayer, even in cases in which such a connection is not explicit. Envisioning the cross was meant to invite God, Christ, or his angels to battle on one's behalf.

The cross was, in fact, capable of staving off a variety of demons. One of the more unusual descriptions of crosses deflecting demons is Evagrius's portrayal of the anti-reading demons.[16] Such demons tend to attack while an ascetic reads Scripture, cooling the ascetic's head and making his eyelids heavy while also provoking yawns. Evagrius explains that such chilling occurs through contact with the moist, icy body of the demon. Once the ascetic is sleepy enough, the demons are said to make themselves small and touch the inside of the ascetic's mouth in order to induce a yawn. Evagrius shares wisdom he received from Abba Macarius about these demons, asserting that making the sign of the cross over one's mouth to thwart demons from entering one's mouth is an "old and mysterious tradition."[17] At stake throughout his explanation is an underlying concern about the porosity of ascetic bodies, particularly through the mouth. By performing the sign of the cross on one's body, an ascetic was sealed against the risk of demonic penetration.

The cross did not just protect an ascetic from demons but might also be deployed actively against them. Like most late ancient people, ascetics believed demons frequently caused illness.[18] Ascetics were thus often sought out to mark ill bodies with the cross, driving the infecting demon out.[19] According to Evagrius, the cross is also capable of driving demons of fornication out of an ascetic's body.[20] Such advice points to the blurriness between demonic onslaught, which could cause impure thoughts, and illness.

And although there are stories of cured individuals returning to their lives, later fifth-century imaginings of such healings sometimes held darker endings, repentance being coupled with death. So, when Abba Ammonas is presented with a woman pregnant illegitimately (presumably made so through the demons of fornication), he merely marks her belly with the cross and proclaims that she will die soon.[21] More troubling is the case of Paësia, the woman who was a hospice owner turned prostitute near Scetis. Provoking repentance from her, Abba John the Little is said to have led her into the desert, made a little sand pillow for her, and signed it with the cross. Then, saying some prayers, John slept. "Waking in the middle of the night, he saw a shining path reaching from heaven to her, and he saw angels of God bearing away her soul."[22] The story is framed to highlight the intensity of her repentance, but it also makes clear that the neatest resolution to a fornicating woman abiding near the brethren (and therefore putting them at risk) was death. In both these cases, prayers conjoined with signing crosses on the women implicitly marks them not only as repentant and returning to Christ but also as about to die.

Evagrius explicitly describes the cross as a weapon in an ascetic's arsenal. In a lengthy section describing prayer, Evagrius compares ascetics to soldiers: "We see soldiers hanging on their houses the implements of warfare—swords and spears, bucklers and breastplates—to reveal their occupation; as for us,

God gives us arms not made from gold and silver, brass and iron, but rather from goodwill and steadfast faith."[23] Such imagery of an ascetic with an arsenal of arms makes sense if the ascetic self is envisioned as perpetually at war with demons. Evagrius elsewhere allegorizes such weapons. So, in his more esoteric *Gnostic Chapters*, he evokes battle imagery of sword and shield, symbolizing "spiritual word" and "practical knowledge.[24] But for our current purposes, what is most noteworthy is that Evagrius frames the description of ascetics as soldiers with references to the cross. While the passage concludes with the suggestion to mark one's food and drink with the cross prior to consumption to ward off the Devil in a basic evocation of the cross's apotropaic function, the section opens with a discussion of how the coupling of the performance of crossing oneself with prayer prepares the body for the desert. Evagrius advises, "When you exit the door of your cell, make the sign of the cross on your forehead and confess God in your mind. Thus, having taken up arms, then indeed walk along, sealed by the cross with your heart's confession. When you return again to your cell, make many and frequent offerings to the Lord."[25] As with the epigraph that began this chapter, the scenario involves the dangers inherent in stepping outside one's cell. The implicit backdrop to both pieces of wisdom is that the desert beyond one's cell is a space fraught with danger from demons. The mark of the cross and a mind focused on God are explicitly described by Evagrius as the ascetic's weapons.

A final example from Evagrius highlights how intertwined the cross and prayer were in the struggle against demons. Evagrius relays a story told by Bishop Epiphanius, which is received through a chain of transmission.[26] Apparently, the son of a certain widow was possessed by a Pythian demon.[27] The widow, understandably distraught, is described thus: "When his mother was rendered humble by her grief, thanksgiving cooled the passion that had hung her soul from the cross, and the demon was cast from the child through her prayers."[28] The story goes on to flesh out the details of this brief précis. It concludes with the mother "weeping bitterly and beseeching Christ, and making the sign of the cross" such that "the demon fled swiftly from the child before so many lashes of the whip." The story opens and closes with the coupling of prayer with cross imagery. At the start, it seems to be her own soul that is crucified, while by the end it is the performative ritual of making the sign of the cross that helps to dispatch the demon from her child. Each time, the cross appears within a larger matrix of prayer framed as a mixture of humility and thanksgiving. But while her prayers are humble and full of gratitude, they also are portrayed with a decidedly violent edge. As in the vignette from the *Life of Macarius the Egyptian* that began Chapter 1, prayer is envisioned as a whip that might be used to lash a demon. In both instances, as in many of the examples offered above, signing the cross (over oneself or another) is one ritual component of the larger praxis of prayer. It is not only the cross that is weaponized but also prayer itself.

Defining Prayer

Given the centrality of prayer to ascetic life and the violent connotations it might convey, it is worth pausing to explore what precisely ascetics understood prayer to be. Although prayer is mentioned frequently in many ascetic sources, most references either occur in passing while the text focuses on another issue or theorize about how best to prepare mentally for prayer. The ascetic inclination for prayer was rooted in early Christian attempts to interpret and to put into practice the injunction of 1 Thessalonians 5:17: "Pray without ceasing." Although all sources tend to be unified in viewing the passage as requisite to ascetic practice, interpretations of how best to embody this command were many. Questions arose as to whether one should do manual labor while simultaneously praying or whether prayer precluded any work, resulting in wandering and begging lifestyles.[29] Even among non-nomadic ascetics, a variety of opinions about how best to perform prayer coexisted.

That at least one set evening hour for psalmody may have existed in the fourth century is supported by Palladius's description of the ninth-hour psalmody that issued from each individual cell.[30] And if one takes seriously Cassian's witness, as scholars such as Robert Taft, Luke Dysinger, and others have, then the oldest practice among desert ascetics probably entailed two occasions for prayer, one just before dawn and one at dusk (Palladius's ninth-hour psalmody).[31] Such prayer may have involved recitation of twelve psalms, as seems to have been Macarius's habit when walking in a tunnel he dug from his cell to a cave and back.[32] Cassian, in his recollections of his time in Egypt, claims he had learned a tradition of twelve psalms recited twice daily at the time of prayer.[33] Palladius implies that sometimes the monk only recited a single psalm but did so twelve times, as Antony did when he attempted to test Paul.[34]

The later *Sayings of the Desert Fathers* would codify this ambiguity, even while retrojecting a more structured model of prayer. In an apothegm attributed to Abba Poemen, he encourages a brother to maintain specific prayer hours *and* to pray whenever not working.[35] References like Poemen's to specific hours of prayer has led some to see a structured rule of prayer.[36] But as should be clear, Poemen was remembered not as limiting prayer to specific times but rather as making clear that prayer and work were separate activities. A "rule of prayer" is perhaps also implied in the later saying attributed to Abba Serapion, but his description conveys more about how such a practice was organized rather than how frequently it was enacted. Attempting to convert a sinful woman, Serapion utters prayers, psalms, scriptural passages, and then more prayers.[37] Later monks also retained the prescribed number—twelve—of psalms and prayers. Thus, the anonymous abba of Rome is described as reciting twelve psalms during the day and another twelve at night, all while practicing the "rule of prayer."[38] Likewise, when Abba Macarius visits two siblings, they together recite twelve psalms, five by each sibling followed by an alleluia, and a few from memory by Macarius.[39] Thus, we see the later *Sayings* retaining the twice daily prayer praxes described by Palladius and Cassian, even as it retrojects the more structured concept of a "rule of prayer" into the past.

While our fourth-century examples and late fifth-century recollections indicate that twelve seemed to be the set number, they all also witness to the blurred relationship between psalmody and prayer. In fact, they convey far more information about psalmody praxis than they do about prayer itself. Such is not surprising when we realize that psalmody had become for many the prayer practice par excellence during the course of the fourth century.[40] In fact, psalmody often functioned largely as a subset of prayer or served as one mode of praying. Even for Evagrius, who clearly distinguishes the activities of prayer and psalmody by juxtaposing their uniform and multiform meanings, respectively, there remains some ambiguity.[41] So, for example, Evagrius suggests as a short prayer to God that an ascetic utter a psalm verse, Psalm 16:13 [Ps. 17:13]. He writes, "To the Lord concerning the expectation that demons are about to come upon us at night: Rise up, Lord, and prevent them, and cast them down. Deliver my soul from the ungodly, your sword from the enemies of your hand."[42] Praying this verse, an ascetic invokes the Lord's violence through rearticulation of a portion of a psalm, essentially blurring the performance of prayer and psalmody. And as the apothegms cited above make clear, not all ascetics were as thorough in delineating the acts of psalmody from prayer as was Evagrius. Thus, some explanation of psalmody itself is essential to any discussion of prayer more broadly.

Since the mid-1980s, several scholars have noted the invaluable witness of Athanasius's *Letter to Marcellinus* for understanding how psalmody was being taught and understood by late ancient Christians—or, at least, by many of the most educated ones. Athanasius, writing to a certain Marcellinus, describes the wisdom regarding the Psalter he had gained from an "old friend," presumably an abba. The letter goes on to describe how the Psalter contains the entirety of the Bible within it, how it includes verses for every situation, how it ought to be sung, and the ways in which its words serve as a mirror for both reciter and hearer alike. Paul Kolbet argues that Athanasius deployed the Psalter as a Christian version of the Hellenistic philosophical practice of undertaking "spiritual exercises to conform the self to a certain ideal,"[43] in this case the Psalter serving as a means of appropriating Christ's transformed body to reform one's own soul.

Athanasius certainly understood the Psalter as able to transform the self, and Derek Krueger has noted more precisely that the goal of such Psalter use was the construction of a common Christian liturgical identity. Specifically, in the ascetic context, he notes that "the monk became Scripture's mouthpiece, and the Psalms scripted the monk's interior self-reflection and outward self-presentation."[44] Recently, Georgia Frank has laid out *how* Athanasius imagined Marcellinus might enact such transformation. Drawing on rhetorical education models, she shows that Athanasius's letter was meant as a blueprint by which Marcellinus might build a memory palace. Placing various psalms throughout the structure, he would thus be able to quickly move through this imaginary space to extract the needed psalm for a particular emotional experience. Pushing further on scholarship that sees Athanasius as articulating a recreation of the self, Frank claims that the enactment of this memory praxis not only incorporated the Psalter into Marcellinus's body (mind) but also allowed him simultaneously to become the Psalter itself.[45] In this way, the Psalter served as a means of divinizing its speaker, at least inasmuch as the Psalter itself was considered divinely inspired Scripture.

Further, the fact that Athanasius frames the Psalter as a garden helps us understand how the Psalter functioned for Athanasius as a way of accessing the divine. As Frank and others have noted, the image of the Psalter as a garden begins and ends this rich letter. Near the outset of his description, Athanasius distinguishes the Psalter from the rest of the books of the Bible: While every book is like a garden, only the Psalter contains a variety of fruits. As he concludes his advice to Marcellinus, Athanasius once more evokes garden imagery, encouraging Marcellinus to select whichever "fruits" of the Psalter will address his needs. It is helpful to note here that the entire discussion of the Psalter is framed by precisely the sort of vegetative imagery that was incorporated into the later painted crosses at Kellia. Equally noteworthy is that Athanasius's word choice at both ends of the letter is *paradeisos*. As his further explanation makes clear, his intention is to describe a "garden" full of fruits. However, the language of *paradeisos*, as discussed in Chapter 1, would also have resonated with images of paradise and/or heaven. Moreover, the popularity that Athanasius's description soon held among ascetics, combined with his intimate acquaintance with several abbas of the desert, makes it possible that a similar systematic approach to the Psalter (if not this system itself) was known by our ascetics. An apothegm preserved in the *Sayings* echoes such vegetative imagery, asserting that the ascetic who cultivates *hēsychia* (stillness) will internally grow green and lush.[46] Certainly, having moved into the desert with paradisiacal longing, ascetics would have noted the extra resonance that Athanasius's word choice evoked. Their recitation of the "garden" of Psalter verses to thwart demons and invite God and his angels was meant to perform the conversion of the desert or the monk himself into a paradisiacal space.

Beyond specific references to psalmody, more general injunctions to frequent prayer also appear in our sources. Evagrius suggests that prayers best thwarted demonic temptation when they were short and frequent.[47] Perhaps with similar concerns in mind, John the Little is later remembered as encouraging frequency in prayer for ascetic success.[48] But even when psalmody proper is not mentioned, brief evocations of psalm verses might be recommended, as Evagrius's mentor, Macarius the Egyptian, would be imagined a century later as having suggested. In the *Sayings*, Macarius states, "There is no need to speak at great lengths. It is enough to stretch out one's hands and say, 'Lord, as you will and as you know, have mercy on me.'"[49] Here, Psalm 40:5 [Ps. 41:5] is offered as an appropriate prayer. Macarius goes on to say that "if the warfare grows pressing," an ascetic can respond with recitation of another psalm verse, Psalm 93:18 [Ps. 94:18]. The violence imagined in such warfare is made more visible when one recontextualizes this latter verse in the psalm from which it is drawn: Psalm 93 [Ps. 94] begins by seeking the violence of a vengeful God. Such short, frequent prayers served as either the first examples of or precursors to a more structured praxis of monologic prayers, in which a single word or short phrase was recited repetitiously. Certainly, by the sixth or seventh century, a particular form of such monologic prayer, known as the Jesus Prayer, is attested in Kellia, as well as outside Egypt in regions such as Gaza.[50]

It is within this context of brief prayer that the short scriptural snippets Evagrius recommends in his *Talking Back* are best understood. Evagrius's text likely functioned as an extension of his mentor Macarius's practice, memory of which is retained in the saying above. In the text, Evagrius suggests specific scriptural passages for countering particular demons, beseeching God, and self-policing.[51] As I noted in the discussion of demons being lashed by prayers, prayer was viewed as a weapon, if not *the* weapon, in an ascetic's arsenal and so Evagrius's *Talking Back* offers a handy how-to guide to a variety of weaponizable prayers. That such a violent understanding of antirrhetic prayer was not incidental to Evagrius's view of ascesis is confirmed by setting even the particular antirrhetic prayers addressed to God within the larger context of petitions for God to punish the demons elsewhere in Evagrius's writing. For example, while describing the proper way to beseech God, Evagrius speaks of "wielding the staff of supplication to God against" the demons such that they might "instantly be driven far away, invisibly and secretly flogged by the power of God."[52] Thus, Evagrius images God as the great demon flogger.

As several scholars note, Evagrius, like many others of his time, describes prayer as a general category that includes psalmody. However, he is unique for defining a type of prayer he calls "pure prayer.[53] In several of his writings, Evagrius expresses his proclivity for pure prayer as the ultimate goal of ascetic prayer practice even as he acknowledges that such prayer is incredibly rare and that most daily prayer falls along more mundane lines. An article by Columba Stewart remains the best introduction to this aspect of Evagrius's thought. Stewart builds his argument on three Evagrian texts that he argues are a "trilogy on the psychodynamics and theology of prayer": *On Thoughts, Reflections*, and *On Prayer*.[54] At the outset of his *On Prayer*, Evagrius states that "prayer is a communion of the mind with God."[55] He then queries what state of mind is needed for such communion with the divine, using Exodus 3 as a biblical model on which to frame his view: "If Moses, when he tried to approach the earthly burning bush, was held back until he removed the sandals from his feet, how can you, who wish to see and commune with the one who is beyond all representation and sense perception, not free yourself from every mental representation tied to the passions?"[56] Using this image of Moses, Evagrius thus sets out to describe pure prayer as imageless, even as he resorts to biblical imagery. As Stewart notes, Evagrius's writings express "a tension fundamental to his own life of prayer, that between a theology of 'imageless' prayer and the incarnational dimensions of a religion based on sacred texts."[57] It is precisely such a negotiation between sacred text and pure prayer that is present in Evagrius's deployment of Exodus 3. Evagrius thus situates himself within an exegetical tradition of interpreting Moses's sandals as representative of materiality that had already been established by his mentor Gregory of Nyssa in his *Life of Moses*.[58] In this way, Evagrius develops his noetic view of prayer, placing the body in service of the mind's true function.

Stewart's argument further unpacks two major images in Evagrius's rendering of pure prayer: the experience of light and of "the place of God."[59] Evagrius, in more and less specific ways, depicts engagement with or knowledge of the divine as an experience of light in many of his writings, especially in his scholia on the psalms.[60] Evagrius visited "holy John, the seer of Thebes," to ask John's opinion about his experiences of light during prayer.[61] When Evagrius was more descriptive of the light, he tended to describe it as "sapphire,"[62] interpreting a Septuagint version of Exodus 24:10–11. Stewart asserts that more general mentions of light in Evagrius's writings ought to be read through this more detailed description of the "sapphire-blue" light Moses and the elders experienced on Mt. Sinai. The centrality of Exodus 24 for Evagrius's understanding of prayer is also evidenced in the presence of "the place of God" in this passage.[63] As Mt. Sinai had already been established as "wilderness" in Exodus 19, it is not a great stretch to imagine that Evagrius's own inhabitation of the Egyptian desert was meant to resonate with Sinai's wilderness. While the desert was not the true "place of God," it was a physical locale in which the "place of God" might be noetically glimpsed during pure prayer.

For Evagrius, pure prayer was sublime. But such sublimity did not preclude violent imagery. More explicitly, Evagrius claims that "the one who has not attained pure prayer has no weapon for battle."[64] Thus, he uses the imagery of taking captives to describe how "the radiance of prayers" might envelop the lower thoughts.[65] Moreover, Stewart notes that "such experiences [of light] were by no means exceptional either then or later, and were evidently the cause of some consternation among Egyptian monks."[66] For while Evagrius left the richest account of such higher forms of prayer, he is not the only witness to such praxis among the ascetics. A certain Abba Anouph describes the experience of prayer as triggering the "light of my understanding."[67] Thus, perpetual light in his eyes allows Anouph to see "tens of thousands of angels standing before God," "choirs of the just," "companies of martyrs," and "armies of monks."[68] He also sees "Satan given over to the fire."[69] In this case, the tradition around Anouph delineates between the privilege of sensing divine light (*phōs*) and justified punishment by divine fire (*pyr*). Even as he delineates these categories, Anouph makes clear that both are part of the experience or vision offered by such transcendent prayer.

Not all early ascetics so carefully distinguished divine light from divine fire, however. Cassian, who had been a student of Evagrius, also describes a higher form of prayer practice in his *Conferences* 9 and 10. But whereas Evagrius uses light imagery from Exodus 24, Cassian uses fire imagery to describe such higher prayer, likely evoking Moses's earlier theophanic experience at the burning bush in Exodus 3. Cassian seems to evoke Exodus 24 in *Conferences* 10 when he refers to the appearance of Jesus to Moses.[70] But echoes of Exodus 3 emerge when the reference is read in conjunction with a section from *Conferences* 12. While in this passage the focus is no longer on prayer but rather on chastity, Cassian evokes Moses and the burning bush to describe how he understands the well-trained ascetic body, precisely the type of body needed to properly pray.[71] He prescribes limited intake of liquid, just as his teacher Evagrius is purported to have taught,[72] in order to help maintain bodily control. He assures his readers that curbing bodily hydration, as in "that wonderful vision of Moses," will ignite "a cold flame and cause moisture without any fiery heat so that the bush of our flesh may not burn, surrounded as it is with a harmless fire."[73] Here, Cassian describes a type of divine fire that encompasses but does not destroy the rightly managed ascetic body, explicitly equating such a body with Moses's theophanic bush. Cassian continues on to intertextually link Exodus 3 to the youths in the fiery furnace (Dan. 3:27) and Isaiah 43:2 ("When you walk through fire you shall not burn, and the flames shall not set you afire"). In particular, the Isaiah passage itself emerges from a larger context within which God recalls using his wrath and burning with fire disobedient Israel (Isa. 42:25) before ultimately forgiving and promising Israel the ability to walk through fire untouched. While the two types of divine fire are not explicitly distinguished here, it is not difficult to understand how Cassian, who did believe in two types of fire, drew this idea from Isaiah.

Stewart argues that the different exegetical underpinnings of Evagrius and Cassian point to alternative experiences of true prayer, Cassian drawing on fire imagery because of his "more affective and ecstatic" view of prayer.[74] It is true that for Cassian pure prayer occurred when "the mind is inflamed and set on fire and incited to pure and fervent prayers."[75] While he also refers to "heavenly light,"[76] it is primarily the image of fiery prayer that permeates his portrayal. Such prayer is "ardent" and likened to an "incomprehensible and all-devouring flame."[77] As in our earlier discussions, the boundaries between prayer and psalmody might be quite fluid. Thus, Cassian notes that the singing of a psalm verse might induce such "an occasion of ardent prayer."[78] Whereas Evagrius's emphasis on "light" language is more easily situated in philosophical discussions about the relationship between the body and mind, and, in particular, the mind's inherent light, Cassian's more emotive approach represents desert threads that understood the body as more transformable, or at least the soul as more capable of briefly transcending the body. That is, Cassian's emphasis on *ekstasis* as crucial to prayer offered a greater possibility of reaching beyond the body, however fleeting an experience that might be. But we should not press too heavily on such distinctions, for, as we shall see below, Evagrius also tended to distinguish between two types of fire. Despite the difference in terminology, as even Stewart notes, both Evagrius's and Cassian's views of prayer represent desert traditions present in the fourth century.[79] And as emerges from this comparison of Evagrius and Cassian, true prayer (be it "pure" or "fiery") hinged on understandings of human bodies. In turn, the malleability of an ascetic's human body was often refracted through an understanding of angelic embodiment, as ascetics sought to imitate the angels.

Angelic Bodies at Prayer

Understandings of materiality (in particular the body) and its role in divine-human relations were central to ascetic prayer practices. In the previous chapter, we saw demons and ascetics struggling for control of the desert; control of human bodies was essential to this conflict over wilderness inhabitation. And in this chapter, we have seen Evagrius's wisdom about the dangers of demons manipulating ascetic bodies, as in the example of a demon touching the interior of one's mouth and inciting a yawn. Underlying such anxieties was a view of human bodies as porous and malleable—and maybe even transformable. The porosity of human flesh opened it up to the risk of demonic temptation either being transformed into a more demonic form or remaining human but deeply sinful and bound for hell. But the risk of porosity also signified great possibility: The human body might engage angelic beings and be elevated in bodily status or at least be prepared for postmortem heavenly transformation. That is, angels could shape one's present or future body.

In the Bible, angels are imagined as fearsome beings. As any careful perusal of biblical descriptions makes evident, angels were multi-eyed, multi-winged, or even multi-headed creatures willing to enact God's wrath against humanity. Such violence and the potential for destruction are often framed with fire imagery. When Adam and Eve are exiled from paradise (creating the desire for ascetic return to paradise in the first place), a cherubim with a fiery sword is set as guard to keep humanity out (Gen. 3:24). Similarly, when

Daniel meets an angelic messenger, the figure is described as having a "face like lightning" and "eyes like flaming torches" (Dan. 10:6). In Psalm 103 [Ps. 104], a text that ascetics may have known from their psalmody practices, the Lord is described as making "flames of fire his servants" (Ps. 103:4 [Ps. 104:4]). And angels as fiery beings extend into New Testament texts as well. Revelation can describe a specific angel as in charge of fire (Rev. 14:18).

Within the early Egyptian ascetic tradition, Evagrius most fully describes the composition of angelic bodies. Despite warning that one ought not desire to see angels, he follows biblical precedent and portrays angels as beings both of fire and of light.[80] At the beginning of his *Gnostic Chapters*, he offers an explanation of angelic bodies: "A prevalence of intellect and fire is in angels."[81] Fire is elevated as unique among the elements because of "what is alive in it"[82] and is repeatedly linked to intellect and knowledge.[83] Elsewhere, Evagrius describes angels as beings of light[84] and the intellect (the capacity humans shared with angels) as capable of experiencing the divine light.[85] Perhaps most muddying of the distinctions between fire and light is Evagrius's description not of angels but of Christ, who Evagrius refers to as an oil lamp, evoking light and fire simultaneously.[86] In discussing fire, Evagrius distinguishes between two types: one that is capable of burning (earthly fire) and one that is incapable ("divine fire"), instead serving to purify that which it touches.[87] Recognizing that Evagrius delineates between destructive and purifying fires also closes the gap some between Evagrius's and Cassian's portrayals of the highest form of prayer. For, as we saw above, Cassian points to the burning bush as a model of fire that is cold and purifying.

As Ellen Muehlberger has compellingly argued, multiple discourses on the hierarchy of angels and their relationship to the earthbound competed and cross-fertilized in the fourth and fifth centuries, texts usually deemed "ascetic" intersecting with and influencing writings that are often grouped as "ecclesiastic." As she has shown, an important current of thought inherited and altered by monastics was a belief in angelic "guides" who periodically bolstered a monk's endeavors.[88] In particular, during prayer, angelic presence signified both correction and protection while simultaneously serving as that which an ascetic was to emulate and embody. An angel was an ascetic's teacher, whose angelic light was meant to illuminate "those who are in darkness."[89] In fact, angels could access the intellections of humans they guided precisely because angelic bodies were largely composed of intellect itself.[90] By being able to read their charge's thoughts, angels might encourage an ascetic to turn away from demonic temptations and back toward the divine. Such instruction was frequently not gentle but rather violent. Angels might chastise through surprise visits in the middle of the night that terrified their charge or might even resort to injuring their charge with "blows."[91] But ultimately, it remained the ascetic's choice whether to weed out dangerous, demonic thoughts. Moreover, having or gaining such a guide was not a given. Abba Ammonas taught that an angelic guide had to be earned through ascetic toil deemed worthy by God,[92] whereas Macarius the Egyptian indicated that an ascetic received an angel through God's mercy on one's sufferings.[93] Evagrius, engaging such traditions, suggests that each individual was granted an angel from birth, but such a gift was often lost, as impure choices might send one's guardian angel fleeing.[94] It is precisely anxiety about the loss of one's angel that is reflected in Evagrius's warning against the demon of sadness, who invites one to believe that the air is actually not populated with angelic assistants.[95]

As Muehlberger notes, the notion of a "divine guide" flows from exegesis of biblical passages such as Exodus 23, in which Moses himself is promised an angel.[96] Here, the angel's role as guardian and protector is more prominent. God, in giving Moses an angel, assures Moses that as long as he obeys the angel he is guaranteed God's violence on his behalf ("I will be an enemy to your enemies and a foe to your foes" (Exod. 23:22)). A similar sentiment is found in Psalm 90 [Ps. 91], in which the psalmist assures that the Lord "will command his angels concerning you to guard you in all your ways" (Ps. 90:11 [Ps. 91:11]). This verse sits only a few lines later than those Evagrius recommended to Eulogios in the passage quoted at the outset of this chapter (v. 5–6). Thus, Evagrius's evocation of Psalm 90 [Ps. 91] to comfort the novice monk would have carried with it the assurance of a guardian angel soon on its way, an angel bringing light to Eulogios who was lost in the dark.

A richer, later fifth-century vision of such a guardian angel is embedded in a saying attributed to Macarius the Egyptian. While Macarius is living at Scetis, two siblings come to him in order to become ascetics. During a later visit to check on their progress, Macarius witnesses (unbeknownst to the brothers) their secret nocturnal prayer rituals. Awaking in the middle of the night, with hands stretched to the heavens, the two brothers prayed, the elder untroubled, while the younger was defended from demonic onslaught by "the angel of the Lord circling round about him with a fiery sword."[97] While the guardian angel of the elder brother is not visible (or perhaps not present?), the angel of the younger brother, who is weak, is clearly in their midst. His angel is referred to as "the angel of the Lord," perhaps evoking the angel placed at the entrance to paradise. In such a reading, the passage symbolizes paradisiacal longing in the imperfect, demonically tempted body of the younger brother. And that the angel arrived as a violent presence at the time of prayer in particular indicates that the younger brother's prayers were not yet fully weaponized (as were the older brother's) to ward off demonic menace. The saying implies that an ascetic could anticipate being assigned a divine angel as guardian to help bolster the violent power of his prayers against the demons.

In the saying, the younger monk needed his guardian angel active and present at prayer. By contrast, his older brother, more nearly perfect in his prayer practices, did not seem to have an angel present. This absence points to another, more advanced role that angels might play in the ascetic life: as models to be imitated. There was among late ancient Christians reflecting on Egyptian ascetics (as well as among such ascetics themselves) a recognition that ascetic bodies might be read as angelic. For example, the fourth-century visitors who composed the *History of the Monks of Egypt* frame many of the brethren they encountered as "living the angelic life," living "as true citizens of heaven."[98] Rufinus, translating it into Latin at the beginning of the fifth century, expands the implication by speaking of the brethren "who while still on earth lived the life of heaven."[99] In particular, the authors of the *History of the Monks of Egypt* depict abbas Or, Bes, Theon, and Apollo and his brethren as angelically embodied.[100] As Georgia Frank has shown, the Christian pilgrims who sought out ascetics brought with them physiognomic presumptions about what to look for in an ascetic's face.[101] In particular, biblical images of angels aglow created an anticipated ascetic face as angelic, that is, radiant with light. Frank rightly warns that such expectations point to how an ascetic's "face was no longer considered the locus of personal identity."[102] Rather, as noted in the earlier discussion of psalmody, a communal, liturgical identity was meant to efface that of the individual.[103] Given that it was the angels who were understood to sing psalms to God, it should be unsurprising that the face of the ascetic mimicking the angels becomes that of the common, liturgical host and no longer that of a given abba.

While writings of visitors to the desert witness a clear expectation for such a transformation in this life, later Palestinian monks would likewise project such a desire for the angelic onto those who themselves had inhabited the Egyptian desert. As the *History of the Monks of Egypt* indicates, fellow ascetics from other regions could image their revered Egyptian brethren as already angelic in nature.[104] Such rhetorical imagery was magnified by the collators of the *Sayings*. So, a father overhears two brothers discourse about their visits to Arsenius and Moses, God revealing a vision of "Abba Moses with the angels of God, and they were all eating honey cakes."[105] That is, Moses is already among the angels, feasting on divine manna from heaven. Thus, successful mimesis of God's angels was meant to elevate the "true" monk to angelic status, if not angelic embodiment. It is precisely this expectation of angelicized brethren that Evagrius, already in the fourth century, evokes in the opening advice to Eulogios when he refers to the "radiant assembly of the brethren"; even Evagrius believed that an ascetic's body had the ability to change to an angelic state and that such a transformation would occur in the time before the resurrection.[106] But certainly such a transformation occurred postmortem, for he assures his fellow brethren that the saints "have been released from bodies and have joined the choir of angels.[107] So the debate among ascetics was not *if* they were capable of transforming into angelic beings but rather *when* such a process ought to be anticipated. And while Evagrius did not believe such complete transformation was possible in his own time, later authors of the *Sayings* were far more comfortable imagining abbas as already angelic while on earth. Despite seeming agreement on the mutability of ascetic bodies, Muehlberger argues that there was an ambivalence in the tradition about expectations of becoming an angel, citing the famous story of John the Little wandering off to be an angel, only to come back hungry and begging his brother for food.[108] Here, she sees the story as indicating anxiety about claims to angelic status among the desert fathers. The moral of the saying is that John had too eagerly anticipated his status as an angel, being still humanly embodied and therefore subject to the body's requirements. He is not corrected for expecting to become an angel but for presuming he had already achieved such a body. Muehlberger likewise reads a conversation between Abbas Ammoes and Isaiah as reflecting concern about portrayals of ascetics qua angels. In the saying, Isaiah describes Ammoes as an angel, only later to say he sees Ammoes "as Satan. Whatever you say to me I take as a sword."[109] Although she is correct that the exchange reflects a shift in the reading of Ammoes's ascetic body as angelic, I suspect the shift in Isaiah's visionary abilities has less to do with his belief in the transformability of ascetic bodies and more with the fraught ways ascetic formation was routed through violent imagery (the focus of the next chapter).

The ascetic aspiration to divination akin to angels, therefore, renders more meaningful the role of psalmody as a prayer practice in a monk's daily life. Monks were imagined as performing the psalms in communion with the angels who praised God. As we have seen, psalmody was central to monastic life, so much so that memorization of at least a few psalms was critical to an ascetic's ability to pray successfully and (therefore) to his salvation. An explicit link between psalmodic prayer praxis and divinized, angelic embodiment is recorded in Palladius's *Lausiac History*. Recalling his experience of the supposedly five thousand monks who lived at Nitria, Palladius writes, "All these work with their hands at making cloth so that none of them needs anything. And indeed, around the ninth hour, one can stand and hear the divine psalmody issuing forth from each cell and imagine one is above in paradise."[110] This Palladian excerpt clearly evokes a rich image of psalmody as a ritual activity performed as mimesis of and in conjunction with the heavenly host. As noted in Chapter 1, Palladius elides paradise and heaven, which, for him, are both immaterial places. He frames their immateriality by setting them in stark contrast to the faux paradise constructed by the pharaonic magicians Jannes and Jambres. Here, in his portrayal of Nitrian brethren, Palladius again seems to elide paradise and heaven, paradise being "above," while marking such a space as only imaginable and not yet accessible to the earthbound. Thus, the anticipation for paradise/heaven and the longing it evoked (argued for in the last chapter) Palladius now explicitly ties to the angelic-like psalmody and prayer of the brethren. That is, appropriation of the desert in the hopes of its transformation involved an accompanying mimesis of angels with hopes for transformation of the human ascetic body into an angelic one. Embodying and imitating angelic praise of the divine pointed to future divinization. But, as we shall see, while fourth-century texts imply that monks believed such transformation was only available in a postmortem future, the authors of the *Sayings* would amplify the linkage of fire with the ascetic qua angel to mark the so-called true monk while still on earth.

Monks Aflame

At first glance, Palladius's scene tempts a modern imagining of angelic hymning that evokes peace, joy, and unity. But the presence of and desire to be like angels coupled with the content of many psalms muddies this idyllic image. From the earliest biblical narratives, divine presence manifested as fire: From fiery swords to burning bushes, divine fire had both epiphanic and violent purposes. Thus, the author of Hebrews claims that "our God is an all consuming fire" (Heb. 12:29). Likewise, the *Gospel of Thomas* places upon Jesus's lips the following: "Whoever is near to me is near to fire."[111] As noted earlier, in biblical narratives, angelic visitors often appear accompanied by fire, or as so bright that they appear themselves on fire. Thus, constructions of asceticism were rendered through interlocking readings of angelic embodiment and divine fire imagery. The combination of scriptural references to divine fire and angels as fiery beings whom ascetics sought to emulate invited memorialization of monastic self-formation through the powerful and frightening image of fire. Later monastics appropriated fire as a productive metaphor through which to reimagine an earlier generation's violent lifestyle and experiences as conduits of the divine. Fire's consuming abilities offered an especially rich tool with which to etch ascetic identity. Already in the fourth century, monks understood fire as divine presence in the material realm, a presence capable of taking possession of the porous monastic body.

While the notion of angels as fiery and capable of entering the ascetic body was old, the image of monks as aflame is absent from fourth-century sources. Evagrius's suggestion to Eulogios that he might become like the "radiant assembly of brethren" perhaps gestures toward such fire imagery. But if it does so, it is cryptic. By contrast, multiple ascetics of the northwestern desert are remembered as experiencing an all-encompassing divine fire in the late fifth-century *Sayings*. In an apothegm attributed to Amma Syncletica, the desert mother defines asceticism: "It is like those who wish to light a fire, at first they are choked by the smoke and cry, but by this means they obtain what they seek. As it is said, 'Our God is a consuming fire.' So, we too must kindle the divine fire in ourselves through tears and hard work."[112] Syncletica articulates ascetic praxis through Hebrews 12:29, exhorting exegesis as performative embodiment of the scriptural passage. While not all stories are as explicit as Syncletica's, a clear expectation of consumption by divine fire is implied in several other ascetic narratives. Abba Joseph of Panephysis is remembered as openly sharing his refinement through divine fire. He links the identity of the "true" monk to being aflame: "You cannot be a monk unless you become like an all-consuming fire."[113] (The quote thus contains another scriptural allusion to Hebrews 12.) Whereas in Chapter 1 the "true" monk was imagined by later generations as able to live naked to the elements, here the monk aflame becomes the mark of true monkhood. In a later saying, Abba Joseph elaborates through bodily performance: "Abba Lot went to see Abba Joseph and said to him, 'Abba, as much as I can, I say my little *synaxis*, fast a little, pray and meditate. I live in peace, and, to the extent I am able, I purify my thoughts. What else can I do?' Then the old man [Abba Joseph] stood up and stretched his hands toward heaven. His fingers became like ten lamps of fire and he said to Abba Lot, 'If you will, you can become all as fire.'"[114] Here again, echoes of Hebrews 12:29 reverberate through an imagined ascetic body at prayer. Joseph's physicality transforms, flames replacing his fingers, even as his lips pray a scriptural allusion.

But not all were comfortable with openly sharing their divine flame. A story about Abba Arsenius at Scetis portrays him concealing his blazing body. The apothegm relates that a brother had come to visit Arsenius, but that, while the brother waited at the door, God allowed him to catch a glimpse of "the old man entirely like a flame."[115] Although the authorial voice makes clear that the visiting brother was worthy of seeing a fellow ascetic on fire, the story ends with his disavowing his vision to Abba Arsenius, assuring his host he saw nothing. Here, it is not merely Arsenius's fingers that are alight but his entire body. Moreover, his experience of divine possession is marked as a secret Arsenius wishes to hide. Yet God deems that his pyrotechnic abilities are (secretly) meant for the eyes of other worthy brethren. In this way, the literary conceit allows Arsenius's ascetic success (as expressed through consumption by divine fire) to be witnessed and recorded while protecting Arsenius from accusations of pride and the concomitant risk of succumbing to its demons.

All of these stories portray the monastic ideal as embodied performances of divine fire. To be "like a consuming fire" pointed both to a monk's zealous love for and devotion to God as well as to the miraculous bodily transformations such singular focus on the divine might produce. Limited by a material body and human imperfection, ascetics never permanently transformed into an "all consuming fire" like God's angels. But an appeal to the subtlest of the elements, fire, combined with performative exegesis of Scripture allowed the monk to be constructed as capable of being briefly consumed in flame or, at the very least, *like* a consuming fire, making him into an angelic(-like) conduit for the divine on earth. That fire imagery in particular would become more prominent in later memorializations of the lost desert makes sense, for the *Sayings* are refracted through the event of Theophilus's mob setting fire to the desert.

Conclusion

Prayer, so central to ascetic life, had multiple purposes, but within this multivalence the violent aspects of prayer must not be obscured or domesticated.[116]

If prayer was frequently envisioned as a weapon, be it a shield serving as protection from demons or a whip itself capable of inflicting wounds, then violence itself sat at the heart of ascetic formation. That ascetics were later imagined to embody something of the divine fire during psalmody in angelic presence is most clearly expressed in the apothegm of Abba Macarius the Egyptian and the two brothers mentioned above. Recall that Macarius had witnessed the brothers praying at night, the younger one protected by an angel wielding a fiery sword. The following morning, all three pretended to awake and then they began their psalmody. The younger brother went first, and as each verse issued from his mouth Macarius saw "a tongue of flame" emerge and float up to heaven. At the elder brother's turn, his chant resulted in not tongues of fire but in an entire fiery column ascending to heaven, an exegetical performance of Exodus 13 that marked his more nearly perfected state. Abba Macarius concludes by explaining his vision's significance: "So I learned that the first [the older brother] was a perfect man, but the enemy was still fighting against the younger."[117] In this way, Macarius articulates an ascetic view of gradations of divinized embodiment through the extent of fire manifestation.

In the same way that angels offered monks models of divine violence, the psalms themselves led monks to internalize violence. Many of the psalms are full of requests and retellings of God's vengeance and violent punishments. Justified divine fire, in particular, is evoked in twenty-one psalms. For example, Psalm 78:5–6 [Ps. 79:5–6]: "How long, O Lord? Will you be angry forever? Will your jealous wrath burn like fire? Pour out your anger on the nations that did not know you, and on the kingdoms that do not call on your name." The repeated reiteration of psalms as part of a larger liturgical practice was central to ascetic performance. Ascetics were expected to memorize these violent images. The habituation of enunciating such calls for violence undoubtedly shaped ascetic orientation. Considering the heavy imbibing of violent psalms among ascetics helps make sense of how ascetics themselves became violent. Through psalmody, ascetics inscribed upon their bodies again and again the violent desires of their forebearers and God's violent fulfillment as response. That is, violence was central to understanding divine-human relations. Ascetics memorizing and reciting—and thus writing on their bodies—the repeated violence found in the psalms yielded violent, divine-like embodiment. To be divine or close to the divine was not only to invite divine violence upon oneself but also to be capable of great violence on behalf of the divine. Divinized embodiment was understood as inherently violent. The next three chapters will pick up these two threads, Chapter 3 considering the broader violence that monastic identity formation required, Chapter 4 exploring how "barbarians" rhetorically symbolized violence, and Chapter 5 imagining how the violence surrounding monks was deployed in arguments over orthodoxy and heresy that would rock the northwestern desert at the turn to the fifth century.

Chapter 3

Monks and Memory Sanctions

> There was a certain old man in Scetis, hardworking in the body but
> not sharp in thoughts. And so, he came to Abba John to ask him
> concerning forgetfulness.
>
> —*Sayings of the Desert Fathers* (Greek, Alphabetical)
> John the Little 18

Forgetfulness, the question set before Abba John the Little, stood as an essential component of ascetic development, amplifying the violent aspects of this formation process. While the *Sayings* here offers a rough definition of forgetfulness—being "not sharp in thoughts"—how forgetting functioned in ascetic life was far more textured than this brief phrase might imply. As discussed in Chapter 2, focus on God through prayer and psalmody enabled intimacy with the divine, constructing a violent liturgical, communal identity in the process. The Janus face of such formation was the active forgetting of one's individual self. That is, psalmody and prayer that oriented one toward the divine simultaneously sought to do violence to past memories, altering recollections of one's past life and the world. Such worldly memories might be manipulated to draw one closer to God by invoking the deterrence of hell. This chapter deepens exploration of how a violent ascetic identity was constructed and how that process intersected with cultural praxes of memory sanctions.

Despite idealistic claims to the contrary, ascetics continued to engage dynamically the surrounding world that they had abandoned for the desert. Ascetic memory manipulation did not occur in a vacuum. Beginning with a larger exploration of the cultural practice of memory sanctions, I argue in this chapter that ascetic forgetting becomes most comprehensible against this backdrop. I unpack ascetic involvement in the Christianized *damnatio memoriae* that Archbishop Theophilus enacted against numerous pagan temples in Alexandria and its surrounding regions, examining especially the case of the Alexandrian temple to Serapis. As the remainder of this chapter will show, exploration of the logics of *damnatio memoriae* illuminates not only what Theophilus and ascetics understood themselves to be doing in their destruction of the Alexandrian Serapeum but also how central such active forgetting was to ascetic daily life. That ascetic formation involved the violence of enacting memory sanctions against oneself once more highlights how violent the goal of asceticism was. The violent ascetic self that emerges in this chapter engages in acts of violence both outwardly, toward pagan temples, and inwardly, toward one's own past self. The rhetoric used for such violent acts will be examined in Chapters 4 and 5 in relation to attacks against desert ascetics.

Damnatio Memoriae as Cultural Context

The logics of intentional erasure, what scholars have termed *damnatio memoriae*, are particularly productive for understanding the larger cultural logic of forgetting in which ascetics situated themselves. Originally (during the Republic and then continuing into the early Principate), *damnatio memoriae* was a process enacted against political elites, especially senators and emperors. There were a variety of ways in which such damning might be performed. *Damnatio memoriae* might involve the denial of funerals or of commemoration of the dead, the permanent loss of a familial name, the erasure of names in inscriptions, the scratching out or revoking of coinage related to the damned, the beheading or destruction of statues, or the etching out of portraits in stone—all acts that resulted in active public, communal forgetting.[1] Only if an individual's memory was deemed particularly threatening were that person's representative objects ever, on rare occasion, destroyed outright. Rather, the norm was only to deface objects, thus visually marking them as publicly damned. In this way, *damnatio memoriae* emerges as a cultural response to the Roman logics of memory. Whereas particular material objects—inscriptions, statuary, portraits, and the like—functioned to immortalize Roman aristocracy for posterity, *damnatio memoriae* was the undoing of such physical markers, the intentional and public damning of an individual.

Charles Hedrick offers a nuanced and clear rendering of the cultural process of *damnatio memoriae*. As he notes, "*Damnatio memoriae* did not negate historical traces, but created gestures that served to dishonor the record of the person and so, in an oblique way, to confirm the memory" of a damned individual.[2] Roman citizens and subjects were invited by such destruction to *remember* to forget the damned individual, a process that tended to make any obliteration of memory impossible and certainly unintended. Moreover, such damning of an individual's memory was a dynamic cultural performance, not a policy extant in any Roman law. The absence of a single law for enacting *damnatio memoriae*, for Hedrick, points to how the repressive act sat at the heart of an active form of forgetting.

Hedrick's work is especially illuminating for the purposes of this book, as his main case study involves the damning of Senator Virius Nicomachus Flavianus at the end of the fourth century. Not only did this act of damning occur in chronological proximity to the destruction of the Alexandrian Serapeum (more on this below) and purported barbarian attacks on Egyptian ascetics (more on that in Chapter 4), but it also highlights how the act of damning could itself be intentionally obscured through later rehabilitation. Emperor Theodosius's sons, Honorius and Arcadius, chose to order and enact specific *damnatio memoriae* against Flavian and others who had worked with the usurper Eugenius. As Hedrick notes, the penalties were "well defined, aimed only at particular, unauthorized events that occurred during a very restrictive period."[3] Honorius's and Arcadius's behavior highlights the ways in which *damnatio memoriae*'s goal might not be about entirely eradicating the memory of a given individual but instead be about marking explicitly behaviors that were considered illegal or illegitimate. Moreover, the performed destruction of material objects that accompanied such a damning would have been so spectacular as to endure in the audience's memory. Witnessing this type of destruction "must have been an extraordinarily impressive event."[4] That is, it was an explicit performance of the insistence to forget, one that demanded a spectacle that would imprint on viewers the expectation to remember to forget.

But how were the various means of enacting *damnatio memoriae* experienced if one were not present at an object's mutilation, erasure, or destruction? In her recent scholarship, Lauren Hackworth Petersen has sought to answer this question using extant Roman material evidence to interrogate what *damnatio memoriae* did to a passerby's memory. As an individual moved through the city, visual cues stimulated remembrance of powerful figures within the larger history of Rome. She argues that the Roman populace, trained to read such visual cues, would have also registered the visual gestures of an awkward absence or erasure created by *damnatio memoriae*. "The emptiness itself functions as a sign that points to the memory of the damned individual,"[5] for the emptiness is never total. Rather, *damnatio memoriae* left traces of the act of erasure itself.[6] Similarly, when a material, such as a portrait head, was reworked rather than utterly destroyed, the viewer often would have detected the palimpsest present, seeing both what had been displaced and that which displaced it.[7] That most victims of such destruction leave traces of their former selves or awkward empty spaces that cue visual recognition of an absence point to the way that *damnatio memoriae* was an active form of forgetting, a conscious and continual remembering to forget. On the rare occasions when objects were completely smashed or melted, literary regalings of the *damnatio memoriae* event might themselves serve as trace reminders of the destruction.[8]

The logics of intentional and incomplete erasure deeply influenced Christian behavior. By the late fourth century, many Roman elites had converted to Christianity, usually maintaining their considerable power.[9] Senator Flavian, Hedrick's *damnatio* example above, was among these elite Roman Christians. *Damnatio memoriae* as lived experience and real threat was as much a part of Christian life as any other aspect of the Roman imperial milieu. Moreover, Christians took it upon themselves to rework the practice of *damnatio memoriae* for Christian purposes. As Peter Stewart has argued, Christians shared a "common cultural vocabulary" with their pagan counterparts, including the cultural logics of *damnatio memoriae*.[10] Christianity adopted and adapted these logics in order to produce a new Christianized world. The ways in which representations (names and images) functioned to point to a deceased imperial figure or to a current imperial ruler became easily transposable to the mortal Christ, who in his incarnation had been a material instantiation of an otherwise inaccessible God. And, as Stewart argues, Christians reoriented *damnatio memoriae*, turning it from a weapon to brandish against political elites to one directed against pagan demons. In this way, it became "a kind of *damnatio* of evil" that was primarily "manifested in the abuse of pagan cult images."[11] As I have argued throughout this book, such an understanding of one's relationship to evil is precisely what amplified the violent identity ascetics assumed in their warfare against demons.

Further, Stewart's work includes a helpful description of the methods by which Christians tended to enact *damnatio memoriae* against statues, in particular. While no official law existed to prescribe praxis, extant archaeological remains help illuminate the dialogic relationship between rhetorical portrayals of such events and how the performances may well have occurred. He argues that, despite some variation, there was a general continuity of practice, with many if not all of the following steps present in the destruction of a statue.[12] Such destruction was initiated through chanting that erupted among a gathered crowd. This negative, derogatory chanting functioned as the ritualized inverse of the chants that were proclaimed during imperial and religious processions through a city. Usually when a political elite or a temple deity was celebrated, the pomp included a procession that involved active participation by the crowd voicing their acclamations of support and adoration. When the deity or imperial representative was later damned, the crowd undid the previous elevation through acclamation by verbally mocking the figure. The chanting not only served as an oral toppling but also mobilized the crowd to then physically pull down the statue, understood in Roman culture as a materialized representation that pointed toward the actual individual or god. Once the statue was down, the crowd began a cycle of mutilation and dragging. While the mutilation symbolized the damning of the figure, the dragging ritually undid the previous ceremonial processions and the honor they conferred. Once the statue had been successfully damaged, the crowd concluded the act through the disposal of the statue fragments as refuse and the assertion that the world had now been turned upside down. While disposed pieces of statues might be reused, sometimes *damnatio memoriae* was completed by disposal of statuary pieces in neighboring latrines, serving as a final act of desecration.[13] The public performance of the *damnatio* ritual removed the honored deity or political elite from communal identity performed through shared memories and spectacularly represented the disruption and danger the object's presence had caused, thus requiring damning.

Destroying the Serapeum: A Case Study

As noted in the Introduction, rhetorical violence can easily slip into physical acts of violence, and in general violence tends to beget more violence. Given the centrality of violence to ascetic identity described, it should not surprise us to discover examples of ascetics participating in actual acts of physical violence. Moreover, the selective forgetting of one's individual self serves as the flip side of the remembering required to scripturalize an ascetic's body through prayer and psalmody. In the light of such violent patterns of remembering and forgetting, I want to take as a brief focus the tradition that claims ascetics destroyed the Serapeum, the famous temple to Serapis at Alexandria, at the instigation of Archbishop Theophilus. If we take seriously that some ascetics seem to have been involved in the destruction of the Serapis statue and his temple, then we have here an example not just of the broader Christian population mobilizing *damnatio memoriae* but also of ascetics doing so in particular. We shall see that ascetics actively engaged in *damnatio* for the purposes of Christianizing the landscape, an impulse paralleling the ascetic desire to transform the desert into a paradisiacal space.

A later apothegm attributed to Theophilus explicitly claims that desert ascetics participated in the decimation of temples in Alexandria. Moreover, the saying ties the event to prayer, which, as shown in Chapter 2, might be envisioned as violent: "Once some fathers went into Alexandria, summoned by Theophilus the Archbishop, in order to pray and to destroy the temples."[14] Usually this saying is viewed as referring to ascetic participation in the destruction of the temple of Serapis, a momentous move by Theophilus according to contemporary and later historians. The saying continues, describing the archbishop offering the monks veal, which most ate unhesitatingly. Theophilus offers one of the abbas a piece, saying, "Here is a good slice, Abba, eat it." The old man then seems to chastise Theophilus for undermining their previous vegetarian diet, leading all the monks to cease eating the veal. David Brakke has read Theophilus's actions as laying "uncomfortably bare the dissonance between the way of the urban bishop and those of the desert monks."[15] I would argue that Theophilus's behavior toward these ascetics also highlights both the probability that some ascetics were indeed involved in temple destruction and that the later tradition felt much ambivalence toward such ascetic presence. In particular, the problematic eating of veal symbolizes the questionable engagement with worldly matters that temple destruction involved. But we are not forced to rely solely on a later rendering in the *Sayings*, for a contemporary pagan philosopher, Eunapius, describes the presence of the monks during the attack on the Serapeum. He describes them as "behaving like tyrants," undoubtedly a violent image in the late ancient context.[16] While Eunapius is certainly a hostile witness because of the antagonism between pagan philosophers and ascetics qua Christian philosophers, that does not mean his claim is untrue.

While there is more than one literary regaling of Theophilus's destructive bent against Serapis, I would like to attend especially to that of Rufinus of Aquileia, written in the early fifth century. My reasons are twofold: one, his telling accords rather productively with the statue destruction practices articulated by Stewart, and, two, Rufinus wrote his version in the midst of the Origenist controversy, in which he had found himself ardently opposed to Theophilus. Moreover, Rufinus, himself a monk in Palestine, had spent some time among the abbas of Egypt and had been a dear friend of Evagrius, advising his flight to the Egyptian desert in the first place. Given these connections, Rufinus is an especially useful witness, not because he offers any truer of a portrayal but rather because he likely reflects certain ascetic self-understandings of the event. His portrayal can be imagined as consonant with a portion, if not all, of the northwestern desert community, some of whom likely attacked the Serapeum.

Rufinus tells of the destruction in some depth in his *Church History*. Composed at the behest of Chromatius, bishop of Aquileia, the first nine books served as a translation into Latin of Eusebius of Caesarea's Greek *Church History*. While Rufinus certainly amended or adapted Eusebius's narrative, Rufinus's own major contribution comes in books ten and eleven, in which he extends the history on from 325 to 395, to the eve of the Origenist controversy. Halfway through book eleven, Rufinus takes up a larger story of riotous violence in Alexandria. Emperor Theodosius I (himself a Christian) had handed over an old pagan sanctuary to Theophilus in response to a burgeoning Christian population. This shift in property ownership led to violent upset in Alexandria, such that the emperor sent a letter in the hopes of settling the dispute. In the letter, Theodosius clearly confirmed that the non-Christian population had lost ownership of the sanctuary. Christians and pagans met at the Serapeum to hear the letter read aloud. Rufinus describes that "no sooner had the first page been read aloud, the introduction to which criticized the vain superstitions of the pagans, then a great cry was raised by our people, such that shock and fear assailed the pagans," the latter quickly fleeing the scene.[17] An interlude then occurs in the narrative, during which Rufinus describes the temple and the statue of Serapis itself, including the tricks played on the people by the temple's priests to inspire and maintain devotion to the cult. He then returns to the letter's presentation and describes the Christian crowd's response. A brave soldier is the first to strike the statue. Rufinus would have us believe it was the soldier's faith, rather than the axe he held, that felled the statue. Serapis then was struck by men until the head had been removed and all of its limbs shattered. The bits were then dragged to various parts of the city for all to see before finally being burned.[18] When all pieces of the statue had adequately been destroyed, Rufinus concludes: "And that was the end of the vain superstition and ancient error of Serapis."[19] The import Rufinus places on these actions is underscored in his next chapter when he credits this destruction with making possible the disposal of all other idols in the city. He states, "Once this pinnacle of idolatry had been

thrown down, all of the idols, or one should rather say monsters, throughout Alexandria were toppled by a like destruction and similar disgrace."[20]
Thus, Rufinus links the fall of the greatest of these so-called monsters to the
downfall of all. In Chapter 4, I will explore more the linking of demons to
monsters, but for the moment let us quickly note that a logic akin to that
found among the threat of various desert demons is at work here. Ascetics
who gave in to one demon were described as at greater risk of falling prey to
others. There was a logic of cascading and expanding jeopardy that linked the
ascetic's succumbing to demons both to his own salvation and to the potential
loss of a Christianized desert. Here, that cascading logic is turned upon the
idols mediating such demons such that by felling the "pinnacle" of them,
Serapis, all others succumbed to Christianizing violence.

Rufinus clearly portrays Alexandrian Christians as mobilizing a Christianized *damnatio memoriae* in his description of Serapis's downfall. As noted
above, Stewart charts a collection of practices often performed with *damnatio
memoriae* of statuary: chanting, toppling, mutilating, dragging, disposing of,
and claiming inversion of the world order. It is precisely this set of actions
that we find reflected in Rufinus's relaying of the Serapeum's destruction. As
soon as the emperor's support was sensed among the letter's hearers, a "great
cry" was raised by the Christians. Such shouting corresponds to the communal chanting that often occurred at the outset of *damnatio memoriae,* for it
was such public tumult in response to imperial edicts (or perceived imperial
edicts) that often culturally marked the initiation of the performance of violence. That the pagans flee indicates their recognition of the violence that was
about to break out. Despite the perceived power of Serapis (acknowledged
even by the riled up Christian crowd), a brave Christian soldier quickly steps
up, taking an axe to the statue in order to topple it. According to the cultural script, the statue is then mutilated, the head being "wrenched from the
neck" and other members "chopped off with axes." Those fragments are than
"dragged" to different parts of the city so that all devotees of Serapis throughout Alexandria might witness the final disposal of his statuary remains, the
various pieces being burnt into ashes. Having thoroughly destroyed the image
of Serapis, Rufinus's concluding statement about Serapis's end dictates how
this performance is to be understood: The previous world order has been
upended, proper Christian order having been established through the com-
pletion of the *damnatio memoriae* performance. That a Christianized world
order was now dominant was visible by the toppling not only of Serapis but
also of all the other idols in Alexandria after him. For Rufinus, Christianization

of the Serapeum's acropolis is completed with the leveling of the sanctuaries and their replacement by Christian buildings. Thus, he states, "On the one side arose a martyr's shrine, on the other a church."[21] In particular, the martyr's shrine seems to have been important in Rufinus's reading, for he goes on to explain how the relics of John the Baptist had come to be moved from Sebaste (in Palestine) to the acropolis of Alexandria.[22] Thus, across several chapters, Rufinus compellingly narrates the *damnatio memoriae* of Serapis and the subsequent, permanent marking as Christian of the acropolis's prominent locus in the city with John the Baptist's bones.[23]

In my earlier discussion of *damnatio memoriae*, I referred to scholarship that took seriously not only rhetorical portrayals of such violence but also extant physical remains. This discussion pointed to the ways in which written documents intersected with other types of extant materials. While Rufinus articulated *damnatio memoriae* against the Serapeum as Christianizing violence that fully obliterated the temple architecture and therefore memory of past pagan worship, the extant archaeological evidence troubles his tidy narrative of complete desolation. Judith McKenzie and her team, as part of the Alexandrian Architecture Project, have done much to further our understandings of the various building stages and historical uses of the Serapeum site. Combining wall drawings done by Mahmoud-Bey in 1866, excavations by various groups (G. Botti [1894–96], the Sieglin Expedition [1898–1902], and Alan Rowe [during World War II]), and present visible remains, McKenzie and her team offer a compelling reconstruction of the entire Serapis complex.[24] Pertinent for our discussion is the tracing of the Roman-era constructions and post-*damnatio* Christian structures (the Ptolemaic sanctuary having burnt down in the second century C.E.).

Archaeological evidence allows a fairly reliable reconstruction of the site as it would have stood in the third and fourth centuries. Roman-era remains consist of limestone-cement concrete wall foundations, ashlar bricks and mortar, and red and gray granite columns and cornices (red for the temple itself and gray for the colonnaded court).[25] There are also extant sculptural pieces that likely stood within the complex.[26] Sometime between 181 and 217 C.E., the new Serapis temple and its accompanying colonnaded court were built, both significantly widened from those of their Ptolemaic predecessors.[27] A single, large staircase replaced previous entrances from the east,[28] a shift that we can imagine served to heighten and centralize the monumental, visual attraction of the entire complex on the acropolis. A second entrance, to facilitate processional movement through the complex, led out of the northern wall onto a city

street. Along the southern and western walls of the court are the remains of
a number of rooms, some possibly serving as an extension of the Alexandrian
library.[29] The complex also included a remodeling of the Lageion, a combination racecourse and athletic game site, to the southwest of the acropolis.[30]
Near the end of the third century, builders added a large column dedicated to
Diocletian (likely with a statue on top); the base and column are still extant.
The column must have been highly visible on the city skyline, underscoring
how prominent the Serapis complex was in Alexandria. If one wanted to make
a mark on the city, Serapis's acropolis remained the place to do so.

As McKenzie notes, this reconstruction from archaeological remains
largely corroborates the late fourth- and early fifth-century descriptions
found in both Aphthonius and Rufinus. Though Rufinus's portrayal is highly
stylized, it remains quite accurate, reflecting both the actual complex and how
viewers likely experienced it. Rufinus's description has sometimes been seen
as inaccurate because of the numerous remains that continued to stand at the
site. But his full description of the destruction should be read not as rhetorical and unreliable but rather as indicative of his own tenuous social location
during and after the first Origenist controversy. Though he had been opposed
to Theophilus, this did not stop Rufinus from referring to the archbishop
as "the priest of God" in his rendering of the events at Alexandria.[31] Thus,
we should see in Rufinus's text attempts to conciliate his recent opponent
through spectacular claims of total destruction.

Assuming Rufinus's reliability, what does he tell us about later Christian
buildings on the site? As referred to above, Rufinus briefly indicates that a
church and martyrium arose on either side. But on either side of what, the
temple or the complex? Archaeological remains indicate that despite frequent
Christian reuse of temples and tombs in Egypt, such repurposing did not
occur at the site of the Serapeum—an interesting choice for Theophilus given
the site's importance. Moreover, the churches were not built within the colonnaded court at all but rather outside its walls to the west, likely between
the complex's walls and the Lageion. McKenzie notes that this location would
have allowed an orientation of the church to the east, as was customary for
many Christian churches in Egypt.[32] Arguably, it also may have offered the
possibility of visually trumping the Serapeum's remains when approaching
from the city port, marking the space as now Christian. McKenzie reads
the Serapeum as the final Alexandrian temple to close and thus indicative
of the final stage in the Christianization of the Alexandrian landscape, the
other temples having been abandoned already. Rufinus's description both

corroborates and troubles her reading. The world order was indeed upended, Alexandria being claimed for Christianity, but Serapis's destruction marked for Rufinus the beginning of the dismantling of these temple sites. Such a process would have been quite simple if the sites were already empty, a point that Rufinus conveniently obscures.

As noted above, given the deep symbolic importance attributed to the destruction of the temple of Serapis, it is noteworthy that Theophilus chose not to reuse or build on top of the ruins. Despite the pagan Eunapius's claims that only the floor stones remained because they were too heavy to steal, it seems that in fact much of the masonry and many of the columns remained on site, the columns only being removed when Saladin used them to reinforce the city walls along the seashore in the mid-twelfth century.[33] Theophilus's decision not to reuse the interior of the Serapeum, coupled with the lingering of many remains on the site despite the popular reuse of *spolia*, indicates that such action, or rather inaction, was intentional. In the spirit of the tradition of *damnatio memoriae*, Theophilus left the ruins as a trace reminder meant to invite the Alexandrian populace to remember to forget Alexandria's pagan past. As discussed above, complete erasure (here, reuse or building on top of the temple) would not have carried the same cultural threat that lingering visual traces would: Christianity had conquered paganism and would enact violence against it again if needed.

The tension between rhetorical regalings of utter obliteration and the lived reality of Christian buildings alongside the Serapeum's ruins highlights the partial nature of *damnatio memoriae* both in theory and in practice. As we shall see in the remainder of this chapter and across the next, the desire to historically narrate utter ruin echoes a similar tension found in ascetic literature itself, both in its demands to forget one's past and in its rhetoric around moments of violence within the northwestern desert communities.

Memory Sanctions Toward an Ascetic Self

If we accept that ascetics were indeed participants in Theophilus's campaign of destruction (first against the Serapeum and afterward against other temples), then it becomes clear that ascetics engaged in the cultural enactment of *damnatio memoriae*, albeit in a newly Christianized mode. Beyond the participation of ascetics in Alexandrian temple destructions, ascetics stretched the cultural logics of *damnatio memoriae* into their own daily lives, an activity

I describe with the phrase "memory sanctions." That is, they extended this cultural logic beyond punishment of cult statues to include ascetic formation of self. In the same way that the poor, human monk and the dry, uncivilized desert pointed toward angelic figures and the space of paradise itself, ascetic logic of remembering relied on representation's gesture toward an absence, just as the erasure of inscriptions and statuary left a trace of what was to be forgotten. As we will see, using the lens of memory sanctions reframes seemingly contradictory instructions across ascetic literature that demand an ascetic to both forget and not forget the world and his past life in it.

As the story of the Serapeum's destruction highlights, abandoning the world was a difficult and perhaps even impossible task. Ascetics might be invited into the city and its politics by bishops such as Theophilus. But the barrage of the world was more persistent even than the occasional call to urban violence. The orientation of ascetic cells (discussed in Chapter 2) pointed monks not only toward the east but also, in closer proximity, toward the Nile and the many villages that lay along its western bank. This village-life vista (whether real or only remembered) undoubtedly risked wrong orientation of the ascetic gaze. And if literally facing the world were not challenging enough, there was an endless barrage of visitors, either brethren or lay tourists traveling through the northwestern desert. At least a small fraction of such visitors aided ascetic inhabitants in surviving the desert, bringing bread, fruit, and other vital supplies, as well as carrying away an ascetic's handiwork to sell in the world. In all of these tangible ways, an ascetic remained inextricably bound to interactions and remembrances of the world, even as he sought to forget it. Thus, like the eschatologically anticipatory ascetic goals of transforming the desert into paradise or the ascetic individual into a liturgical, angelic-like being, permeating ascetic literature are injunctions to forget the world and its entrapments. Evagrius, in fact, could define ascetic life through such erasure of one's past: "Therefore, do you want, beloved, to take up the solitary life for what it is and to run after the trophies of stillness? Leave there the concerns of the world, the principalities and powers [that is, demons] set over them (Eph. 6:12). Stand free of material concerns and passions, beyond all desire, so that, having become a stranger to the conditions deriving from these, you may be able to foster stillness properly."[34]

While the goal of ascetic life here is stillness (a concept to which we shall return below), the process through which stillness is acquired is active abandonment of one's past life. Only through forgetting might an ascetic hope to succeed.

Such forgetting was necessary because of the inherent danger worldly memories, especially of one's own past, posed to an ascetic.[35] Whether the memories arose of their own accord or were triggered by demons, the concomitant passions that memories evoked ensured demonic onslaught. If we take seriously that Evagrius's advice in *Talking Back* is based on years of discussion with fellow brethren, then a few types of memories posed especially insistent threats: family, wealth, inheritance, clothes, social acquaintances, food, and desired bodies (both those of young boys and women).[36] Mentions of familial issues and recollections occur in his discussions of the demons of gluttony,[37] fornication,[38] love of money,[39] sadness,[40] anger,[41] acedia,[42] and vainglory.[43] Recalling tables flush with delicious food and drink might not only invite gluttony but also evoke memories of the family members with whom the table had been shared. Remembering and desiring a woman might tempt one to establish a family. And recollecting one's kinsmen frequently induced concerns about lost money, inheritance, and status. Depending on the nature of an ascetic's departure, thoughts of family might also induce sadness over lost bonds and their mutual consolation. Or, one's departure may have produced volatile emotions, so recalling could trigger the re-experiencing of anger. Memories of family might also invite attacks by the demon of acedia, who recommends either permanent abandonment of one's cell or at the very least a short reentry into the world to visit relatives. Such visits to family might not only lead one to desire one's past life but also result in an ascetic being weighed down by worldly matters or being tempted to pontificate about the goodness of ascetic withdrawal and thus suffering from the demon of vainglory.[44] All of these examples highlight how precariously reliant ascetic life was on forgetting, since recalling food or one's family invited a cascade of other worldly memories that led to demonic violence.

Moreover, while family might remind an ascetic of the inheritance he lost, other desires for wealth might also tempt an ascetic.[45] Among the things an ascetic left behind were his home—quite often a much nicer space than his current cell. Demons or an ascetic himself might conjure memories of his former, resplendent abode, recollections that suggested his present cell was "detestable" and should be abandoned, sometimes resulting in the ascetic perversely moving into an even less hospitable locale.[46] Ascetics remembering past wealth might decide to once more seek money and belongings, justifying their behavior with claims to offer it as alms or hospitality. Or memories of money, inducing fear of lack, might lead an ascetic to justify hoarding wealth as a way to be prepared and not burden others with assisting him, especially should he develop an illness.[47] But as Evagrius warns, all of these behaviors were temptations inspired by demons. That he also recommends scriptural passages to thwart extortion of or stinginess toward brethren indicates not only a desire to scripturalize the ascetic self (as seen in Chapter 2) but also that such temptations were real and persistent, issues that in turn inevitably led to anger, grudge-bearing, and other such hostile emotions among brethren.[48] Acting on any such thoughts would only result in succumbing to the demons of love of money and anger, ultimately drawing an ascetic back toward remembrance of and involvement in the world.[49]

Failing to forget worldly memories, especially of one's own past, might in particular encourage an ascetic to hoard food and wine out of fear of deprivation.[50] Such fears are part of the danger underlying the story of the ingestion of meat by the monks supping with Theophilus before the sack of Serapis's statue. Ascetics were to be especially wary of conversing or living with "men who were materially focused and enmeshed in the world,"[51] whether they were past acquaintances or current brethren, precisely because of the temptations and concomitant demonic assault that could ensue. Thus, the tense exchange between the old abba and Theophilus about the archbishop's menu choices resonates with the risks the older abba believed had been brought upon the brethren by visiting Theophilus and engaging in his campaign. If an ascetic caved to temptations regarding food and drink, as several of the brothers had to Theophilus's veal, the brother soon found himself subject to the onslaught of the demons of fornication, as food was understood to warm the body, in turn arousing a monk's sexual desires. Demons of fornication often materialized in the shape of a desired body that dared to touch the ascetic or else incite his imagination.[52] Failure to forget objects of sexual desire offered fodder for demons to force an ascetic to practice voyeurism. Evagrius seems to draw on his own past when he speaks of the temptations brought on by visiting with or remembering a married woman.[53] Explaining the unfolding approaches of the demons of fornication, he articulates the violence of an ascetic's counterattack: "To the Lord concerning the demon of fornication that, when it cannot humiliate us through the desire of our body, then shows us in our intellect a monk performing the obscene sin of fornication: The swords of the enemy have failed utterly, and you have destroyed cities. *Their memory* has been destroyed with a noise, but the Lord endures forever" (Ps. 9:7–8, emphasis added).[54] Through artful scriptural interpretation, Evagrius compels his fellow brethren and his readers to internalize and perform Psalm 9:7–8 in order to violently destroy such obscenity.[55] Only through willful, intentional forgetting could an ascetic hope to avert his gaze from the erotic. As Evagrius makes clear, the eradication of memories and their concomitant desires was essential to forgetting the world. The physicality of the images triggered underscores the enduringly material nature of ascetic experience. Even as ascetics sought union with the divine by remembering God, they were attacked from all sides by demons and the coarse reality of their lived desert situation.[56] Thus, an ascetic found himself forcibly attempting to remove past memories from his person, spending day and night fighting to forget them.

It is especially telling in the example above that Evagrius's scriptural selection from Psalms couples the "destruction" of memory with the image of a city's destruction (full of clamor and violence), precisely the type of physical destruction *damnatio memoriae* would have entailed. Thus, Evagrius, himself once a worldly aristocrat, repurposes the cultural logic of *damnatio memoriae* with a twist. Violence is no longer to be turned outward against physical representations but rather inward toward the mental representations of past memories, "idols of the world," that invite demonic attack.[57] In fact, the snippet of Psalm 9 uttered against demons of fornication recalls the chants of *damnatio memoriae* that signaled an imminent attack ("noise"). In the next section, I occasionally note resonances with Stewart's collection of *damnatio* practices, even if they are not clearly ordered in this broadened use of memory sanctions toward ascetic self-construction. Only by violently removing idolatrous memories could an ascetic defeat the demons and become an angelic-like conduit for the divine.

Asceticizing Memory Sanctions

In his definition of asceticism above, Evagrius centers forgetting of worldly things on the purpose of forming an ascetic self that is capable of stillness, as remembrance of one's past was antithetical to stillness. The Greek term translated as stillness above is the rich concept of *hēsychia*. *Hēsychia* is translated not only as stillness but also often as silence or tranquility. And although the term evokes a sense of peacefulness, *hēsychia* resembled ascetic prayer in that it was weaponizable in the battle for the desert, serving to "bar the gates of your soul" against "the phalanx of the demons."[58] *Hēsychia* was a goal for ascetic life because it was simultaneously the requisite state for achieving pure prayer and the gift that resulted from an experience of pure prayer, functioning in both spheres on a literal and figurative level in its conceptualization.[59]

Such dynamism between literal and figurative registers of meaning likewise occurs in the apothegmatic tradition. In particular, as Nienke Vos has recently argued, the systematic collection's section on *hēsychia* illustrates how *hēsychia* frames the entire ascetic process from beginning to end, creatively warbling between literal and figural stillness in order to weave them together as inextricably linked.[60] So it would be inaccurate to imagine that Evagrius was anomalous in his portrayals of *hēsychia*. Rather, he ought to be understood as himself participating in and reflective of the larger ascetic traditions of Egypt. Acquiring *hēsychia* allowed a form of prayer that might usher in a new paradisiacal world order. Thus, claims of experiencing *hēsychia* resonate with the claims of inverting the world found in standard *damnatio memoriae*.

Moreover, this concept of *hēsychia* was located in a dense network of ideas that included not only forgetting but also exile (*xeniteia*), an idea that also appears in Evagrius's definition of ascetic life above, when he suggests becoming a "stranger" to one's past. A dynamic body of scholarship has recently emerged on ancient notions of exile, but the importance of forgetting for exile and related concepts has gone largely under-theorized.[61] As others have noted, Evagrius recommends becoming a stranger in order to attain the goal of *hēsychia*. He always couples this recommendation, however, with warnings against wandering from one's cell.[62] So, a bit of "dragging" oneself around to perform humility was good, but too much was dangerous. Evagrius's anxiety reflects his awareness of the dangers present outside the cell. His advice to the novice Eulogios (quoted at the start of Chapter 2) highlighted how scary the desert might be (particularly at night), as demons and other animals might frighten a young ascetic away from his goal of becoming luminous like his elders.[63] Evagrius encourages the newly minted brother toward courageous battle through prayer and psalmody. But despite his confidence in addressing Eulogios, it is clear that while Evagrius defined ascetic life through *hēsychia*, *xeniteia*, and damning the memory of one's past, anxieties lingered about the risks inherent to one's *hēsychia* and ability to forget the world if one embodied *xeniteia* too fully. It is not hard to imagine Evagrius worrying that ascetics who remained outside their cells too long would (through fear) fail to forget the world and lose their stillness, experiences that in turn might produce heightened demonic violence and a loss of divine-like luminosity.

Anxiety over preserving stillness is retained by the later monastic generations in a saying about Abba Isaac the Theban. An apothegm relates that Isaac regularly ran "as if pursued by fire" at the end of communal gatherings with the brethren. The tradition assures that Isaac did so not to avoid the other brothers but "to maintain mastery over the stillness from the brethren's gathering." When pressed by brothers to explain his antisocial behavior, Isaac asserts he is avoiding demons, not the brothers, and concludes by comparing himself to a lamp: "For if someone has a lit lamp and stands lingering in the air, it is extinguished as a result of his behavior. Thus also for us, being illuminated by the holy offering, if we linger outside the cell, our mind is darkened."[64] While brethren were described through language of luminosity in the previous chapter to point toward their angelic-like endeavor, here Isaac evokes monks-as-lamps to gesture toward the dangers inherent in lingering outside one's cell. Although Isaac has become a luminous monk, such a shift attracts demonic onslaught, leading him to flee to his cell and avoid distraction from the brethren. Even though he explicitly blames demons, it becomes clear that interaction with the brethren counts as worldly interaction that might in turn result in demonic attack.

Such a pairing of stillness and forgetting the world is also found in the traditions surrounding Abba John the Little. The dense networks among the brethren in the northwestern desert make it hardly surprising to discover that Evagrius knew John. In the latter half of his treatise on prayer, Evagrius uses John as an example of someone he has seen so full of stillness during prayer that John did not respond as a demon manifesting as a dragon chewed off and vomited John's own flesh.[65] While fascinating for a variety of reasons, Evagrius's story is important because it makes clear that John the Little was known among the brethren as a pinnacle example of stillness, one whose authority as embodiment of stillness Evagrius evoked in his own articulations of proper prayer. Although Evagrius's story about John does not explicitly use language of forgetting, it is part of a series of stories in which Evagrius highlights how ascetics who pray truly forget to be aware of their bodies, their selves being fully enthralled with God. These examples can be read as successful "topplings" of worldly concerns, including the annoyances of embodiment. Evagrius is more explicit elsewhere in his writings about the opposition between stillness and being in the world. So, he asserts that "the mind that is touching upon the Holy Trinity will forget everything that is created."[66] In both these texts, Evagrius makes clear that forgetting the created world and all that is in it is essential to being able to pray with true stillness and, thus, to commune with the divine.

As mentioned above, stillness and forgetting are particularly and deeply intertwined in traditions around John the Little. While Evagrius explicitly evokes John to image stillness, John similarly appears in the *Sayings* as the individual about whom forgetting is most frequently invoked. Two apothegms often found alongside one another tell stories of other people's interactions with a forgetful John. The first saying describes a camel driver who comes to collect John's handiwork (in this case, rope) in order to sell it on his behalf. The saying makes clear that because John was deep in prayer he continually forgot to bring out the rope to the camel driver. Only on his third attempt was John able through the use of the repeated mantra "rope, camel" to remember this worldly affair. Here, John is offered as a model of forgetfulness of the world.[67] Though the camel driver disturbs John, John's struggle to remember his errands highlights his recognition that he was still enmeshed in the world and not able to entirely forget it for God. That is, the residue of remembering the world, the necessary failure to fully forget the world, is the requisite predicament of human embodiment.

A passage often coupled with the preceding passage (perhaps another version of the same story) likewise portrays John as forgetful of worldly matters. In the second variation, John is passing along to another brother some baskets he has woven. The brother repeatedly approaches John for the baskets, but John forgets his task each time as he enters his cell. We can only imagine the possible frustration of the brother as Abba John asks him yet again, "What do you want, brother?" and he responds, "The basket, Abba." The major distinction in this version is that the third time John forgets, he does not force himself to remember worldly cares through a mantra but instead drags the other brother inside his cell, saying, "If you want baskets, take and go, for I do not have time."[68] Abba John remains largely unfazed in both encounters. While John is explicitly described as disturbed by the camel driver, we may hear in the second story hints of frustration with the fellow brother who wastes his time with such a worldly concern. It does appear that certain insider-outsider boundaries are policed, as the brother is allowed into John's cell, while the camel driver is not. The distinction reflects the hierarchy of feared distractions: A brother is far less likely to disrupt the sacred space of one's cell than is a worldly camel driver. Both narratives highlight the tensions between worldly engagements (in these cases, the economics of selling one's handiwork) and the ascetic ideal of forgetting the world to focus fully on God. That the tradition retained both variations is worth noting, making clear that neither version on its own was adequate. When coupled, they highlight the boundaries between ascetic and secular while heightening the image of John as divinely forgetful. John, who had wrongly thought himself already an angel early in his ascetic career,[69] knew as much as any ascetic that the goal of forgetting the world was always only partial.

Despite John's willingness to allow another brother to enter his cell, the Abba Isaac saying discussed above implied that brethren themselves might endanger one's stillness. Brethren behaving badly might contaminate other brothers with their grudge-bearing, anger, or other such negativities, opening an opportunity for demons to attack. Thus, the ascetic tradition proffers a model for proper behavior after witnessing a fight. While the Greek traditions tend to attribute the story to John the Little, the Coptic version attributes it to "one of the great men in Scetis." For clarity, I refer to John, but we should not lose sight of the fact that the story was popular in multiple languages and, while tied to John in particular in Greek, was more generically linked to an exemplar living in Scetis in Coptic. In the story, John retreats rapidly from "the church in Scetis" upon overhearing an argument between brethren. Having arrived back at his cell, John circumambulates his cell three times before entering. His behavior strikes his contemporaries as odd, and his brethren visit him seeking an explanation for his actions. In answering, John (and the tradition relaying his story) has the opportunity to explain how circumambulation might serve a cathartic, apotropaic function to extinguish any lingering anger he carried from witnessing the brethren's disagreement. By circling his cell three times (probably a Trinitarian gesture), John is able to "dispose" of the recollected anger so as to enter his cell "with stillness of mind."[70]

Evagrius witnesses to the presence of similar logics already in the fourth century, warning that a person's irascibility tends to cooperate with the demons, leading to forgetfulness of the saints and inability to truly pray.[71] He goes on to suggest that a brother recall Psalm 36:8, Ecclesiastes 11:10, and 1 Timothy 2:8, all passages that commend eradication of anger. Beyond evocation of scriptural passages recommending excision of anger from one's person, Evagrius also mentions a "mysterious and ancient custom" that involves driving dogs from one's house before prayer.[72] Rather than maligning this odd practice, Evagrius offers a spiritual interpretation: Dogs as animals represent the animal part of humans, irascibility. Thus, chasing dogs out of the house models exteriorly the interior cleansing of one's irascibility in order to achieve prayer. While later apothegms do not offer such explicit spiritualizing explanations, both Isaac and John model practical approaches to the risks fellow brethren might pose to one's stillness. Isaac flees to his cell rather than linger with the brethren after worship for fear of being tempted into worldly engagements. Similarly, John, upon encountering just such a base, worldly interaction—a fight between brothers—hurries back to his cell. But John, since he had already encountered wrongly oriented anger, required the extra step of Trinitarian circumambulation of his cell to ensure he did not accidentally carry the residue of worldly anger into the sacred space of his cell. While specific language of forgetting is absent, forgetting remains central to Abba John's behavior. What has shifted from the previous stories is the unacceptability of the worldly trace lingering in John's body. In his economic exchanges for the purpose of sustenance, John's affect ranges from neutral to vague annoyance at being distracted from his singular focus on God. While forgetting the world was always incomplete, dangerous residues like wrongly oriented anger had immediately to be exorcised through prayer and bodily rituals. Though easy to overlook, the Trinitarian evocation in John's circling points toward the shift John was hoping for: forgetting of the world and remembering of the divine, coupled actions that enable his progress toward the goal of the ascetic self. Even as ascetics sought a liturgical, divine identity through remembrance of Scripture and the Trinity, they were attacked from all sides by demons. The sanctioning of memories, including the "mutilation" of their concomitant desires (here, the excision of anger associated with memories) was essential to forgetting the world and forming an ascetic identity. Thus, an ascetic found himself attempting to violently erase past memories from his person.

And yet, as the stories of John and his handiwork highlight, erasure of one's entanglement in the world was always partial. Indeed, as we will see, it was critical that the erasure of one's past self remain incomplete. While an ascetic might focus on the divine during prayer such that he forgot the created world, such experiences were only ever fleeting. Evagrius, in fact, portrayed forgetting of the shadowy, created world as a heavenly reward that one only fully received at death.[73] While still living, an ascetic was *not* to forget his past, for to do so might result in his forgetting his imperfect human state.[74] In particular, to forget the world and one's past actions in it was to risk forgetting the sins resulting from one's human nature. So, Evagrius can advise the novice ascetic Eulogios to not forget his past life, as it is demonic thoughts that "often make light of your sins and often conceal them with forgetfulness."[75] To forget past sins, in turn, invited forgetfulness of one's impending future judgment, a deleterious risk and an invitation to demon attacks. Evagrius claims that to forget one's sins, or the meaning of the tears such recollections ought to produce, is to risk suffering madness.[76] Not forgetting one's past was crucial to producing a wellspring of tears for the very deserved eternal punishment such sins incurred and for the mercy God might show such a sinner. After a lengthy description of the sufferings that sinners in hell already experience, those they will feel on Judgment Day, and the copious tears such knowledge should produce, Evagrius exhorts, "Do not forget these things, whether you happen to be in your cell or outside it somewhere."[77] Likewise, in his *Praktikos*, Evagrius encourages recalling one's past sins, connecting, *not* forgetting, one's sins to awareness of God "who guarded you in the desert" from the violence of the demons.[78] Thus, ascetics living in the desert might only experience divine protection if they fought against forgetfulness of their past lives. To forget would be to risk one's eternal damnation, producing a dangerous form of forgetting, the kind that sent one into "a pit of forgetfulness," resulting ultimately in one's ruin.[79] All these examples highlight how *not* forgetting the world—and, as a result, not forgetting the divine—was framed through threats of violence. Should one forget, demons might attack one's person, especially if one got too haughty and forgot God. But not forgetting one's sins also carried meaning through the promised violence of God's impending judgment. That is, not forgetting one's past worldliness entailed actual and potential violence as much as sanctioning of one's memories did.

Intentional *not* forgetting is explicitly described as a violent process for the ascetic self in the John the Little passage with which this chapter began. As noted there, another brother queries John about forgetting. The brief epigraph sits in a larger story about the two men, preserved in a late fifth-century saying. The old man ("not sharp in thoughts") receives John's answer regarding forgetfulness only to return to his own cell and forget the message. The old man returns to John's cell "very often" to rehear the message, only to be "ruled by forgetfulness" upon returning to his own abode. At some point, the brother apparently ceases returning, for when he later runs into John, he says, "Do you know, Abba, that I have forgotten again what you told me, but so that I would not disturb you, I did not come?" Whereas the camel driver's disturbing of John seemed a nuisance in the saying examined earlier, here John chides his brother for imagining himself as a disruption. John sends the brother to "kindle a lamp," and then tells him to kindle more lamps from the first. John questions the old man about this exercise: "Is the (first) lamp harmed in any way because you light other lamps from it?" The answer, of course, is no, and John goes on to equate himself with the first lamp. He assures the brother that "if the whole of Scetis came" to him, he would not be hindered from his relationship with the divine, and thus the brother should always feel welcome to seek or re-seek a word. The two brothers endure, presumably in prayer (though the saying does not say so explicitly), and God takes "forgetfulness away from the old man." Thus, through joint effort, the two men are able to invite divine intervention on the old man's behalf.

Despite the generosity John extends to the old man in his lamp lesson, the final line of the saying indicates that the later tradition still understood John's experience of assisting his brother through the lens of violence: "Thus was the daily labor of those of Scetis, to offer zeal to those battling, even having violence done to themselves in order to gain for each other the good." There is no doubt that John's actions are offered as a worthy example of ascetic success in an earlier generation. But it is equally clear that John represents a properly oriented, violent ascetic self. John's "zeal" allows him to assist his "battling" brother. As in Chapter 2, even the less-than-perfect brother is imagined as enmeshed in battle, seeking to more fully enact the ascetic ideal. And though demons are never explicitly referred to in the story, it is not hard to imagine that many in the tradition understood demons to be the reason that the brother was "ruled by forgetfulness" and required John's sharing in his labor. Moreover, that together the two could encourage God's help squares well with Evagrius's vision of God as guardian of ascetics fighting demons in the desert. Together with the brother, John is enmeshed in the violence of battle, as he is described as inviting violence upon himself by his zeal on his brother's behalf. That is, violence is remembered by later Palestinian monks as integral to the removal of forgetfulness and the success of *ascesis* among the fourth-century abbas.

Across the stories discussed in this chapter, John exemplifies the delicate negotiations an ascetic had to make around acts of forgetting. If we take seriously that ascetics adapted the logics of *damnatio memoriae*, then we can better parse the tensions around how to engage the world, as ascetics were commanded to forget and simultaneously to not forget their worldly pasts. Memory sanctions were never an utter obliteration of a memory but rather the performed violent dishonoring of a memory, in this case one's own. John can be imagined, in the spaces between these retained narrative moments, as enacting memory sanctions against himself. The story of John's lesson in humility, having mistakenly imagined he was already an angel that did not require food, conveys that John learned early in his ascetic practice the incomplete nature of his abandonment of the world. Portrayals of John later in life find a wiser, humbler abba who, enthralled in prayer, momentarily is allowed to forget the worldly concerns of baskets, rope, and his own body, even as he models the necessity of continuing to engage in such realities. In this way, ascetics learned to partially erase their past memories, leaving only a trace, like the lingering scratch marks of an excised name. Such violent erasure left only residues meant to remind a monk of his own imperfect human state and the anticipated future violence of God's imminent, final judgment. The result was an ascetic humbled in his relationship to the divine, a newly produced self that was a palimpsest of new scriptural embodiment overlaying past trace memories. In this dynamic interplay between remembering Scripture and dismembering idolatrous memories of one's past, ascetic identity came to be articulated in an ever-heightening zeal for God, like John on the old man's behalf. It is John's successful damning of his "worldly" self as rope and basket maker, a violence against self, that produced his zeal, which itself required John to continue his self-violence anew for the sake of a brother's ascetic success. We can see in John's zeal his anticipation of and answering to God's call to all ascetics to be divinely sanctioned conduits of violence.

John's zealous call and answer with God likewise mimics traditional acts of *damnatio memoriae*, as they often involved dynamic communication between political leaders and the crowd, the crowd sometimes anticipating and at other times responding to political calls for violence. The even mightier call of the divine invited ascetics into a formation process that required violence and, in particular, valued self-violence. Violence against self in turn made possible the violent performance of eradicating demons from the desert, even as demons, as inhabitants of idols, were also being driven from the Serapeum and other temples through the violent rituals of *damnatio memoriae*. As with Theophilus's actions in Alexandria, the ascetic goal was to Christianize the space, as violent ascetics sacralized the desert in the hopes of transforming it into a physical representation on earth of or at least a gesture toward heaven/paradise.

Charged with Violence

Evagrius offers a rich description of the dangers an ascetic might experience if he forgot his "first" or his "human" states through the temptations of anger, pride, or sorrow. Such emotions were often rooted in worldly remembrances or encounters and were welcome fodder for demons in their attacks. Having failed to sanction one's own memories to avoid these passions, an ascetic suffered anew. Evagrius claims that an impassioned individual who attempts anchoritic practice "first sees the air of his cell all afire and lightning flashes at night shining around the walls, then there are voices of people pursuing and being pursued and chariots with horses figured in the air, and the whole house is filled with Ethiopians and tumult."[80] Rowdy crowds and animals and the threats of lightning and fire—just the type of "tumult" one might encounter in the midst of destroying Serapis's statue, for example—are coupled to provoke fear and humility in the ascetic practitioner. The presence of Ethiopians among this imagined crowd was meant to trigger disgust and shame as correctives to the ascetic self, a technique that relied on ancient notions of ethnicity, as even attempts to control worldly engagements remained deeply embedded in worldly ways of knowing. In this way, the violent image Evagrius conjures simultaneously mirrors the controlled chaos of acts of *damnatio memoriae*, even as it deploys traditional, worldly ethnic stereotypes.

Both the previous chapter and this one have highlighted how acts of remembering and forgetting constructed a violently charged ascetic. Seeing themselves as embattled with demons for control of the desert produced for ascetics a violently charged space. The violent ascetic located in a violent desert embodied the divine promise of an angelicized self and a paradisiacal, heavenly space. But such intense, violent focus also created a highly combustible context. Given the centrality of the tight link between, on the one hand, remembering and forgetting in the desert and, on the other hand, ascetic meaning making, it should not be surprising that a perceived rending of this bond through moments of violence in the desert resulted in both ascetic anxiety and a narrativizing of a Golden Age of asceticism and the death of the desert. The multiple modalities of violence that ascetics experienced and enacted made them targets not only for demonic onslaught but also for the theo-political struggles of their own day. As we shall see in the next chapter, worldly violence could slip into the desert.

Chapter 4

The Desert and the Discourse on Barbarians

> When Scetis was abandoned, he left crying, and said, "The world
> ruined Rome utterly, and the monks Scetis."
> —*Sayings of the Desert Fathers* (Greek, Alphabetical)
> Arsenius 21

The preceding chapters have laid out the violence inherent in ascetic constructions of the desert, the demons, and the monastic self. The intersection of these violent threads led to actual moments of violence in and out of the desert. The discussion in Chapter 3 of probable ascetic involvement in the toppling of Serapis serves as an example of ascetics leaving the desert to participate in acts of religiously motivated violence. Working in the other direction, the epigraph to this chapter is often cited as evidence of violence occurring in the desert, in particular the ruin of Scetian asceticism through "barbarian" assault. Discussions of raids on Scetis and the events of the first Origenist controversy often unfold in scholarly discourse with little reflection on the close chronological proximity between Theophilus's raid on Nitria in 400, on the one hand, and the purported Scetian raids, dated to 407–8 C.E., on the other. While Theophilus's confrontation with the monks in the desert is the focus of the next chapter, this chapter questions the dominant scholarly narrative that a series of barbarian raids across the fifth century destroyed a monastic way of life and thus brought the Golden Age of desert asceticism to an abrupt close. Certainly, people of differing ethnicities did live in portions of or on the edges of the northwestern desert, and some of them may even occasionally have robbed the brethren. But discourse on barbarians, especially as violent, has served to deflect blame for acts of violence and, more generally, to obscure the very violence of northwestern asceticism itself.

This chapter is at once historical and historiographical. It attempts to imagine the historical past of the northwestern desert of Egypt (as in previous chapters) and later rememberings of that past in the fifth century, as well as to analyze more recent historiographical renderings of the desert by scholars. As in previous chapters, this chapter once again invites us to recognize the sayings not as reflections of historical events but rather as later refractions. As noted in the Introduction, the *Sayings* have a long history of being taken as a historically accurate portrayal of asceticism in fourth-century Egypt. Placing such trust in the *Sayings* is crucial to the scholarly narration of a barbarian raid on Scetis. When we recognize the rhetorically constructed nature of the sayings and their later composition date, they become harder to take at face value. As this book suggests, sources written by actual witnesses from the late fourth and early fifth centuries need to be given preference and only then placed in conversation with the *Sayings*, as it was written roughly a hundred years after the fact.

To imagine what evoking a barbarian raid on Scetis meant to late ancient peoples, this chapter begins by describing the other beings that populated the desert: monstrous beasts and so-called barbarians. The desert as an Other space hosted not only animals but also imagined, fantastic creatures such as centaurs. These varieties of monsters, outside the reach of Roman and local law, threatened ascetics with the risk of violence or death. At the same time, visitors to the desert and ascetics themselves reflect anxiety about the blurry boundaries among ascetic, demonic, and monstrous bodies. The presence of desert barbarians likewise represented risks both for violence and for identity confusion. The presence of these various bodies in the desert, each defined in relation to the desert's reputed power, inevitably led late ancient people to sometimes confuse ascetics with these other beings. The case of Abba Moses the Ethiopian in particular highlights how muddled the distinctions among monster, barbarian, demon, and ascetic could be. This chapter concludes with a reassessment of the traditional scholarly narrative of a barbarian raid on Scetis and asserts that the evidence assembled by Hugh Evelyn-White is thin and problematic. As part of this reassessment, I return again to examine the figure of Abba Moses the Ethiopian as the only named person killed in the raid. If barbarian raids did ever occur, they were not events that vastly altered the history of Christian monasticism.

Lawless Monsters?

As we saw in Chapter 1, the desert was imagined as a powerful place, one constructed in opposition to urban life. My focus in that chapter was on understanding the desert itself and its demonic inhabitants, as well as the ways in which both carried inherently violent connotations. In the intervening chapters, I have also sketched out ascetics as violently seizing and inhabiting the desert. As part of that land grab, the ascetic strove to emulate (if not attain) an angelic body, a nonhuman type of body. But there were yet other bodies present in the desert, and they are equally crucial to understanding the rhetoric that developed around acts of violence committed there. In the desert, one might find a variety of animal inhabitants as well as more fantastical beasts that might be termed *monstra*, such as satyrs, centaurs, and other hybrid beings. There were also supposedly uncivilized, *apolis*-ed people, often referred to with the generic term *barbarians*. Because they lived in the otherworldly desert, these bodies could not be understood through the normal rules governing the world.[1]

As we saw in Chapter 2, demons sought to interrupt ascetic prayer, and ascetics, in turn, weaponized psalms and prayers against them. While the wiles of demons were many, one of their strategies was to play on ascetic fears of real desert-dwelling beasts. Distinguishing between actual animals and demonic embodiments of animals was problematic for an ascetic, as is reflected in our texts. Interactions might be as straightforward as snakes biting or scorpions stinging an ascetic's body. Or, the experience might be remembered as more otherworldly (since that was what the desert was supposed to be). Near the end of Chapter 3, I discussed Evagrius's story about John the Little as the ultimate example of ascetic stillness.[2] What marked John's amazing maintenance of stillness was his ability to ignore a beastly attack. Rapt in prayer, John did not respond to a dragon biting hunks of his flesh and vomiting them back at him. Here, what draws our attention is the unsurprising presence of a beast (probably reflecting the prevalence of snakes in the desert) being cast as a monstrous dragon. The horrific behavior of the dragon is not Evagrius's focus, as we might expect, but rather serves to highlight John's stillness. Evagrius's telling implies that dragons were a common nuisance to the ascetic. Thus, when a demon takes the form of a dragon and antagonizes John, the presence of the dragon-demon is noteworthy only because of John's exceptional nonresponse. The implication, of course, is that most brethren would not have been able to ignore such a terrifying and painful experience, regardless of whether they were in prayer.

The desert was also imagined as home to more mythical creatures. Perhaps the most famous example is Jerome's hippocentaur in his *Life of Paul*. In this text, usually dated to the late 370s or the early 380s (when Jerome was still a novice to ascetic life and had not yet become embroiled in controversies), Jerome tells of Paul, who preceded even Antony in the desert. Most scholars agree that Jerome here seems to be playfully, perhaps even competitively, engaging Athanasius's *Life of Antony*. Viewed in this light, his text offers a window into visions of the desert that were held by Romans elsewhere in the empire. Much scholarship has recently explored how Jerome's hippocentaur serves him in his imaginings of the Egyptian desert. Virginia Burrus has pointed to how such "monsters," as Jerome called them, functioned in hagiography to construct an ascetic identity that was oversaturated and therefore itself monstrous.[3] Patricia Cox Miller sees in the figure of the centaur a hybrid creature, one that marks ascetic identity and its relationship to the desert as likewise hybrid. In particular, she, too, sees the multiplicity of ascetic identity, the blurring of the idealized and the barbarous.[4] Engaging the work of Gloria Anzaldúa on *mestiza* consciousness, Peter Mena has also unpacked the hippocentaur in Jerome's *Life of Paul*, highlighting how all the animals function in the narrativized desert to construct the ascetic as *mestiza*.[5] Anzaldúa's *mestiza* functions for Mena to point to the multiple, hybrid identity of the ascetic vis-à-vis the desert, an identity that exceeds simple definition. Each approach seeks to untangle the multiple meanings of ascetic identity constructed by Jerome through the image of the hippocentaur: the ascetic as barbarous, the ascetic as monstrous, the ascetic as wild and bestial. What was particularly troubling about figures like the centaur is that they seemed to partake of *some* humanness and yet were *not* human, a description that, as we shall see in the next section, resembled Roman renderings of the barbarian. As previous scholarship emphasizing hybridity, or *mestiza*, identity indicates, there was often troubling overlap between identities.

So-Called Barbarians

Despite the rich imagining that served ascetic discourse so well, the desert was not solely an otherworldly place of the sub- and superhuman. It was also home to other human beings, despite Roman claims to the contrary—Austuriani,

Ethiopians, and Mazices, so-called barbarians, who lived along the edges of Egypt or in neighboring Libya. Much scholarship in recent years has nuanced our understanding of non-Roman peoples living in and on the edges of the empire.[6] Archaeological finds coupled with acknowledgment of the role of rhetoric in ethnographic construction have done much toward offering a more just historical rendering of these communities than easy acceptance of Roman stereotypes had yielded in previous generations. When we attempt to speak of barbarians in the northwestern desert of Egypt, however, the evidence remains very limited, and what is extant tends to be highly fanciful. In what follows, I treat each major "barbarian" ethnic group mentioned in our sources in order to understand them as much as possible in their own right and to contextualize how they were used to symbolize violence in Roman rhetoric.

The Austuriani are those about whom least is known. They are referred to in multiple letters of Synesius as a community that repeatedly raided Cyrene and neighboring cities at the start of the fifth century.[7] They seem to have emerged as a people from somewhere west of Cyrene, but nothing more is known of their precise locale of origin. The tendency in Synesius to depict a vicious and violent people, full of greed and bloodlust, coupled with scholarly tendencies to elide the Austuriani with modern Berber peoples (thus constructing a colonialized and timeless Berber) has left only the merest traces of an actual community. The best scholarly attempts have sought to situate the Austuriani among other tribal communities of late antique North Africa, acknowledging that they lived in a complex cultural system (and thus, were not monolithic or undeveloped), even if such systems are now largely lost to us. Some scholars have followed Denis Roques in his speculation that the Austuriani were actually tribal communities allied to Gildo, a Roman general who as the *comes Africae* sought to undermine Honorius as western emperor.[8] Such an urge among these tribal communities makes sense only two decades after Emperor Valentinian's *magister militum*, Theodosius (the father of Emperor Theodosius I), slaughtered tribal allies to Firmus (more on which below). Other scholars, however, have rejected Roques's thesis as implausible, instead situating the Austuriani within an African tribal confederation later known as the Laguatan, an alliance that survived into early Islamic rule.[9] In this view, the Austuriani/Laguatan were those tribal communities who found themselves in alternating cycles of support and contestation with one another and with neighboring Romans. During times of extreme Roman pressure, they might join forces against the larger Imperial threat. In either approach, the Austuriani are only glimpsed as yet one among many African tribal communities of late antiquity that might incite violence on behalf of or against Rome. In the eyes of the Romans, the Austuriani were synonymous with violence.

By contrast, the most mentioned and perhaps best-known "barbarians" of the region are the Ethiopians, those people living further up the Nile, south of Egypt. The term *Ethiopian* functioned on two registers in late antiquity. It was used both to denote an actual community, those living in and south of Nubia (descended from the Kush kingdoms) and to refer generically to anyone with a dark skin tone as part of "ethno-political rhetoric"[10] that had little interest in the lives of the actual Ethiopian people. It seems that sometime across the fourth century, many of the regions termed "Ethiopian" began to convert to Christianity. Little evidence remains for fourth-century Nubia, but when evidence reemerges in the mid-fifth century the Nubian kingdom is decidedly Christian. In contrast, we have fourth-century evidence of the Aksumite kingdom to Nubia's south, peoples who also were sometimes referred to as Ethiopian in Roman literature. Evidence for Christianity in Aksum surfaces in the late fourth century when king 'Ezana is said to have converted, leading Athanasius to appoint a bishop for 'Ezana's people.[11] Although we cannot presume full-scale conversion to Christianity, it does mark the beginnings of a gradual cultural shift. Thus, it is not unreasonable to imagine Nubia being exposed to Christianity in the fourth century as well, situated as it was between Egypt to the north and Aksum to the south, both Christianized regions themselves. That the kingdoms of Nubia and Aksum began to strengthen over the course of the fifth century also points to the very real economic and military threats Ethiopians could pose to the Roman Empire.

Romans elsewhere in the empire sometimes confused Ethiopians and Egyptians. This blurring resulted in Egyptians anxiously separating themselves from Ethiopians, Egyptians noting what they clearly viewed as recognizable (and distinguishable) physical differences, especially as regarded skin tone.[12] Even if other Roman citizens could not always distinguish Ethiopian from Egyptian, their portrayals of Ethiopians likewise relied on a perceived somatic legibility that rendered the Mediterranean Roman body as ideal and variations from that norm as defective. Climatic realities not only darkened skin hue but were believed to thin blood, making Ethiopians ineffectual warriors against the Romans. Rather than reflecting any reality in Romano-Ethiopian political relations, such stereotypes functioned as an ethno-political discourse that elevated and valorized Roman self-understandings. Such a reading of Ethiopian discourse is particularly amusing given that Romans accused Ethiopians of self-delusion. As Gay Byron has so eloquently argued, references to Ethiopians in the Greco-Roman milieu, including in Christian texts, are not a straightforward gesture to the peoples of Nubia or Aksum but rather represent a complex network of meaning.[13] One way in which Ethiopians functioned was as geographic boundary markers, delineating the limits of the known world, a role that in turn marked them as mythical, sub- or superhuman peoples. For our purposes, Ethiopians also served (especially in Christian, monastic discourse) as symbols of sexual excess, their bodies capable of exceeding the boundaries of sexual propriety and evincing promiscuity.[14]

While Ethiopians marked southern boundaries in the Roman imaginary, the west included the Roman regions of Libya and Cyrene as well as a vast expanse of desert dotted with oases around which a people known as the Mazices lived. While there are far fewer references to the Mazices than to Ethiopians, the distance between their actual identity and their rhetorical presentation is similarly vast. Ana de Francisco Heredero offers a picture of the Mazices as a seminomadic people who, through their engagement with Roman colonization of Cyrene, came to be sedentary.[15] Based on literary and epigraphic evidence, it seems likely that the Romans recognized as *praefectus gentis* several leaders among the Mazices across the fourth century. The writings of Ammianus Marcellinus seem to indicate that some Mazices participated in the revolt of Firmus against Emperor Valentinian I (mentioned above).[16] Ammianus's urge to valorize Theodosius as a great general points to his own ethno-political purposes in describing the Mazices. Reading against the grain of his text, it seems likely that the Mazices had allied with Firmus as a means of allying with Rome; both Firmus and his father had already been closely connected to the empire. As even Ammianus betrays in his explanation, Firmus (and potentially the Mazices with him) were revolting against the crimes and neglect of the appointed *comes Africae*, Romanus, who was abusing the surrounding populace and failing to protect them from attacks by neighboring peoples not in alliance with Rome. That is, the point of alliance with Rome—protection—was being denied them, leaving them little choice but rebellion. Moreover, in this instance, Theodosius was willing to forgive Firmus but not the Mazices who had supported him, going on to slaughter many of their people. Thus, we can imagine the Mazices learned the dangers of allying themselves with Rome.

Yet it is clear that by the sixth century, the Mazices and Romans continued to have a relationship of mutual respect that allowed trade.[17] What is less certain is how to understand the relationship between the Romans and the Mazices in the fifth century. Synesius, Palladius, and John Cassian, all writing in the early fifth century, refer to the Mazices, but in each case the rhetorical advantages of evoking the Mazices obscure our ability to discern actual information about this community. Writing in 405 to Simplicius, a powerful military figure at the Constantinopolitan court, Synesius refers to the Mazices as "semi-barbarian" people. As is well attested in scholarship, Synesius was quite capable of partaking in vitriolic rhetoric against barbarians. The most famous example is his strong critique of integration of so-called barbarian peoples into military and court leadership in his *On Kingship*, written in the late 390s or early 400s.[18] Thus, it is noteworthy that he conveys a more nuanced understanding of his neighbors, the Mazices. Through the language of "semi-barbarians," Synesius acknowledges that some communities, particularly the Mazices, inhabited a liminal identity between Romans and barbarians, capable of at least some cultured, civilized behaviors according to Roman norms.[19] For Synesius, that the Mazices did not fully participate in Roman culture is evidenced by their betraying to another neighboring people, the Austuriani, that the defenses of Cyrene were weakened by an ineffectual military leader, Cerialis. Thus, the Mazices' partial barbarity makes them an easy scapegoat in Synesius's writings for the attacks of the Austuriani on Cyrene and surrounding regions. That is, even when Synesius seems to offer nuance, he ultimately understands all barbarians as inevitably inclined to ally with each other against Rome. A fairer reading of the Mazices would seem to indicate they were a community living on the edges of the Roman Empire who attempted to negotiate (as Synesius's own language betrays) living in the places between empire and other tribal communities, often successfully and thus relatively unnoticed.

Palladius likewise shows some awareness of the Mazices but only deploys them for rhetorical gain. His brief mentions occur in his *Dialogue* and his *Lausiac History*. In each text, the Mazices merely serve as boundary markers, corresponding to the Ethiopians to the south, and indicate extreme distance. The *Dialogue* describes the exile location (a result of condemnation as "Origenist") of his fellow bishop, Demetrius, as at an oasis neighboring the Mazices.[20] In this case, Demetrius's exile is meant to parallel Palladius's own extreme remote exile location at Syene, near the Ethiopians. The Mazices represent the western limits of civilization just as the Ethiopians do the southern. As noted in Chapter 3, there has been a great deal of scholarship on exile throughout the Roman Empire in recent years.[21] Here, it is worth noting that exile was a political performance designed to cut an individual off from civilization. For our purposes, placing himself and Demetrius alongside Ethiopians and Mazices rhetorically functioned for Palladius to mark the extreme nature of their exile. For his rhetoric to work, Palladius had to presume his references to Ethiopians and Mazices would code for his audience as pointing to uncivilized barbarians.

Palladius's second reference, in his *Lausiac History*, comes a decade and a half later. While even briefer a mention than in his *Dialogue*, Palladius's past use of the Mazices as a rhetorical tool should remain in the backdrop. It is striking that in his presentation of the monks at Nitria a reference to the Mazices arises, once more in conjunction with Ethiopians, as a way of marking the extreme limits of the desert that the monks of Nitria are attempting to inhabit.[22] As before, the presence of Ethiopian and Mazice bodies is meant to delineate uncivilized hinterlands. Here, they serve as foils for the monks, marking as miraculous the lives of the ascetics in Nitria. In Chapter 2, I highlighted how Palladius could evoke heavenly expectations for the Nitrian desert, describing the ascetics singing psalms like angels. But Palladius's framing in reference to Ethiopians and Mazices reminds his reader, however unintentionally, that there were also so-called barbarian bodies already in the desert.

By far, the most extreme rhetoricizing of the Mazices occurs in Cassian's *Conferences*.[23] While Synesius clearly knew something of the Mazices as a people, and Palladius may have, Cassian seems only to know them through the rhetorical trope of violent barbarians. In attempting to trace the importance of discretion to proper ascetic practice, Cassian relates the story of two brethren who wandered deeper into the desert without food, trusting in God to provide for their needs. Their lack of provision leads them to the brink of death. Only an encounter with some Mazices, who help them recover, saves them. But, for Cassian, this story cannot be an indication of the goodwill of the Mazices as a people but rather of divine intervention. He describes the Mazices as "a race that is even more savage and ferocious than almost all wild tribes, for they are not driven to shed blood (as other tribes are) from desire of spoil but from simple ferocity of mind."[24] Cassian's portrayal of the bloodthirsty Mazices indicates nothing about the nature of the actual people; in fact, Cassian works hard to counter the perception of them as helpful or peaceful, as the story of the abbas indicates. Here, the Mazices are only a product of rhetorical imagination, standing in as the savage foil to the disciplined ascetic (even the foolish one) that only divine grace can transform.

All such references to Austuriani, Ethiopians, or Mazices rely on cultural expectations of barbarians as lesser humans, as Romans' Others. And, as we have seen, even when authors do use more precise ethnic terms, what they are describing is not necessarily separable from more generic bombast regarding

what and who barbarians are. Even though Ethiopians were portrayed as incapable of matching Roman military prowess, generalized references to barbarians subsumed more particular northern (Scythian) and southern (Ethiopian)
characterizations. Thus, barbarians became timeless figures inherently inclined
toward violence. In such rhetoric, the barbarian is imaged as savage and wild,
more comparable to beasts than to humans, and therefore dangerous. As this
chapter continues, it is important to remember that the authors cited tend
to refer to this Roman imaginary construct rather than to any actual groups
of people.

Monstrous Ascetic, Barbarous Ascetic

While not all desert inhabitants were described as monsters, their presence
in the desert did signal that they were supposed to be beyond Roman and
local law, living outside the nearest city's legal reach. Their presence, as we
have seen and will see below, was supposed to allow them to embody super-
or subhuman forms, marking them as beyond the laws of nature, much like
Jerome's hippocentaur. Such performed lawlessness carried both great possibility and great risk for ascetics. As Foucault notes in his discussion of the
monstrous (which violates law by its very being), the monster provokes an
extralegal response, one that, though it occasionally expressed pity toward
the monster, more often was a response of violent suppression.[25] While law
in antiquity was decidedly different from our own modern notions, Foucault's
linking of the monstrous to lawlessness is productive for thinking through
not only how monstrous bodies proper were viewed but also how all bodies
inhabiting the desert were imagined in late antiquity as beyond the law.

The range of bodies that occupied the desert meant that distinctions
between them sometimes blurred. As we saw in revisiting the story of John
the Little and the demonic dragon, boundaries between demons and monstrous animals could be collapsed in the service of constructing the prayerful
ascetic. Evagrius similarly deploys a conflation of demons and barbarians while
describing to Eulogius the ascetic who has succumbed to the demonic temptation to pride. He writes, "Such a person is a slave of a barbarian mistress . . .
but he who defeats the spirit of honor with humility will destroy the whole
legion of demons."[26] Here, Evagrius portrays caving into the demon of pride
through the image of serving a "barbarian mistress." Thus, being ruled by a
"barbarian" (and a female one at that) illustrates how deplorable and low on

the social scale is the demonically induced individual who enjoys the esteem of others. Barbarians, rhetorically imagined as uncivilized, immoral, promiscuous, violent, and consequently as *not* fully human, served well as a foil to the heaven-inclined, virtuous, chaste ascetic. Thus, barbarians and demons could simultaneously serve as an ascetic's Other, the distinctions between barbarians and demons dissolving.

In Chapter 1, I also briefly noted Dag Endsjø's scholarship on Athanasius's evocation of Greco-Roman traditions regarding *eschatia*, the "uncultivated or improperly cultivated" spaces that began at the walls of a *polis* and stretched to the ends of the earth.[27] Endsjø argues that "the primordial ambiguity of both the *eschatia* itself as well as those who were found there meant that anything could be something different from what it appeared to be."[28] That is, as the antithesis of the civilized, ordered world, the desert lacked ordered separation, the past bleeding into present, the living intermingling with the dead, the superhuman blurring with the subhuman, the wondrous with the horrendous. As we have seen in this and in previous chapters, underlying spatial (world and desert) and somatic (Roman, barbarian, angel, demon, beast, and monster) distinctions was a belief that an individual's spatial location was capable of transforming his embodiment. So, the desert, a space unbound by particularities coded in laws (political and natural), might produce bodily alterations, "leading one either close to a divine existence or down to the level of the beasts,"[29] producing either a superhuman (divinized) or a subhuman (demonic, monstrous, barbarian) body. In this light, literary portrayals of unkempt, wild ascetics who lacked the common markers of civilization (Roman clothing, housing, jewelry, etc.) encountered in the desert landscape take on new meaning.

Despite the fact that ascetics were *meant* to construct their identities in contrast to all these other bodies, the boundaries between an ascetic and all the others could be porous and sometimes elusive. In Chapter 1, we considered a story about Macarius the Egyptian's definition of the true monk as part of the larger, later Jannes and Jambres garden traditions.[30] The saying indicates that Macarius was traveling from Scetis to Nitria to visit Pambo and other brethren. After Macarius's arrival, the Nitrian brethren sought a word from him. To illustrate the true monk, Macarius recounts an encounter he had with two monks in the deep desert, who he claimed had greater endurance than he and thus were true monks in contrast to his strivings. Although Macarius's description in Chapter 1 served as an example of how central self-violence became to later fifth-century imaginings of fourth-century ascetics, his narration of the two true monks is worth revisiting in the light of the more populated desert that we explore in this chapter. The two monks Macarius discovered were Egyptian and Libyan, rather wild-looking, and lived naked in the midst of animals. The self-violence required to be like these two monks was more than Macarius could himself bear; nevertheless, he held up such self-violence as the ideal for ascetic life. Standing in the desert heat and cold, the two completely abandoned markers of civilization such as clothing, choosing instead to bare their skin like the animals with whom they lived.

While the image is meant to evoke the peaceable, heavenly kingdom into which ascetics strove to transform the desert, we can also imagine that their bodies might have been read as barbarous rather than ascetic by anyone besides the wise Macarius who might have encountered them. It is also telling that the backgrounds of the two monks remained important. Extended exposure to the sun undoubtedly would have deeply darkened their exposed flesh. That they needed to be marked as Egyptian and Libyan and presumably *not* Ethiopian underscores the possibility for misreading their bodies as savage barbarian ones rather than as the exemplary Roman ascetics they were. As we saw above, barbarians might be described as bestial, constructed as closer to animals than humans. Macarius's extensive description of the two monks belies that these two naked, dark-skinned bodies living with animals would have been read as barbarous. Thus, Macarius's true ascetic required self-violence to the point of erasure of easy delineations between barbarian and ascetic. By the late fifth century, to be a true ascetic was to be a barbarous ascetic.

Already in the early fifth century, we find evidence of such a reading of monastic behavior. A letter of Synesius witnesses to how other late ancient peoples might interpret ascetic bodies as barbarian. While Synesius would end his life as a Christian and as bishop at Ptolemais, much of his career was spent in non-Christian philosophical circles and in political posts both in Constantinople and in the region of Libya. In a letter addressed to Hypatia written sometime between 400 and 404 (during the same years as the first Origenist controversy), Synesius responds to critics, including "some in dark cloaks," that is, ascetics.[31] Elsewhere, he describes them sarcastically: "Already I have observed even barbarian men from both of the best races undertaking contemplation, and because of this they are both apolitical and without fellowship with men, in as much as they are eager to set themselves free from nature."[32] He continues, more mockingly, to describe an ascetic's singular, unrelenting, "barbarian" focus on basket-weaving, marking their behavior as distinct from that of their more moderate Greek counterparts, describing them as "violent and unyielding."[33] Synesius's polemical portrayal relies on his audience's knowledge of the rhetoricized barbarian. It also trusts that his fellow Romans would have recognized the *apolis*-ed nature of ascetics as barbarian and their emphatic focus on basket-weaving as a further marker of their violent, barbaric nature. Moreover, we must imagine that such portrayal of ascetics as violent and barbarian no doubt resonated among non-Christians with the concurrent monastic destruction of the Serapeum in Alexandria in the early 390s (discussed in Chapter 3). Although Eunapius, a pagan philosopher who recounts the attack on the Serapeum, does not use the term *barbarian* in his depiction of the monks, he seems to participate in such rhetoric, derisively describing the monks as "men in appearance" but actually "swine," acting in an "unseemly fashion in public," behaving like tyrants.[34] Eunapius clearly does not valorize extreme asceticism as Macarius does, yet once more the true ascetic is the barbarous or animalistic one.

The confusion between demons, barbarians, and ascetics is perhaps most poignantly expressed, though, in the figure of Abba Moses the Ethiopian (or "the Black"). An apothegm portraying his ordination as a priest plays on Abba Moses's dark skin, having the archbishop (most likely Theophilus) proclaim him "entirely white" post-ordination.[35] The remainder of the saying riffs on the dichotomies of white/black and inner/outer ascetic disposition. The archbishop and other priests "test" Abba Moses by casting him out of the sanctuary because he is Ethiopian. But Abba Moses responds with humility: "They have acted rightly toward you, ashen-skinned, black one. Not being human, why do you come among humans?"[36] David Brakke notes that "Moses accepts both the equation of blackness with being nonhuman (demonic?) and the separation from non-Ethiopians (that is, human beings) this entails," suggesting that reference to Moses's nonhumanity may point to the blurring of Ethiopian peoples and "Ethiopian" demons.[37] While Abba Moses's Ethiopian nonhumanity could be (and probably was) read at times in relation to Ethiopian demons, his nonhumanity also would have registered in relation to traditional "barbarian" rhetoric, especially as "barbarian" and "Ethiopian" might be used interchangeably to describe certain non-Roman peoples. As we saw above, the stereotypical "barbarian" nature was often described as one that was lacking in civility and therefore full humanity. The double meaning of Abba Moses's self-declaration as not human, both in the sense of nonhuman demons and less-than-human barbarians, as was Evagrius's discussion of demons as barbarian, intensifies the slippage among ascetic, barbarian, and demonic bodies in ascetic discourse.[38]

Late ancient portrayals and scholarly considerations of Moses the Ethiopian see his presence in the desert as unusual as he posed the possibility of barbarian bodies being transformed through ascetic practice. Depictions of his body were meant to symbolize how the humble virtue of a true ascetic could overcome even violent, barbarian impulses. Such views relied on clear demarcation between ascetic and barbarian. In Palladius's portrayal of him, Moses comes to represent not only the conversion of his own "barbarian" body but also the promise it held for conversion of other such problematic bodies. As discussed further below, Palladius asserts that Moses's well-known past as a robber made him an especially powerful witness to the power of asceticism and especially capable of convincing other robbers to likewise convert to the monastic way of life.[39] Although Palladius refers not to Moses's "barbarian" ethnicity but rather to his robberhood, the ambiguity of these categories—barbarian as violent robber—allows the possibility that Palladius understood Moses's Ethiopian body as uniquely capable of converting the other regional robbers, who were often deemed barbarians. Despite this nexus of readings of and expectations for Moses's body as ascetic, the death of the desert is often deemed by modern scholarship as caused by violent barbarian bodies incapable of conversion. As we shall see, Moses, as symbol of the barbarous ascetic, would continue to produce anxiety, as later strains of the ascetic tradition foreground him as the primary victim when barbarians purportedly first attacked Scetis at the beginning of the fifth century.

So-Called Barbarians in Scetis

As noted at this chapter's opening, the traditional scholarly explanation for the flight of monks from the desert relies on ancient reports of barbarian raids, the attacks marking the end of a golden age. In his expansive, three-volume study, *The Monasteries of the Wâdi 'n Natrûn*, Evelyn-White argues that three distinct barbarian raids occurred in Scetis in 407–8, 434, and 444. He reconstructs these three occurrences by drawing a variety of sources together and producing a neat and tidy narrative of Scetis's history. Evelyn-White's reconstruction, often repeated by subsequent scholarship, relates that a certain tribe of barbarians (sometimes conjectured to be the Mazices) attacked the monks living at Scetis, causing the monks to flee for their lives or stay to be slaughtered. And yet, despite the devastation, Evelyn-White goes on to argue that Scetis was capable of being sacked again a few decades later, and then a third time ten years after that.

As with earlier scholarship on barbarians in and beyond Egypt (especially on the Mazices), Evelyn-White's work betrays as much about his own historical context as about the northwestern Egyptian desert in the fourth and fifth centuries. In describing Scetian raids, Evelyn-White portrays the early fifth-century barbarians: "At all times the people of this remote region have borne the same character. So soon as failure of their own resources impels them, or governmental embarrassment or weakness allow them an opportunity, they descend upon Egypt using the various oases as stepping-stones across the desert . . . so, too, in late years the embarrassments raised by the European War invited the Senussi attack on Egypt in 1915 by way of the coast and the Wadi Natrun on the north, and the Oases of Dakhleh and Khargeh on the south."[40] In Evelyn-White's own context, recent struggles between Europeans and natives have brought embarrassment to the West. Reading his historical moment back onto late antiquity allows Evelyn-White to align himself with idealized, civilized monks against the raiders, who are portrayed as an orientalized, unchanging, subhuman Other. Given the above exploration of the rhetoricized barbarian and Evelyn-White's colonialism, a reconsideration of the prominent role scholars assign to a barbarian raid is in order.

Of particular interest is the first supposed raid on Scetis, as scholars tend to situate it around the end of the first Origenist controversy, in 407–8 C.E. John Chrysostom's death in 407 opened the way for offers of amnesty to be made to many of his compatriots in the following years. As Peter Van Nuffelen has argued, Chrysostom's passing removed from the negotiations the thorny issue of accepting his deposition.[41] The so-called Origenists now only had to renounce their adherence to Origen's writings in order to be reinstated; bishops were even restored to ecclesial seats. Thus, Synesius, as newly minted bishop, could write to Theophilus in 411 seeking advice on how to handle deposed bishops who still refused to return to their ecclesial thrones.[42] The years of 408–9 also saw the publication of Palladius's vitriolic *Dialogue* in defense of John, as it mentions his recent passing.[43] Thus, the years 407–11 contained much theo-political turmoil as the first Origenist controversy slowly drew to a close. And yet, not one among Palladius, the more temperate Ps.-Martyrius, and Synesius mentions a barbarian raid on Scetis. While Evelyn-White acknowledges Theophilus's raid on the desert, he problematically asserts that the absence of references to Origen's texts in

Scetis indicates immunity for the Scetian monks from the larger violence and aftershock of the attack.[44] But Theophilus's behavior did require a response, as he wrote a letter to the monks of Scetis in the aftermath.[45] Evelyn-White's quick dismissal of likely the largest theological issue of the day (Origenism) in order to reconstruct a barbarian-raid narrative has resulted in scholarship that continues to read these events as separate, unrelated matters.

It is also noteworthy that all the sources for the first barbarian raid of Scetis, except Augustine's letter (which, as we shall see, is somewhat vague), come from the mid-fifth century or later. That is, almost every source Evelyn-White points to for the barbarian raid on Scetis describes it through later moments of turmoil, including the sack of Rome in 410, larger ethnic shifts in the Roman Empire that happened across the fifth century, and the highly contested theological outcomes of the first council of Ephesus and then of Chalcedon. This refraction has important consequences for how we make sense of references to abbas leaving the desert because of violence.

As just noted, Augustine's *Letter* 111 serves as the earliest reference to some Egyptian brethren incurring violence. Writing in response to the worried presbyter Victorianus in 409, Augustine laments, "For a short time before, even in the solitude of Egypt, where monasteries are separated from all clamor, as if securely set apart, some brothers were killed by barbarians."[46] It is Augustine's "a short time before" (*nam ante parvum tempus*) that led Evelyn-White to situate the raid in 407–8. Shifting the date away from 395 C.E. (as was suggested by Sebastien Lenain de Tillemont and others), Evelyn-White argues that Augustine could not have meant a whole fourteen years earlier with this turn of phrase. Bolstering Evelyn-White's position was his assertion that Palladius and Cassian, still living in the desert in 395, certainly would not have left such a devastating event out of their later narrations. And yet, reconsiderations of the dates of when Palladius and Cassian wrote their texts produce precisely the same problem for Evelyn-White's date, as both the *Lausiac History* and the *Conferences* are now thought to have been authored post-407–8 C.E.

When we find Augustine discussing the many calamities wrought by barbarians, we would do well to locate his depiction within the larger rhetorical practice of stereotyping barbarians as described above: Augustine deploying such tropes doubly to portray these communities as the Romans' ethnic Other and as the Christians' heretical Other. In this light, Augustine's references to the recent slaughter of Egyptian brethren should be reconsidered. As just noted, what Augustine means by "a short time before" is a matter of interpretation. Depending on the speed by which such information traveled, the event may have been several months or several years earlier. Moreover, he reports that the attack was on "some brothers" (*fratres*) living "in the solitude of Egypt" and expresses no notion of the specific deserts of Egypt in which the brothers were slain, a point worth noting as we have evidence of ascetic inhabitation throughout desert regions of Upper and Lower Egypt. The reference is further situated in a long list of other horrors (including attacks in Italy, Gaul, and Spain), all ultimately minimized by the greater horror of Donatist Christians. Thus, though Augustine indicates awareness of the slaughter of some ascetics, the story merely serves as another example among many of the tragedies besetting the late antique world, all of which Augustine used with good rhetorical force to highlight the greater tragedy with which he himself was beset, that is, his struggle against the Donatists.

Another reference to barbarian encroachment into Egypt is found in Philostorgius's *Church History*. Preserved as an epitome in Photius's ninth-century *Library*, Philostorgius's text was meant to cover the history of the church up to 425. Presuming that Photius accurately reflects Philostorgius's original, this mention is the next datable reference to violence in Egypt. Akin to Augustine's *Letter*, Philostorgius situates his reference to barbarians in Egypt within a litany of horrors that beset the empire. Philostorgius rhetorically frames the many calamities as justified divine retribution for Emperor Theodosius's expulsion of Eunomius. That is, when we read his witness, we must be aware that he is deploying barbarians within a larger theo-politically charged agenda that sought to denigrate Theodosius's reign. Having articulated a variety of horrors that had recently taken place, Philostorgius continues, "But not only that, for both the Mazices and Austuriani (who dwell between Libya and Africa) desolated Libya to their east, and utterly blotted from memory no small part of Egypt, and invading the Africans to the west, accomplished the same."[47] As the discussion above noted, despite rhetorically heightened portrayals (like Cassian's) of the Mazices as bloodthirsty, actual neighbors like Synesius recognized the Mazices as fairly peaceable and merely "semi-barbarous." But here, as with Synesius, we have a coupling of the Mazices with the Austuriani. It would seem that Synesius could delineate the Mazices from the Austuriani, the former only truly guilty of giving the Austuriani information about Libya's vulnerability, while Philostorgius could not.

For Evelyn-White, Philostorgius's obliteration of "no small part of Egypt" was proof that barbarians sacked Scetis. Considered in relation to Synesius's witness, we know that the Austuriani (and perhaps some of the Mazices) besieged much of Libya, and thus it is perhaps reasonable to imagine

Philostorgius is correct that these communities went on to strike a good portion of Egypt as well. Given the location of monks in the northwestern desert, it is possible that these settlements might have suffered from some of the incursions into Egypt. But it seems unlikely that such attacks would have been restricted to only the monastic settlement of Scetis. Rather, if this encroachment of the Austuriani extended beyond Libya into Egypt, it would be better to imagine that damage would not have been limited to Scetis but would have befallen any ascetics living anywhere in the northwestern desert. But Synesius's *Downfall of Cyrenaica*, written in 411, complicates even such a generous reading of Philostorgius. In his text, bemoaning the attacks of the Austuriani, Synesius notes that the Austuriani had in fact been briefly repelled from Pentapolis (in the western regions of Libya) by the Roman general Anysius and his men. Forced to retreat, the Austuriani ceased attacking as a mob and instead encroached as "marauding bands."[48] Only after Anysius's death had Pentapolis finally fallen to the Austuriani. This description of the unfolding battles is important because it indicates that Pentapolis itself was still very much the focus of the Austuriani through 411. If it was so difficult for the Austuriani to successfully capture Pentapolis until after seven years of siege, it seems unlikely indeed that they had already reached the northwestern desert ascetics of Egypt in 407–8 C.E.

Evelyn-White's dating also relies heavily on several apothegms about Abba Arsenius, trusting them as both chronologically and historically accurate.[49] As I discussed in the Introduction, such trust in the *Sayings* would seem misplaced in the light of scholarly realization concerning how the textual tradition of apothegms was collected at a later time in a much different place and context. In the Introduction, I also problematized what we can know about a historical Abba Arsenius (Arsisius)—very little. As the saying at the opening of the chapter reveals ("When Scetis was abandoned, he [Arsenius] left crying, and said, 'The world ruined Rome utterly, and the monks Scetis'"), desertion of the desert would eventually be read through the sack of Rome in 410.[50] In Evelyn-White's translation of this saying, the order of places was reversed, Scetis and then Rome, reflecting the chronology of these destructions. Such a claim is highly speculative. If Scetis's position ought to be at the beginning of the pair, such a position may well reflect the primary focus of the ascetic community on themselves, and the secondary focus (if at all present) on concern for the world they are supposed to have left behind. Evelyn-White likewise leans heavily on Arsenius 42, which lists the various places Arsenius lived across his life (Scetis, Troë (near Memphis), and Canopus).[51] Trusting in the historical reliability of the *Sayings*, Evelyn-White presumes that the mention of Arsenius living in Scetis forty years is meant to be largely a continuous duration, with the exception being Arsenius's brief flight to Canopus to escape the barbarian raiders. It is worth noting, however, that the only saying attributed to Arsenius that mentions him experiencing barbarians actually explains how Arsenius came to live in Lower Egypt (fleeing Troë for Scetis), not how he came to leave it.[52] When a reason is given for his departure, the apothegm claims it is his being "continually disturbed" that leads him to abandon Lower Egypt.[53] Such disruption echoes stories of Arsenius avoiding visits by Theophilus and brethren, and his cursing of a wealthy woman who insists on visiting him.[54] It is Daniel alone who is supposed to have left because "barbarians invaded Scetis."[55] Seeming to despair about God's care for him, Daniel then walks into the midst of the barbarians, presumably in order to accept death by their hands. Miraculously, Daniel walks through the barbarian crowd unscathed and then acts "human" and flees "with the fathers." If Daniel is supposed to have stayed with Abba Arsenius until his death, usually set in 449, then neither he nor Arsenius left Scetis in 407–8. As another apothegm of Daniel makes clear, Daniel continued to engage other abbas living in Egypt under the episcopacy of Theophilus's successor, Cyril.[56] If barbarians entered Scetis in a way that affected Daniel's life there, it happened closer to the mid-fifth century.

In fact, most references to barbarians at Scetis come from late fifth-century sources.[57] The first is in John Rufus's *Life of Peter the Iberian*, usually dated to the later fifth century. Peter is said to have sought out "a man from the great holy ones of Scetis."[58] The explanation offered for the old abba's presence in Palestine rather than in Scetis is that a "band of robbers of the Mazices" who "fell upon the monasteries there [Scetis]" led the monks to depart.[59] There also are two stories in the *Sayings*, one found in the Greek tradition (and attributed to Anoub) and one in the Coptic (attributed to Dioscorus). In the saying of Anoub, the setting is a time when "the Mazices came and desolated it [Scetis] the first time."[60] The Dioscorus saying is much expanded and has "barbarians from the east" who enter Dioscorus's cell, scaring a brother with him and stealing his things, only to return his knife before leaving. In this latter saying, the barbarians are given voice, asserting that "we are not going to kill either of you."[61] In these passages, the Mazices or generic barbarians are once more blamed. But, as repeatedly noted throughout this chapter, the Mazices or generic barbarians here seem to be invoked more as a violent rhetorical trope than as actual peoples. Moreover, when the three stories (of Peter, Anoub, and Dioscorus) are read together, it seems that these supposedly violent Mazices or generic barbarians really behave as small robber bands, murdering no one. Lack of physical harm to the monks resonates with the saying of Daniel above, in which the point is that he walks through the barbarians unscathed.[62] While the Daniel saying would like the focus to be on God's continued concern for Daniel, we might also see in this saying barbarians who were willing to let the monks walk away. Thus, these collected references to barbarians trouble the notion of a clear and ruthless swarm of barbarians descending on Scetis. Rather, taken individually and together, it would be better to read these references to so-called barbarians within the larger discourse around occasional robberies of the monks in the northwestern desert. On the whole, most robber narratives in the *Sayings* rhetorically function to highlight how detached an abba was from his belongings. So, when Macarius the Egyptian encounters a robber stealing his own belongings, Macarius actually helps the thief load the goods rather than confront him.[63] And, as with many such stories, Macarius's actions are given scriptural justification, as both 1 Timothy 6:7 and Job 1:21 serve as the models that his peaceful engagement with the robber followed. That monastic encounters with barbarians are mostly recorded as being sporadic, mild, and nonviolent indicates that the boundaries between robbers and barbarians in the desert were also blurry. Many of the other passages that Evelyn-White gathered to argue for a barbarian raid on Scetis warn about or refer to loss of Scetis but make no mention of barbarians.[64] One saying thus offers abandonment of Scetis as the explanation for Abba Theodore's move to Pherme.[65] Recall from Chapter 1 that Pherme was a satellite community further into the northwestern desert, closer to the so-called barbarians. It thus becomes hard to imagine Theodore moving deeper into barbarian territory to flee barbarian destruction of Scetis.

Other texts that predict the demise of Scetis lean not on barbarian rhetoric but rather on overpopulation, excessive vegetation, youths, and fire imagery to explain its abandonment. So, Macarius the Egyptian is depicted as interpreting the presence of cells built in close proximity to the marsh as merely a warning of Scetis's desolation, while the subsequent access to water and ability to plant trees marked the desert's imminent demise. For Macarius, the loss of Scetis would only truly be certain when the community began to have youths in its midst.[66] Here we find echoes of the concerns about population density discussed in Chapter 1. In that context, growth in the ascetic community meant development of satellite communities deeper into the desert. By contrast, while Macarius partakes in anxiety about the proximity of brethren, it is architectural development in the direction of water, symbolic of the world, that is the problem. The many stories referred to in Chapter 1 told of ascetic individuals inhabiting ever more arid, remote locales. On the contrary, in this saying, Macarius is anxious about how close to water, represented by the marsh and trees, new settlements are.

The most damning concern in Macarius's foretelling, however, is the presence of youths. A similar linking of young bodies and the loss of Scetis's four churches is evidenced in a saying of Isaac.[67] Young male bodies represented sexual danger, potentially inviting the demons of fornication to upset an older abba's equilibrium.[68] But I would suggest there might also be another resonance possible in the image of youthful bodies—one of violence. As noted in the Introduction, youths (alongside enslaved individuals) were hired often as muscle in theological struggles. In that discussion, Palladius's portrayal of Theophilus's attack and his caricature of these youthful bands makes clear, such young boys had set the desert afire.[69] The young bodies tied to Theophilus were not sexual temptation but markers of impending violence.

Such fire imagery also characterizes one of Evelyn-White's final sources—though here, again, there are no barbarians described raiding Scetis. This shorter mention is an anonymous apothegm about an old abba who usually built cells for the brethren with great joy. One day, the elder arrives to his work filled with sorrow. When queried by the brothers about his sadness, he replies, "This place shall be abandoned, children. For I have seen a fire kindled in Scetis, and the brothers seizing palm branches, striking it, put it out. And again it was kindled, and again it was put out. But a third time it was kindled, and it filled all Scetis, and no longer was it possible to put it out."[70] Evelyn-White finds in the thrice-fiery Scetis image an evocation of the three barbarian raids of Scetis mentioned above, though no reference to barbarians is ever made. Again, there is evidence for only one actual fire—that set by Theophilus's youths at nearby Nitria.

The actual fires set by Theophilus and his bands, however, do not fully explain the presence of fire imagery in the *Sayings*' vague prophecies about Scetis's demise. Beyond actual, destructive flames, fire imagery should be read as symbolizing heresy. Although in Chapter 2, fire was often of divine or angelic origins, there was also a contemporary tradition that saw heresy as fire, rapidly spreading and hard to extinguish. We find such use in the writings of Epiphanius, one of the era's best-known heresiologists, and in those of Archbishop Theophilus himself. Both writers were some of the most vocal anti-Origenists during this period of doctrinal and ecclesial dispute. When the apothegm above is set alongside this tradition, it becomes clear that the fire that is remembered as repeatedly breaking out in the desert is not multiple barbarian attacks but rather repeated heresies that result in theological controversy. Much recent scholarship has explored Epiphanius of Salamis's *Panarion* and its use of medical and ethnic imagery to order and name so-called heresies.[71] While the image of heresy as fire is not similarly prominent in such scholarship, it is relevant that fire appears in his description of the rise of Arianism, a so-called heresy that had first emerged and become popular in Alexandria and its surrounding areas, including the desert regions of our anonymous abba. Epiphanius portrays Arius's wrongheaded and dangerous teachings as a fire that spread, consuming almost "the whole Roman Empire."[72] Read in conjunction with the apothegmatic tradition, the images of Arian heresy as all-consuming fire and some unspecified fire repeatedly reigniting at Scetis invite an interpretation of the fire at Scetis as a heretical blaze. Theophilus echoes his ally Epiphanius's language in his depiction of Origenism as a heresy spreading in the desert. In his first synodal letter to his own community, he appeals to medicinal imagery by describing Archbishop Heraclas as a doctor who, with the "divine two-edged sword," removed the "terrible ulcer" that was Origen in a previous era.[73] But, in his synodal letter to the bishops of Palestine and Cyprus, Theophilus chose instead to depict his opponents as ruffians who "prefer to be consumed by fire, rather than see Origen's writings condemned."[74] The fire imagery here symbolizes both the quick spread of heresy and the concomitant eternal condemnation in hell in which such heresy would result. Heresy imaged as fire likewise occurs in Theophilus's festal letter of 401, where he likens himself and his side to the three children in the fiery furnace, surviving the Babylonian blaze of the Origenist heretics unscathed.[75] Taken together, these examples show that fire was a common way to evoke the threat of heresy and that our anonymous abba's vision is better understood in this tradition of interpretation.

The final generic passage that Evelyn-White makes much of is found in the *Virtues of Macarius*. The text has been varyingly dated to pre-451 for its lack of Chalcedonian rhetoric, or else to the seventh or eighth centuries. Even if we accept the earlier date, the text articulates a backsliding in monastic practice over three generations, not an attack.[76] Furthermore, only two devastations are mentioned, and both have to do with immoral behavior, not with violent barbarians. In the passage, Macarius narrates the origins of Scetis, when all the "laws and commandments" of Christ were kept by the brethren. The first suffering is prophesied as a future event that will occur because of passions, presumably wrongly oriented ones. Again, Christ will give the brethren a chance if only they will keep half his commandments. And the last generation will no longer even be required to keep any commandments but must merely "dwell alone." At each stage of this foretold future, destruction occurs because of communal misbehavior, but, in each case, Christ forgives the ascetics and restores them to Scetis. Given that the subsequent passage has Evagrius ask Macarius about free will, it seems far more plausible that we have here a nostalgic narrative of decline since the first generations.[77] By elevating the earliest monks, the author can critique the perceived weaknesses of the present community, here imaged as failing to keep commandments and caving to passions. Such nostalgia requires a perceived loss of moral upright-ness among the brethren but makes no appeal to barbarian violence.

The reassessment of Evelyn-White's evidence above calls into question the perpetuation of a barbarian-raid narrative for the first decade of the fifth century. As I have shown, it seems quite unlikely that barbarians raided Sce-tis in 407–8, as has been often repeated by scholarship since Evelyn-White's argument first appeared. *If* barbarians entered the desert, Scetis was probably not the sole locus of assault. Moreover, the evidence above suggests that the experience of barbarian encounters would have been akin to other instances of robbery—treacherous, but contained to a small group of raider-robbers and monk-victims.

So-Called Barbarians and an Ethiopian Abba

One crucial source for the first barbarian raid remains: the traditions around Abba Moses the Ethiopian. Abba Moses's mistreatment at his ordination by Theophilus and brethren was noted above. In the discussion, Moses's Ethiopian body posed a challenge to the desert project. While he could be acclaimed as an exemplar of asceticism's ability to transform, his contin-ued Ethiopianness linked him both to generic notions of barbarians and to demonic appearances. This ambiguously located Ethiopian abba is also a main witness to and martyr of the supposed barbarian raid on Scetis. Although six other brethren are said to have perished alongside him, his is the only name remembered. The evidence for murder by barbarians is depicted in two, late fifth-century sayings. In the first saying, Moses proffers a warning to the brethren: "If we guard the commandments of the fathers, the barbarians will not come to this place, but if we do not guard them, the place will be deserted."[78] As with earlier examples, ascetic obedience or disobedience to the monastic Fathers' commandments can lead to safety or to the desertion of the desert. Here, Moses links ascetic behavior (obedience or disobedience to the monastic Fathers' commandments) in particular to the risk of barbarian attacks (and having or losing God's protection during the attacks). In the Coptic version of this apothegm, the verb for "will be deserted" is the root *shwf*, meaning to desert or destroy. This same root sits behind one of the rarer Coptic words for desert. In Chapter 1, it was this term for desert that was used by the demons who complained to Macarius about losing their "desert places." As noted there, the root evokes a desolate, ruined landscape, available for demonic inhabitation. Similarly, then, this language of desertion/ destruction in Moses's mouth would have evoked reminders of the desert as home of demons. Although the desert has begun to be transformed into a sacred locus, Moses reminds his brethren that possession of the desert is tenuous, contingent upon proper ascetic practice. Moreover, the invocation of so-called barbarians as the agents that would revert the desert from its paradisiacal possibility to demonic locus rhetorically heightens the risk of disobedience. Even here, where it is not explicit, we can see in word choice a potential blurring of demon and barbarian bodies—and even those of ascetics. In their failure to follow the commandments, the ascetics have lost an essential marker of distinction between themselves and all the other bodies inhabiting the desert. And, in the process, the desert itself is once more transformed from a place of paradisiacal hope to one of danger.

In the apothegm that usually follows this one, Abba Moses's prophecy comes true. Of all the passages cited by Evelyn-White, this is the only apothegm that explicitly describes the Scetian sack. Thus, it is worth examining more closely.

> Once when the brothers were sitting with him, he said to them, "Look, today, barbarians come to Scetis, but arise and run away." They said to him, "And you, do you not flee, Abba?" And he said to them, "For many years I have expected this day, so that the word of the Lord Christ might be fulfilled, saying, 'All those who take a sword, will die by a sword' (Matt. 26:52)." They said to him, "We do not run either, but we will die with you." He said to them, "I have nothing to do with the matter. Each decides to remain." There were seven brothers and he said to them, "Look, the barbarians are near the door." And entering, they [the barbarians] killed them [the brothers]. But one from among them hid behind the ropes. And he saw seven crowns coming down and crowning them.[79]

Abba Moses begins by once more predicting the barbarians' arrival, only now it is imminent, "today." While there is a fair amount of space devoted to dialogue, the actual act of violence is rather brief: "And entering, they killed them." Such brevity points to the rhetorical purposes to which Moses's death is being put. By neither testing God as Daniel had done before moving to Lower Egypt nor running away as John the Little was said to have done in later traditions, Moses remains in harm's way, an act that results in martyr crowns for him and his unnamed companions.

Moses's scriptural evocation of Matthew 26:52 to support his self-sacrifice alludes to his past life; as both Abba Arsenius and Palladius note, before he was a monk, Abba Moses was an especially violent robber.[80] As noted earlier in this chapter, robbers did occasionally appear in the desert among the brethren, and the boundaries between barbarian and robber could be quite blurry. Once more, Moses's body serves as a prime example of the problem of delineating boundaries: He is a barbarian by way of both his Ethiopian identity and his former life as a robber. The saying suggests that the only way to distinguish Moses's multiple identities was for his violent past to be fully purified by barbarian-inflicted violence.

But both of these stories were written down in the late fifth century in Palestine. If there are not contemporary witnesses to Moses's death, how historically trustworthy are the two apothegms? As one might anticipate, there are problems with relying on this story as a witness to a Scetian raid. First, how does Moses end up in Scetis, available to barbarian attack? While he certainly began his ascetic career in Scetis, the *Sayings* tradition otherwise indicates that Moses, distracted by constant visitors, moved from Scetis to Petra.[81] Whether this Petra is the ascetic community across the Nile River and into the eastern desert or another more remote location in the western desert remains uncertain. Cassian situates Moses not in Petra but in a deeper region of the western desert he calls Calamus.[82] Perhaps the apothegms that move Moses out of the northwestern desert do not accurately reflect Moses's location, as Palladius never mentions Moses abandoning Scetis, and Cassian only has him retreat deeper into the wilderness. Recognition that the *Sayings* is not in fact a historical window into fourth-century Egyptian asceticism requires a reassessment of the narratives around Abba Moses's life.

Palladius, too, recounts a story of Moses encountering robbers, but the outcome is different from the martyrdom reflected in the *Sayings*. In his rendering, Moses defeats four robbers, bringing them before his fellow brethren, saying, "Since I may not hurt anyone . . . what do you recommend I do with them?"[83] These robbers do not kill Moses but rather are converted to the ascetic life because of his example. Palladius's Moses, in fact, is never murdered, instead living in Scetis to an old age, leaving behind seventy pupils. If we are to believe that Palladius left exile in Syene and began heading toward Alexandria in the years immediately following both John Chrysostom's death and Moses's supposed murder in 407–8 C.E., it seems highly unlikely that he would have heard of John's death but not of Moses's demise. The question that lingers is, if Moses was indeed killed by barbarians, why would Palladius contradict other accounts of Moses's murder in the desert?

Whereas the *Sayings* fashions Moses's death at the hands of barbarians as a scriptural indictment of his past, for Palladius Moses's past becomes a conduit through which other robbers might also be converted into ascetic disciples. That is, while one thread of the tradition finds Moses's body only redeemable through violent death, another fashions his impossibly asceticized barbarian body as transformative of other barbaric bodies. As noted earlier, the *Sayings* preserves a clear witness that Moses's body posed a problem not only for many of his brethren but also for Archbishop Theophilus. Thus, it is unsurprising that the same tradition would view Moses's former robber-hood as marking him worthy of murder. By contrast, Palladius's mention of Moses's former banditry amplifies the power of his conversion; a violent, barbarian robber can be converted to Christian asceticism and can, in turn, convert his former robber compatriots. If Moses was killed by Theophilus, it would have served Palladius, who was trying to rehabilitate his fellow Origenists in writing the *Lausiac History*, to have glossed over the episcopal attack and instead to have portrayed Moses as living to a ripe old age. In all the traditions, Abba Moses acts as a signifier for the violent barbarian, albeit turned monk, within the monastic community. He symbolically represents an uneasy tension between the promise of Christianity in its ability to convert even the Other and the perceived risk inherent in the Other's presence within the community—a tension that holds within it the potential for destruction and death.

Conclusion

The later fifth-century tradition remembers only Abba Moses and his companions as dying at the hands of barbarians. Given how much Abba Moses's Ethiopianness troubled Theophilus and some in the ascetic community, it is a rather neat solution that Abba Moses would fall prey to other (presumably dark-skinned) barbarians, helping to remember the community into a less ethnically diverse ascetic population. Such a deployment of barbarian rhetoric would have been completely in keeping with Roman literary tropes with regard to ethnicity, as evidenced even in ascetic texts. Moreover, Palladius, as an actual acquaintance of Moses, offers a counternarrative with a natural end of life for Moses. Given Palladius's own return from exile in the years immediately following 407–8 (an exile he notes placed him near Ethiopians), it challenges the imagination to believe that he would not have heard about so traumatic a raid on a former mentor and neighboring ascetic community.

The piecemeal nature of Evelyn-White's evidence for a raid coupled with these competing traditions calls into question the death of Moses at barbarian hands—and, likewise, the notion of a barbarian raid concluding the Golden Age of the desert.[84] This is not to say that barbarians never came among the monks and robbed them. But the meager evidence for actual violence calls into question Evelyn-White's reconstruction, given that the sole targets were Abba Moses's problematic Ethiopian body and those of his disciples. That Archbishop Theophilus is remembered in the later *Sayings* not only as being among those who mistreated Moses but also as the perpetrator of the only known major act of violence in the northwestern desert at the turn to the fifth century should heighten suspicion toward the notion of Moses's murder by barbarians.

Evelyn-White asserts that "the storm of controversy concerning Origen's works, which had burst with such dire results over the Mount of Nitria and Kellia, had not seriously disturbed the calm of Scetis."[85] Given Theophilus's violence against the Tall Brothers and their brethren, as well as later recollections of his mistreatment of Moses, the references to barbarian raiders, including those who murdered Moses, should be reconsidered in the light of violence at Nitria, perhaps even as coded references to Theophilus's attack on the settlement. By later in the fifth and into the sixth century (when most of our sources are dated), it was a far different world for Christians in the Roman Empire. In the aftermath of Theophilus's clear victory in the first Origenist controversy, it would no longer be prudent to remember his acts of violence. The discourse on barbarians constructed those living on the edges of the Roman world as potentially violent, regardless of what a given people was actually like. Barbarians imagined as violent made them believable agents of actual acts of violence. Over the course of a century, the narrative shifted from blaming an ecclesial leader to offering traditional barbarian scapegoats to improve the memory of a blessed archbishop. Given the actual influx of barbarians and violence elsewhere in the empire, such as the sack of Rome by Alaric and his Visigoths a few years later, a rereading of the loss of the northwestern desert to barbarians would have been easily fabricated. As the apothegm of Arsenius that opens this chapter notes, such a memorialization was not straightforward historical remembering but rather a remembering of a lost ascetic sacred locus and self-understanding through appeal to barbarian violence.

Chapter 5

Reordering the Desert

And if God's grace had not restrained the attack of the mob, what
normally happens in riots would have occurred. For people break
out into such criminal foolhardiness, or rather insanity, that even
monks leading a holy way of life and normally the mildest of men
cannot hold back their fury.

—Theophilus, *Second Synodal Letter to
the Bishops of Palestine and Cyprus* 6

We saw in Chapter 3 that monks acted out the violence of memory sanctions
against the statue of Serapis at Archbishop Theophilus's goading. Theophilus was more than happy to rile up the "mildest of men" when the object of
"their fury" was his pagan opponents. In this chapter, Theophilus as inciter
of violence once again plays an important role, though the location of this
provocation is no longer the city of Alexandria but rather the monastic desert itself. While Chapter 4 interrogated the narrative of so-called barbarians
attacking the ascetic communities of Scetis, this chapter considers the only
clear historical record of violence in the northwestern desert—Archbishop
Theophilus's attack on the monks of Nitria, first mentioned in the book's
Introduction. Even if we were to accept that so-called barbarians did raid Scetis
(although, as argued, there are good reasons not to), the attacks would have
been most immediately legible through Theophilus's incursions into the desert
a few years earlier. In the epigraph above, Theophilus attempts to manage the
narrative of the fight he engaged in at Nitria by portraying the monks who
stood against him as foolhardy, maybe even insane. As we shall see, Theophilus's assertion of his own authority in the desert had important implications
for how the desert was read by subsequent generations of Christians.

Theophilus's entrance into the desert threatened the monks through the violence of pillaging their belongings, burning their buildings, and perhaps even murdering their inhabitants. But equally devastating would have been what Theophilus's action represented: the incursion of the urban sphere of legal control into the spiritual wilderness of the desert, the attack of Roman *oikonomia* into monastic *eschatia*. As argued in Chapter 1, the desert garnered its powerful Otherness from its lawless difference from the worldliness of Rome, especially as expressed in nearby Alexandria. No longer outside the bounds of earthly law, the desert after Theophilus's attack was perceived by some monks to have lost its power.

This chapter begins by reconstructing the fight between Theophilus and the Tall Brothers. While the book began with Palladius's narration of the conflict, here I juxtapose the competing extant accounts in order to imagine what might have happened and to understand the purposes violence and violent rhetoric served in each iteration. I then return to the accusations cast against Theophilus and argue that Theophilus's men may indeed have killed some Nitrian monks. Within this examination, I reconsider the story of Abba Moses and suggest that, given the problematic evidence to which Hugh Evelyn-White appeals, if someone violently slaughtered Moses and his followers it was either a small band of robbers or Theophilus and his band of youths and enslaved Ethiopians. I then briefly trace how Theophilus's violent reputation cast a long shadow on his episcopal successors in the fifth century. Across the same decades, the exiled monks and their subsequent students were forced to reimagine their history. The Tall Brothers and their followers fled the northwestern desert and, having resituated in Palestine, greatly influenced Gazan monasticism in part through their importing of tales of their lives in Egypt. I consider how, in this Gazan milieu and beyond, the loss of the desert was and was not retold across the fifth century, including in the construction of the *Sayings of the Desert Fathers*. I close by arguing that a Greek alphabetical *Sayings* collection was compiled in Gaza in the late fifth century as a memorializing response to a century of violence, one that sought to obscure the attack of Theophilus and to remember an idealized monastic past.

Civilizing the Desert?

As noted in the Introduction, Palladius's rendition was meant to be a compelling argument, not a historical recounting. As Demetrios Katos has argued,

Palladius was trained as a forensic practitioner, and his concerns in the *Dialogue* directed his rhetorical skills toward the rehabilitation of John Chrysostom and his own ecclesial and ascetic comrades, especially the prominent Tall Brothers whom Theophilus had attacked.[1] Palladius's politico-legal training was necessary in his face off with Theophilus. Building on Norman Russell's rendering of Theophilus as forensic practitioner in his own right, Krastu Banev argues that it was Theophilus's own great skill in rhetoric and particularly judicial argumentation coupled with an intimate awareness of monastic piety that led to his successful smear campaign against a long-dead Origen and many living so-called Origenists, including Palladius.[2] Thus, we find several bishops (most prominently, Theophilus, John Chrysostom, and Palladius) as well as several ascetics embroiled in a "legal" battle that blurred boundaries between theology and politics. Beyond recognition of the education bishops might have had in traditional rhetorical and judiciary methods, the spatial resonances of the desert as Other to the civilized Roman world render legible how this struggle unfolded. Theophilus violently thrust worldly legalism into the lawless desert so that the subsequent proliferation of the Origenist controversy became embedded in judicial rhetorical styles.

In addition to the contrasting defenses by Palladius and Theophilus, the event was also narrated to a lesser extent in the *Dialogues* of Sulpicius Severus and the *Funerary Oration for John Chrysostom* of Ps.-Martyrius. Sulpicius Severus's *Dialogues* portray a character named Postumianus who travels through Egypt and who, during his visit to Alexandria is invited to be a guest of Theophilus. Written sometime between 403 and 406, the *Dialogues* reflect an almost contemporary witness to the violence at Nitria, especially as an attempt to portray the event in the midst of the larger controversy. The *Funerary Oration*, its author now lost, was written just a year or two later, in the immediate aftermath of John's death in 407, as a replacement for a proper funeral eulogy. While its primary focus is on John's struggles, it offers another contemporary narration of the conflict between Theophilus and the Tall Brothers, one that tends toward hostility against Theophilus. In the attempted reconstruction in this chapter, each of these texts is cited where it offers nuance or an alternative explanation of the events that unfolded.

The violence that erupted between Theophilus and the Nitrian community was first triggered by some fiduciary concerns arising between Theophilus and the prominent priest Isidore. Although Isidore had been ordained by Archbishop Athanasius, he continued to serve as "guest-master of the church of Alexandria," first under Archbishop Peter, then his brother Archbishop

Timothy, and finally the new archbishop, in 385, Theophilus.[3] As late as 396, Theophilus still so trusted Isidore that Isidore acted as Theophilus's emissary to Epiphanius, bishop of Cyprus, and John, bishop of Jerusalem, as the first rumblings of the Origenist controversy began in Palestine. Moreover, Theophilus attempted to place Isidore on the Constantinopolitan ecclesial throne instead of John Chrysostom in 397, seeking to situate an ally near the court. Theophilus's actions make clear that Isidore was his valued confidant for almost a decade and a half, until their falling out sometime in 398 or 399.[4]

Palladius asserts that the argument between Isidore and Theophilus occurred because a wealthy widow gave Isidore money to clothe poor women in the city but requested that Theophilus not know of the money for fear he would spend it on building projects instead. When Theophilus found out about Isidore's secret, he "became swollen in body in his anger," going on to trump up charges of sodomy against Isidore.[5] Theophilus, of course, portrays his charges as legitimate: A woman had accused Isidore with a serious crime, and then Isidore bribed the woman into silence by enrolling her as a widow of the Church.[6] Theophilus assures his fellow bishops that Isidore's unwillingness to present himself before the Alexandrian and Egyptian clergy indicates his guilt.[7] While it is impossible to know for sure whether Palladius or Theophilus is presenting a fairer reading of Isidore's quandary, both stories indicate that Isidore's interactions with a widow and his use of money in relation to her permanently damaged his relationship with Theophilus.

Isidore's plight is important because his subsequent retreat to Nitria, where he first practiced asceticism, ultimately triggered Theophilus's violence against the desert monks.[8] Their hospitality toward Isidore ruined not only Theophilus's relations with Isidore but also Theophilus's previous respect for the Nitrian brethren. Ps.-Martyrius likewise has the Tall Brothers suffering "the penalty of loving a brother."[9] The text deems kindness shown to Isidore as the impetus for Theophilus's hostility. Palladius claims that the ascetics' reception of Isidore led Theophilus to send letters to neighboring bishops ordering the excommunication of several monks in charge of the monasteries. In this way, Palladius focuses blame solely on Theophilus, whereas Ps.-Martyrius also draws into his rendition the Egyptian bishops who followed Theophilus in passing judgment on the Tall Brothers. In Ps.-Martyrius's hands, Theophilus becomes an erratic tyrant, terrorizing his bishops and "illegally changing their sees."[10] So traumatized were the bishops that they behaved more as slaves than men of power in the church. The *Funerary Oration* argues that the bishops' "half barbarian" names—retaining references to

ancient Egyptian gods—were symbolic of their "completely barbaric" character.[11] Deploying barbarian rhetoric, Ps.-Martyrius implies that the bishops
are unfit to rule, much less to pass judgment on the monks of Nitria.

Palladius goes on to assert that the excommunication orders gave no
reason for the action, so several monks and their priests went to Alexandria
seeking an explanation. Palladius paints Theophilus as being so angry that he
appeared like a "dragon" or a "bull."[12] In the story of John the Little and the
dragon (discussed in Chapters 3 and 4), the presence of a dragon was both
a bestial and a potentially demonic image. Given Palladius's portrayal (more
on which below), it is not unreasonable to see him as imaging Theophilus as
animalistic and maybe even demonically possessed. Palladius further purports
that Theophilus, in his rage, choked and punched the old monk Ammonius
until his nose bled. Without their answer, the monks stumbled back into
the desert. Thus, Palladius envisages a raging Theophilus as the instigator of
violence, claiming that he physically struck the brothers first.

Although Theophilus corroborates that some monks approached him in
Alexandria, his portrayal of the event differs starkly. Theophilus articulates
his viewpoint in his *Second Synodal Letter*, written to the bishops of Palestine
and Cyprus, in order to have it "arrive" ahead of the monks in Palestine. It
is from the end of this letter that the chapter's epigraph—depicting monastic mob violence—is drawn. Warbling between harsh criticism of Origen's
"heresy" and monastic defense of Isidore, Theophilus links the two without
ever adequately explaining their relationship.[13] Rather, the rhetorical structure of the letter is meant to invite conflation of the two issues. He argues
that "certain people bearing the name of monks" had formed a band, using
"material inducements" to gather "a number of destitute people and slaves."[14]
With a quick turn of phrase, Theophilus implicitly claims the right to delineate between true monks and those in name only. He returns to the matter
later in the same letter, assuring his audience that he only involved himself
with such monks to "correct their error" that they might "live in a manner
worthy of their name so that those who are called monks, if they really want
to be what they say they are, may love silence and the catholic faith."[15] As I
discussed in Chapter 1, the monastic tradition reflects ascetic definition of the
true monk through embodiment in the desert. Here, Theophilus's ecclesial
power encroaches into the desert, the archbishop asserting that he has the
power to delineate the true monk from the pretender. In the latter quotation,
he does so through claims of catholicity; he as archbishop has the legitimacy
to speak, while the brothers should be quiet (a rather creative appropriation

of ascetic valuation of the silence (*hēsychia*) needed for prayer). Moreover, he condemns the monks for not coming alone but instead bribing a band of undesirables (poor and enslaved peoples) to accompany them and pressure Theophilus, in his own see, on the matter of Isidore.[16] Thus, Theophilus portrays the monks as entering his territory in order to threaten him, the accompanying band intimating the violence Theophilus might suffer.

Whereas Palladius has the beaten, bleeding Ammonius and his companions retreat peacefully into the desert, Theophilus makes no mention of injury to any of the monks. Instead, he claims that the monks, displeased by Theophilus's reception, sought to incite violence in the city before heading home. In particular, Theophilus asserts that they tried to arouse the pagan populace against him, particularly attempting to reignite violence in response to the recent destruction of pagan temples. Theophilus quotes them as having shouted that "[outrages] against the rights of temples have not been [committed] in the Nitrian monasteries!"[17] He claims the monks denied any involvement with the temple destruction that happened, for example, at the Serapeum. If some of the monks actually did participate in the Serapeum's demise, this later attempt to rile up the Alexandrians by reminding them of their lost temple would indicate that the violence was still a sore point for some of the Alexandrian populace almost a decade later. As noted in Chapter 3, the later apothegm that links the monks to Theophilus's destruction of pagan temples also indicates continued ambivalence among the monks about their involvement in such violence. Thus, Theophilus may be accurate in his portrayal of the Tall Brothers and their entourage publicly denouncing Theophilus's violence against the temples. However, Theophilus's accusation may well be fabricated, as it denies these monks any share in his glory of Christianizing the landscape and instead portrays them as sympathizing with pagans over their own bishop. Given Isidore's loyalty to Theophilus, his intimate relationship with the Nitrian monks in the early 390s (when the Serapeum was attacked), and Rufinus's positive rendering of the Serapeum's destruction, it is all the more likely (as argued in Chapter 3) that some of the monks from the northwestern desert (whether Nitria, Kellia, or Scetis) were indeed involved in *damnatio* against Serapis. The ambivalence of the ascetic community about its own involvement would ultimately crystallize in the *Sayings* in the rather unsympathetic portrayal of Theophilus serving the abbas veal.[18]

Despite Theophilus's accusations against the monks of inciting violence after his meeting with them, he claims that he later visited "the places themselves" (that is, the desert) only at the invitation of "the holy fathers and presbyters who are the superiors of the monasteries."[19] His justification appears a bit odd given that the Tall Brothers and those who followed them filled many of these prominent roles. While such a request may just be an invention by Theophilus, if one expands inquiry to the northwestern desert more generally, it is plausible that some of the more prominent members of Scetis vocalized concerns to Theophilus about some of the Tall Brothers' more speculative teachings. Such becomes more imaginable when we take into account Sulpicius Severus's witness that the "strife raging between the bishops and monks" was caused by multiple "crowded synods" decreeing "no one should read or have the books of Origen."[20] His depiction attests to a concern among the ecclesial authority about the growing popularity of studying Origen. Theophilus's letter echoes Sulpicius Severus, as he claims he entered the desert so rapidly out of fear that these "rabid" brothers' heresy might contaminate more of the brethren. Theophilus goes on to warn the bishops of Palestine and Cyprus against the monks' "insane attacks," assuring them that he has "not done them any harm" or "acted aggressively" against them.[21] His need to assert that he did the monks no injury likely belies his knowledge of the charges being brought against him.

Attempting to counter their narration of his "visit," Theophilus defends himself in a passive-aggressive way. Although he claims he will "pass over the rest, how they have attempted to murder us," he in fact does not abandon the topic but instead describes in great depth the violent behavior of the monks. The brothers, occupying the church at Nitria, blocked the entrance of Theophilus and his company, including other bishops, by filling "strategic parts of the church."[22] He accuses them of hiring and arming "freedmen and slaves" to fight on their behalf.[23] Playing on their palm branches as symbols of peace, he asserts that they used the palms to hide not only "cudgels and staves" but also the desire for "bloodshed" that lay in their hearts.[24] Although he portrays the monks as secretly violent monsters, Theophilus acknowledges that no riotous violence actually occurred. Such restraint was due not to the monks' nature, however, but rather to the grace of God. Constructing the monks through rhetoric akin to that used to describe barbarians allows Theophilus to make the same move Cassian made against the Mazices. The monks could not restrain themselves from violence; only God could intercede against such inherently violent creatures.

Here, again, there is overlap with Palladius, who corroborates that Theophilus came into the Nitrian community. But Palladius in his *Dialogue* (in a passage already discussed in the Introduction) narrates a starkly different perspective. Having bloodied Ammonius's nose in Alexandria, Theophilus is portrayed as calling a synod of bishops against the Tall Brothers as an act of further vengeance. Whereas Theophilus insists that he called a synod only against Isidore (who refused to appear), Palladius claims the synod was also against three of the Tall Brothers, that they were given "no chance to speak," and that Theophilus "pretended there had been a perversion of doctrine" that led to his denunciation of the monks, when Theophilus was actually angry about their support of Isidore.[25] Once again, we catch a glimpse of how Theophilus's letter about the Tall Brothers was meant to paint them as heretics while masking Theophilus's own actions. Palladius similarly obscures legitimate concerns about Origen's writings by painting them as mere pretensions to mask an act of revenge. In this way, both figures use their judicial rhetorical training to good effect, exaggerating the errors of their opponent while erasing their own potentially infelicitous behaviors.

Palladius goes on to accuse Theophilus of having bribed five monks from the monastery (perhaps Nitria) to tender false memoranda against the Tall Brothers by offering them ecclesial positions (one bishop, one priest, and three deacons) in exchange for their treachery. Palladius derisively mocks the lying monks as "little men" who would never have been chosen for a position of power among the brethren, and Theophilus as foolish for considering himself "another Moses."[26] Notably, Palladius's assertion of the monks' illegitimacy also leaned on the non-Egyptian backgrounds of these five brothers—that they were from Libya, Pharan, Alexandria, and Paralos—allowing him to imply that no actual Egyptian would side with Theophilus. Having gathered the signatures of these five to the memorandum Theophilus himself wrote, Theophilus is said to have approached the local prefect, seeking military force to expel these brothers. Such a legal maneuver was meant to legitimate Theophilus's intended violence against the monks. The law, embodied in Theophilus and his band, was about to enter the monastic desert. This aggressive move is partially corroborated by Sulpicius Severus. In his account, he notes that the "zeal" of both sides had caused such unrest that "the governor of the city was called upon to regulate the discipline of the church by a perverse precedent."[27] The governmental force struck with such terror that all were said to have fled. What Sulpicius Severus does not have Postumianus (his dialogue character) say is equally important: Who called in the governor? Given Postumianus's visit to Theophilus in the immediate aftermath, the implication is clear—Theophilus had invoked governmental violence. Thus, it would seem that Theophilus was granted local imperial military support or, at the least, permission to gather his own muscle.

Entering the desert with drunken youths and enslaved Ethiopians, Theophilus set about ordering acts of violence against the brethren.[28] He had Bishop Dioscorus (one of the Tall Brothers) thrown from his ecclesial chair, adding insult to injury by having unbaptized, Ethiopian slaves perform the demotion. Here Palladius again invokes Ethiopian bodies as markers of theopolitical meaning. As noted in Chapter 4, Palladius uses Ethiopians to mark the boundaries of the civilized Roman world. Reading Palladius's portrayal of Dioscorus's deposition with these intertexts underscores the chaotic, uncivilized behavior Theophilus brought into the desert. Having Roman (or local) law behind him, Theophilus seems to have likewise seen himself as imitating the biblical patriarchs—in particular, Moses. He explicitly links his actions in the Origenist controversy with Moses in his *Sixteenth Festal Letter*, suggesting that "[we] beseech God for our detractors, emulating Moses."[29] Palladius inverts Theophilus's self-fashioning as a law-delivering second Moses, Palladius imaging Theophilus as uncivilized and lawless through association with enslaved Ethiopians. Palladius asserts that Theophilus continued his violence, ordering his band to raid the brothers' cells, stealing their property, and setting fire to Scripture and other sacred books. As the most outrageous accusation (so much so that even Palladius hedges on its validity), Palladius recounts that some even claimed the group had burnt a young boy to death alongside the Eucharistic elements. While Theophilus's youths and enslaved Ethiopians may indeed have done much damage, the survival of the Tall Brothers requires an explanation. Thus, Palladius claims that throughout this onslaught, the three Tall Brothers hid in a cistern, only being able to slip away once Theophilus's fury had been satisfied.

Ps.-Martyrius echoes Palladius's characterization of Theophilus's actions as unjust. For Ps.-Martyrius, the monks were "holy men who had pursued a solitary life" their entire lives without learning "of the evils in cities."[30] This is a rather hyperbolic portrayal given that some of the monks most interested in Origenist speculation were non-Egyptians like Evagrius who had taken up residence in the desert as adults. Once again, Sulpicius Severus is more circumspect in his accusations. While he attributes the enactment of violence against the brethren to the governor and claims Theophilus warmly welcomed Postumianus, Postumianus is still loathe to remain in a place where "devastation of the brethren," "especially by bishops," had so recently occurred.[31] In this rendering, not only Theophilus but also all the bishops were culpable for the expulsion of the monks, tacitly including Theophilus without explicitly blaming him. These varying narrations each indicate that the Tall Brothers were violently exiled by Theophilus, and unjustly so.

On the one hand, it is perhaps not surprising that violence would erupt in the desert, given the violence inherent in ascetic identity construction, daily life, and engagement with the desert and its various inhabitants that we have seen thus far. On the other hand, we should not confuse imaginable violence with anticipated violence. Regardless of whether ascetics agreed or disagreed with Theophilus's theological reversal of his stance with respect to so-called Origenism after his *Festal Letter* of 399, it seems plausible that his violent antics against the Tall Brothers and many of their brethren would have come as a shock to ascetics throughout the northwestern desert. Ascetics might travel to Alexandria and other cities to participate in ecclesial violence, but such attacks were not supposed to happen in their own desert. While assaults from demons, beasts, and perhaps even barbarians were expected, violence from neighboring bishops was not. Theophilus's actions effectively broke the mystique of the desert as a lawless, *apolis*-ed Other space. Rather than being a utopia, different from the world, the desert—as Theophilus performed for the entire empire—was subject to Alexandria and the Church in particular just like any other place. The desert could be civilized.

Maintaining Control

Set alongside one another, the tales of Palladius, Theophilus, Ps.-Martyrius, and Sulpicius Severus allow trace glimpses of what may have actually occurred. But before we attempt such a reconstruction, we must briefly set it in the larger narrative of the Roman Empire and its neighbors from the 380s until the death of Theophilus in 412. Understanding the military and political threats from neighboring peoples as well as the ecclesial power struggles within the empire will better illuminate the violence at Nitria and the rhetoric depicting it. Theophilus's actions are legible, as are the counteractions of the Tall Brothers and their community (including Palladius), within the larger theo-political realities they had to navigate.

Starting in the 380s allows an understanding of the immediate precedents to the first Origenist controversy. In 382, Emperor Theodosius I had negotiated peace with the Visigothic people, whom his predecessor had repeatedly battled.

Such peace was tenuous at best, for Alaric was soon stirring up troubles, leading a group of Visigoths into battle against Theodosius by the early 390s. But
Theodosius was able to press Alaric back into the service of the Roman Empire,
such that Alaric led troops on Theodosius's behalf in 394 against the western
usurper, Eugenius. When Theodosius died the following year, however, the
Gothic people abandoned their peace with Rome. Thus, the delicate stability
Theodosius had maintained collapsed, and violence between the Romans and
their "barbarian" neighbors increased. Within a year of the Tall Brothers' flight
to Constantinople, Alaric would successfully invade Italy. Moreover, across the
entire course of the first Origenist controversy, the Austuriani would repeatedly raid portions of Libya. All the while, the Hun people pressed from the
northeastern edges of the empire. And, as we saw in Chapter 4, the Ethiopian
kingdoms increasingly gathered power from the beginning of the fifth century
on. The pressure of new peoples entering the empire could truly be felt on all
sides. Anxiety about the loyalty of such peoples to Rome, but also about the
loyalty of the imperial government to these new inhabitants, would result in
both the execution of the semi-"barbarian" military leader Stilicho in 408 (once
the guide of Emperors Arcadius and Honorius) and the sack of Rome by Alaric
in 410. Distrust of the Other repeatedly resulted in political violence.[32]

It is precisely in this era of instability that the first outbursts of the
first Origenist controversy emerged. Shortly before Theodosius's death, in
393 C.E., Epiphanius, bishop of Cyprus, visited Palestine, ostensibly as a
guest of John, bishop of Jerusalem. It was an encounter that quickly turned
sour. Epiphanius, mocking and undermining John from John's own pulpit,
slandered him with accusations of Origenism.[33] Epiphanius had already established himself as a staunch opponent of Origen two decades earlier, arguing,
among other things, that Origen's subordination of the Son to the Father
begat the Arian heresy. As Elizabeth Clark has shown, when Epiphanius
returned to refuting Origen in the 390s, his theological assertions took a
decidedly new edge, addressing contemporary ascetic debates around reproduction, the potential redemption of the devil, and the presence of God's
image in humanity.[34] Despite anger at this disrespect, John seems to have
avoided making any statements that might have implicated him, but his alliance with Rufinus indicates John may indeed have had some sympathy for
aspects of Origen's writings. Regardless, Epiphanius's initial efforts to provoke
John failed, and he headed home.

But, as with all aspects of the controversy that would unfold, issues of
authority and boundaries equally played a role. Within the year, Epiphanius

had the opportunity again to incite John. When several monks from Jerome's monastery came to visit Epiphanius, the latter took advantage of the moment. Transgressing John's ecclesial territory, Epiphanius ordained Jerome's brother Paulinian.[35] As noted in passing above, Isidore was then sent (around 396) by Theophilus to negotiate between Epiphanius and John. It was this act of questionable ordination that sparked Theophilus's involvement. At this juncture, Theophilus seemed more inclined to ally with John. While scholars (and some of Theophilus's contemporaries) have often read this alignment as indicative of Theophilus's Origenist sympathies, the juridically trained Theophilus was likely more distressed by the encroachment of one bishop upon another's jurisdiction. Epiphanius's behavior signaled a disordered usurpation of another's authority.

Yet Theophilus would learn valuable lessons from this encounter. For, despite Epiphanius's distasteful behavior, Theophilus's ambassador Isidore was not able to broker peace because of the sloppy conveyance of his own letters. And, while John initially had governmental backing for his excommunication of Jerome and his brothers for their involvement in the ordination, the murder of the local prefect set to enforce it made such imperial support meaningless. Beyond this misfortune, the dissemination of a letter of Epiphanius, ostensibly written to John to justify his action, smeared John with lengthy accusations of Origenism.[36] In these results, Theophilus astutely saw the extra care required in communicating with colleagues through letters in this fraught political moment, the governmental force that could be legitimately mobilized against monks, and the efficacy of blurring actual narration of events and charges of heresy in epistolary form. He undoubtedly also recognized the malleability of charges of Origenism, which was not yet a specified heresy. Such flexibility meant that bishops were able to affiliate any number of beliefs with heretical anxieties of the time.

Theophilus would put all of this knowledge to good use in his fallout with Isidore and the Tall Brothers. Having seen that governmental muscle might be invoked against the brethren, he enlisted state power (or at least permission) before he set out into the Nitrian desert. Such a decision was meant to give credibility to Theophilus's actions. Ever the legal stickler, Theophilus could point to his actions as merely upholding imperial order. And his convincing of local authorities no doubt rested on his own attempts to quell instability within the church during an otherwise unstable time in the empire. We can imagine Theophilus linking political and theological instability in juridical terms that would have held legitimate meaning for the governor who approved his encroachment into the desert. Likewise, in the aftermath of what happened, Theophilus took care to send the exact same letter in his own defense not only to one party of bishops but to two separate regions. The *Second Synodal Letter to the Bishops of Palestine and Cyprus* is in fact two near identical copies of the same letter, one addressed to Palestinian bishops and the other to Cypriote ones. And in the letter, as noted above, Theophilus successfully toggled between describing his version of events and his denunciations of Origen's works, effectively tying what he viewed as the illegitimate behaviors of the monks to heretical teachings.

As discussed earlier, the precise nature of what caused the fallout between Theophilus and Isidore is unclear, but one may speculate that central to the disagreement was Isidore's unwillingness to bow fully to Theophilus's authority around treatment of the unnamed widow. Given Theophilus's emphasis throughout his episcopacy on hierarchical order and proper use of authority, it is not a stretch to imagine that Theophilus saw in Isidore disobedience (however minor) that could not be tolerated in an unstable age. When the brethren of Nitria offered hospitality to Isidore, Theophilus undoubtedly saw this action as a spreading insurrection against his episcopacy. We might imagine the spreading disobedience as an uncontrolled fire, precisely the type of imagery used by ecclesial figures to speak of heresy (as noted in Chapter 4). Theophilus would make clear that such was no longer permissible. Thus, taking into account the imperial and ecclesiastic politics leading to Theophilus's incursion into the desert allows us to see how Theophilus would have understood and justified his actions vis-à-vis questions of authority and the appropriate use of violent discipline.

All versions seem to corroborate aspects of the following chain of events: Upon entering the desert, Theophilus and his group arrived first at the church of Nitria, where Dioscorus served as a bishop. Several brothers, viewing Theophilus's actions and group as illegitimate and threatening, may have sought to bar their entrance to the Nitrian church, seeking to protect their own beloved bishop and sacred space. That a few brothers from the monastery had chosen instead to ally themselves with Theophilus likely implies division, however slight, within the community. While Theophilus understood himself as archbishop with ecclesial authority over the Nitrian church, the brothers who defended the church clearly did not acquiesce to his assertions of power over the desert community. Theophilus's own repeated declaration that no violence occurred perhaps masks the violence of his own band, which must have successfully entered the church in order to cast Dioscorus from his seat of honor. But how violent the deposition actually was is masked by Palladius's appeal to "violent barbarian" discourse in his version.

Notably absent from Theophilus's rendering of events is any mention of further interaction between the two factions. Although he acknowledges that no one from his band was hurt, he claims he and his group fled for their lives, fearing they would be murdered.[37] Palladius likely speaks accurately when he notes that Theophilus or at least his band continued their encroachment into the desert, Theophilus's ruffians not leaving until they had received the spoils of their labor—the opportunity to pillage and burn the brothers' cells. While Palladius undoubtedly rhetorically heightens his rendering of the violence, his description of this continued violence aligns with the common behavior of such youthful bands. Brent Shaw has compellingly argued within the context of North Africa that bands of young men were frequently employed in regional ecclesial struggles in the fourth and fifth centuries. Derisively (and perhaps inaccurately) mocked as Circumcellions by Augustine, Shaw has shown that such *Agonistici* or *Agoraioi* were known throughout the empire.[38] As evidence from North Africa indicates, such young men were usually read as either "holy fighters" or "robbers," depending on one's perspective.[39] Likely seasonal workers who were recruited for particular enactments of social violence on behalf of the church, these youths tended to be paid with alcohol and loot for their muscle, their violent acts often consisting of torching property and beating individuals.[40] While Palladius's rendering of the event is certainly hostile toward Theophilus, this does not mean the presence of youths is mere literary flourish. As Shaw also notes, such gangs had taken on an increased role in Christian anti-pagan violence in the 380s and 390s.[41] While there are no explicit references to youths in Rufinus's account, it is highly probable that Theophilus had a group of youths among the crowd who destroyed the Serapeum. And it is likely that Theophilus brought just such a recruited group of youths with him to Nitria.

An important aspect of situating Theophilus's band within broader late ancient ecclesial trends is recognition that Theophilus's behavior, though horrifying to Palladius and his contingent, was a standard practice of the day. In fact, Theophilus's description in his *Second Synodal Letter* seems to hint that the monks who first sought him in his see had likewise gathered such a band. Whereas Palladius's rendition has the party consist of only monks and priests, Theophilus claims a band of monks as well as poor and enslaved peoples had arrived in Alexandria to threaten him and incite violence. Here, the poor and enslaved likely parallel the day-worker youths and enslaved Ethiopians that

Theophilus is portrayed as employing. In fact, both sides probably participated in the common practice of hiring extra muscle for defense and as a
threat to the opposing party. And, though it was a common practice, both
sides also recognized the unsavoriness of their youthful and enslaved bands,
Palladius and Theophilus each erasing their respective community's involvement in such hired violence.

Theophilus claims that only a few brothers and transient pilgrims fled
the desert, but his letters about the Tall Brothers and Theophilus's dramatic
actions against Archbishop John Chrysostom for supporting them belies
what a threat to Theophilus's power the group truly was.[42] Theophilus's
lengthy *Second Synodal Letter* betrays his anxiety about the potential fallout
for this clash. Theophilus's worry likely also indicates that the exiles were
both more numerous and more connected than Theophilus was willing to
admit. For Palladius, Theophilus's violent entrance into the desert traumatized not only the three sought-after brothers but also a large portion of the
monastic community present, as "three hundred worthy monks" and several
priests and deacons joined the three persecuted brothers in their flight from
Egypt to Palestine.[43] Palladius's substantial number is likely exaggerated, but
it does indicate that the group was sizable, certainly more than Theophilus's
three monks and handful of pilgrims. Even if there were not quite as many
as three hundred who fled the desert, the group was large enough to represent
the damage Theophilus's encroachment into the desert had caused.

Equally important to consider is how the remaining, neighboring monastic communities viewed Theophilus's actions, even if they allied themselves
with his theological denunciations of Origenism. When scholars imagine Theophilus's incursion, they often focus only on the ascetic community at Nitria.
But, as Chapter 1 showed, the regions of Nitria, Kellia, Pherme, and Scetis
were tightly connected, with borders between them being sometimes quite
porous. As we have seen repeatedly throughout this book, most ascetics rarely
stayed put, traveling and moving among these locales as well as beyond them.
And, as noted in the Introduction, ascetics of differing theological positions
were capable of living alongside one another.[44] A letter from Theophilus (only
partially extant), written to the brothers of Scetis, indicates that the community (which may have included many who supported Theophilus's theological
stance against Origen's writings) must have questioned his violent attack on
Nitria.[45] In the fragment, Theophilus seems to be defending himself, asking, "Is
it right to tolerate such people?"[46] One can imagine these brothers, who tended
to live peaceably alongside one another while holding different theological

beliefs, pressing Theophilus to explain why he did not just leave these other brothers alone, isolated as they were in the desert. Even if the Scetian brothers never officially addressed Theophilus, the fact that he bothered to send a letter points to his own awareness that his behavior might be read as unjustly violent even by his theological allies. To justify his actions, Theophilus aligns Origen's Christology with that of the heresies of Arius and Eunomius, claiming that to allow these misguided brothers to continue in their beliefs would have encouraged other heretics as well as pagans.[47] In this rhetorical move, Theophilus not only forms a heretical genealogy for Origenism but also once more invokes the danger of pagan renewal. While certainly a rhetorical strategy to deride so-called Origenist monks, it also invited the Scetian monks to remember their own possible involvement in violence against pagans, such as the destruction of the Serapeum. Thus, we hear echoes of Theophilus's invitation for these monks to share in the glory of his Christianization of Egypt, something he had denied the Tall Brothers in his *Second Synodal Letter*. But acceptance of such a position placed the unruly, violence-prone monks squarely under Theophilus's authority as bishop. The archbishop expected obedience from those below and did what was necessary to maintain his control.

The "Dangers" of Barbarous Abbas

If governmental control could impinge on the desert, then the presence of barbarous bodies in it demanded a response. The encroachment of Alaric and his community, as well as other neighboring peoples, resulted in a heightened fear of violent barbarians permeating the Roman Empire. Theophilus's "civilizing" of the desert would have undoubtedly expanded that fear to the desert, even without any actual incursions from neighboring Austuriani, Mazices, or Ethiopians. While Chapter 3 framed ascetic involvement in the destruction of the Serapeum as participation in cultural praxes of memory sanctions, such an interpretation does not preclude readings of ascetic political behavior as potentially posing a threat to the larger, Roman social order akin to other barbarian incursions on the edges of empire. Their violent involvement in a common cultural practice was allowable only inasmuch as they were subjected to Archbishop Theophilus as representative of Roman political and ecclesial legal order. Even then, Theophilus's power was tenuous, as Theophilus himself admits that recollection of the Serapeum's destruction many years later still threatened to lead to pagan mob violence.[48]

And, as we saw in Chapter 4, clear delineations between barbarians and monks were often not easily discernible. The unruly, uncivilized ascetic body could be and was read as barbarous. The desire to perform an otherworldly, paradisiacal body made ascetics susceptible to confusion with the barbarian neighbors who also populated the desert. As the witness of Synesius indicates, even someone who would ultimately be ordained as a Christian bishop saw the ascetics' singular focus on basket-weaving "as violent and unyielding."[49] Such basket-weaving was a popular handiwork among monks because baskets provided some financial support while allowing the monks the opportunity to continuously pray. Yet, given the discussion in Chapter 2 of prayer and psalmody as violent, Synesius was not entirely wrong in reading their basket-weaving as violently tinged. Such violent behavior, however, registered most powerfully in the symbolic body of the barbarian.

Theophilus understood his role as archbishop to be one that aligned imperial and ecclesial power. His actions against the Serapeum, and subsequently other pagan temples, underscore how he viewed himself as an agent of governmental and divine power simultaneously. Thus, the biblical figure of Moses as law-giver and law-enforcer served as a perfect scriptural model for Theophilus. While Palladius mocked him in *Dialogue* 7 for acting like a fool, Theophilus undoubtedly understood himself as a second Moses meant to usher in order in an unstable era. That he was able to garner imperial and local support for his actions is confirmed in his success at the Serapeum. But such success was precarious and required strict control of those beneath him. Any perceived slight against him might open up dissension among all those who had found his attacks against the temples barbaric, non-Christian and Christian alike.

Theophilus's swift and brutal response first to Isidore and then to the Nitrian community corresponds well to his self-fashioning. Krastu Banev has noted how insightfully Theophilus activated his knowledge of ascetic emphasis on obedience in his own demands for compliance from the monastic brethren.[50] Expanding on Banev's point, I would argue that, in coupling reverence of obedience and silence (*hēsychia*) among the brethren with regard to his own agenda, Theophilus sought to muzzle ascetic protests against the enforcement of his "law." Given what Theophilus understood to be at stake, it is not wrong to imagine him as capable of ruthlessness in the service of the greater political and ecclesial good. He makes clear how far he is willing to go, telling the bishops of Palestine and Cyprus that he is "prepared to defend the faith to the death."[51] While Theophilus wants to claim that he and his band faced the ostensible risk of being murdered, Theophilus's language (and even more so his actions) call into question whose lives were really endangered. It is in this light that we must return to Palladius's claim that Theophilus and his mob may even have murdered a young boy at Nitria.

Palladius's uncertain accusation against Theophilus of a single murder has been read either as an indication that Theophilus did cause the death of a single young boy or as mere hyperbolic slander on Palladius's part. Most recently, Banev asserts that no contemporary witness accuses Theophilus of murder and sees Palladius's hesitancy as "a colourful touch" to his slander, which even Palladius knew he could not defend.[52] Banev's position allows him to discredit the Constantinopolitan *Synaxarium*, which includes a reference to Theophilus murdering monks, as later hagiographic imagination.[53] The entry on July 10 commemorates "the myriad holy fathers in the caves, who Theophilus, archbishop of Alexandria, handed over to bitter death by smoke and fire because of Isidore the presbyter."[54] It is true that the language of "myriad" may invite amplification of numbers and that the source may be situated in a tradition that favored the monks over Theophilus, but Banev is wrong that the mention of monks dying "is absent from all contemporary sources."[55]

Once more, the writings of Sulpicius Severus and Ps.-Martyrius complicate the picture. While Banev does note that Sulpicius Severus's *Dialogue* describes Theophilus's behavior as "persecution," he ignores the immediately preceding line from the *Dialogue*. Here, Sulpicius Severus explains that despite Theophilus's hospitality, Postumianus did not wish to remain "where recently a grudge had blazed to the point of devastation of the brethren."[56] The Latin underlying the phrase "devastation of the brethren," *fraternae cladis*, might alternatively be rendered "massacre of the brethren." How one chooses to render *cladis*, the violent connotations of which range from injury to death, depends entirely on context. The language of persecution that follows does little to clarify the matter, for persecution likewise encompasses both beatings and murder. A few lines earlier, there is a reference to the governor being called in to enact violence that caused the brethren to flee, but again this does not preclude the possibility of death for some of the monks. Sulpicius Severus, perhaps cautious about explicitly describing the violence in Alexandria, leaves an ambiguous witness that may or may not plausibly corroborate the claims found in the *Synaxarium*.

More explicit support for Theophilus and his band killing some of the brethren is found in Ps.-Martyrius. As I have already noted, similar to Palladius, Ps.-Martyrius is decidedly hostile to Theophilus. But while Palladius hedges in his reference to a single youth's death, Ps.-Martyrius more clearly indicates that witnesses came forward from the fleeing Nitrian brethren with accusations of murder. When the exiled brothers approached the emperor for assistance, they were then provided with an imperial "escort" for their hearing before the bishop. The emperor's protection points to the perceived danger the monks were in and that violent retaliation was indeed a possibility. Ps.-Martyrius asserts that it was at this moment that Theophilus desperately began to trump up charges of heresy against them. But it is the reason Ps.-Martyrius gives for Theophilus's heightened animosity that is most of interest: Theophilus, recognizing the imperial support, realized "his affairs had come to rest on a razor's edge, for there had been added to the charges against him the murder of monks and the burning of monasteries."[57] This passing reference indicates that charges not just of burning the monks' cells but also of murder of multiple brothers were leveled against Theophilus. If such charges were true, then the witness of the *Synaxarium* rightly commemorates the murder of several monks by Theophilus.

When one includes these other sources, Theophilus's own repeated assertions in his letters that he did the monks no harm, and considering what was at stake for Theophilus, it seems hard not to imagine that Theophilus was implicated in the murder of a few monks. While he did not successfully lay hands on any of the Tall Brothers except Dioscorus, his hired band likely brutally beat and burned as was their custom, with incidental deaths perhaps occurring in the process. What precisely Dioscorus suffered at their hands remains obscured, but it should be noted that, although he successfully fled to Constantinople, he was dead within a year or so.[58] The brutality that surrounded contested depositions and subsequent exile would likewise lead to John Chrysostom's death a few years later.[59] Moreover, the very fact that Theophilus was so careful in managing the narrative on his way to Constantinople indicates he was fully aware that charges of murdering monks had been added to those about improper ecclesial procedure. With this reframing, the memorialization of the *Synaxarium* may exaggerate, but it does not fabricate that Theophilus had allowed the slaughter of monks he found disobedient.

Banev's urge to rehabilitate Theophilus as brilliant and not devilish is a noble one and not something I wish to undermine. The harder truth, as the discussion of bands of hired muscle above highlights, is that Theophilus was merely acting in ways expected from imperial leaders. Given the increased blurring of lines between government and church across the fourth century, Theophilus as a leader of the church had merely acted as anyone in charge would have. The difficulty for him was that his behavior had left him in a very bad light indeed. It is not merely that scholars have too readily accepted Palladius's depiction of Theophilus; in the fifth century, negative portrayals of Theophilus were published, both during his own lifetime and in the decades following his death. That even Sulpicius Severus, a moderate voice in the midst of the Origenist controversy, depicts Postumianus as eager to leave the company of an otherwise friendly Theophilus because of his actions indicates that Theophilus's deeds may have been legal but were deemed by many of his contemporaries as deeply unsettling.

But if the monks were behaving barbarously, leading Theophilus "appropriately" to discipline them like a second Moses, one ascetic in particular was ripe for Theophilus's abuse: Abba Moses and his Ethiopian body. As we have repeatedly seen, both positive and negative renderings of ascetics left them open to being (mis)read as barbarian. Thus, Moses's body necessarily most fully represented the dangerous blurring of boundaries between ascetic and barbarian. Moreover, as discussed in Chapter 4, it was Theophilus who was remembered as using his position of power as archbishop to abuse Abba Moses during the ordination process. In these events, Moses was humiliated in front of the brethren for his dark skin, the archbishop imaged as linking skin tone to sinfulness. That Moses accepted the abuse marked him as properly modeling obedience. Given that Moses's Ethiopian ethnicity would have already linked him to negative barbarian stereotypes, Theophilus successfully disciplining such a person would have resonated as marking his authority over even the most unruly of bodies.

The *Sayings* and later the *Alexandrian Synaxarium* remember Moses as having been killed by barbarians, and this is indeed possible.[60] But, as Chapter 4 showed, no major barbarian incursion likely occurred during Moses's lifetime. Only the faint possibility of Austuriani penetrating beyond Libya into Egypt can make Hugh Evelyn-White's position viable. If so-called barbarians killed Moses, it was far more likely a small robber band. All other stories of robbers stealing from the monks are either tales of an abba helping load up his belongings or at worst the robber beating an abba. Moses again would be the sole memory retained of an abba dying at the hands of a robber. As noted at the end of Chapter 4, given memories of Theophilus's mistreatment of Moses, it is worth entertaining the possibility that Moses was among the monks Theophilus killed. While such can only remain conjecture, that both Palladius and Cassian sought to claim Moses's legacy ties him however loosely to the so-called Origenist circle, making it impossible to rule out Theophilus's involvement. If it was Theophilus who caused Moses's demise, his success at defending himself and slandering John Chrysostom in Constantinople would have quickly made it difficult for subsequent writers to memorialize Theophilus's victims—especially Moses. Rather than, with Banev, reading Palladius as slandering Theophilus, we should perhaps read in his hesitant mention of a possible murder recognition of his own precarity, as he was recently recalled from exile. Unlike Ps.-Martyrius and Sulpicius Severus, who were able to note Theophilus's acts of violence, Palladius as a prime opponent of Theophilus did not have such a luxury. Palladius might write many hostile things about Theophilus, but the charge of murder, especially of monks, quite plausibly would have found Palladius back in exile among barbarian peoples he equally disliked. No major player in the Origenist battle wanted to be linked with uncivilized, "barbarian" behavior.

Echoes and New Rumblings Across the Fifth Century

Revisiting the events at Nitria highlights how ecclesial violence slipped from Alexandria into the ascetic wilderness and the ramifications Theophilus's actions would have had for interpretations of the desert. While Theophilus intended to civilize and stabilize what he saw as an undisciplined monastic faction, the instability he caused by reaching into the desert with imperial force drove away a great number of monks and likely troubled many of those who remained. By fashioning himself a second Moses and extending the law into the lawless wilderness, Theophilus damaged or destroyed the mystique of the desert as Other. For those who had fled, their desert was dead. Even if some robbers did attack and kill Abba Moses and some of his brethren, Theophilus's violent incursion into the desert would have been the more traumatic violent experience for the monks and would have led some to see the desert as robbed of its power and the Golden Age of asceticism lost.

In the chaotic context of the early fifth century, Theophilus's attack on the ascetic desert was enough to drive away many of the ascetic leaders and, in some cases, cause them to complain about their plight on a global stage. One might ask why such an event finds its way largely only into a few polemical tracts and letters and leaves only a trace (by my reading) in the *Sayings*. The answer can be found in the reactions of fellow Christians, for what ensued between holy men and bishops seems to have upset many involved. Sulpicius Severus's extreme discomfort with what had occurred likely represents the assessment of many Christians throughout the empire. The international, ecclesial situation soon demanded that disputes be forgiven and forgotten, though not without leaving some traces.[61] Once John Chrysostom's name was reinstated on some of the diptychs and exiled bishops like Palladius began to return, the need to establish peace between rival parties would only have increased. How to narrate what had occurred would indeed have been a delicate matter. It is possible that some of the references to barbarians noted in Chapter 4 (and relied upon by Evelyn-White to reconstruct the fate of the desert) are re-rememberings of Theophilus's drunken youths (who behaved violently like barbarians were imagined to) and enslaved Ethiopians (who were perceived as barbarians) attacking Nitria so that the memory of Theophilus's violence became displaced by a new narrative of barbarian onslaught. Such would have been an especially easy rhetorical move to make. Similarly, Augustine, often quite savvy in ecclesial political matters, may in his *Letter* 111 have blamed "barbarians" for the deaths of some brethren rather than explicitly linking Theophilus to the violence.[62]

While this can only remain speculative, the Coptic apothegm attributed to Dioscorus (mentioned in Chapter 4) can perhaps, likewise, support such an interpretation. In the saying, a small band of barbarians assures Dioscorus they will not kill him, but they then rob him of all but his knife. The possibility of having multiple individuals with the same name (here, Dioscorus) is a notoriously thorny issue for the desert tradition. But another Dioscorus who is well known from the era is the bishop of Nitria, one of the Tall Brothers, who Theophilus had thrown from his ecclesial throne and then chased out of the desert. If the apothegm describes the same Dioscorus, we would now find "barbarians from the east" chasing him from the desert rather than the revered archbishop of Alexandria. If it is Dioscorus the Tall Brother who is robbed here, then the tradition may have reimagined Theophilus's attack on Dioscorus as a barbarian raid. Given the Coptic tradition's continued valorization of Theophilus, such a retelling would have been especially helpful.

Beyond embarrassment about the unsavory interactions among Theophilus, John Chrysostom, and the abbas, the growing prominence of the Alexandrian patriarchate across the first half of the fifth century would have increasingly precluded polemicizing against the blessed Archbishop Theophilus's memory. Theophilus had successfully defeated John Chrysostom and the Tall Brothers, even if all remaining Origenist-inclined Christians were eventually welcomed back. Moreover, his successors until the Council of Chalcedon would continue to garner increasing power and imperial support for the ecclesial throne of Alexandria. First, his nephew Cyril, who replaced him as archbishop, succeeded in defaming another Constantinopolitan archbishop, Nestorius, at a council in Ephesus in 431. Such was possible both because of his intimidation of the opposing party through hired muscle and his use of similar violence to press for imperial support. While Cyril no doubt had to address his uncle's legacy vis-à-vis both the divided monastic community and a troubled imperial court, it is equally true that he was able to navigate successfully his disagreement with Nestorius because of the power his uncle had garnered to the Alexandrian ecclesial throne.[63] Edward Watts has suggested that, early on, Cyril intentionally "choreographed a number of actions to evoke Theophilus."[64] Moreover, in the florilegium that Cyril presented at Ephesus, he included two excerpts from Theophilus as a valued father of the Church to support his argument against Nestorius.[65] Thus, given how large his uncle's legacy loomed across his episcopacy, it would have become increasingly difficult to mount any critique of Theophilus and his actions.

But memories of Theophilus as volatile certainly do seem to have continued in certain sectors. Two letters written by Isidore of Pelusium to Cyril hint at continued criticism of Theophilus among fellow bishops. Sometime shortly after Cyril became archbishop, Isidore urged him to return John Chrysostom's name to the Alexandrian diptychs. In the process, Isidore suggests that Theophilus's actions were really done out of "private vengeance" rather than ecclesial necessity.[66] While Isidore does not outright name Theophilus, it is clear whose behavior he is criticizing. That Cyril never reinstates Chrysostom's name indicates his continued alignment of his tenure with his uncle Theophilus's legacy. More explicitly, Isidore warns Cyril in the midst of his struggles with Nestorius that some who have come to Ephesus for the council are speaking ill of Cyril. He notes that they claim Cyril is imitating Theophilus, for Cyril "falls into a rage" against a holy man.[67] Here, more than two decades later, fellow bishops still recall what they saw as the unjust actions of Theophilus, seeing in Cyril's feud with Nestorius a reenactment of Theophilus's fight with John Chrysostom and the Tall Brothers. Isidore's warnings indicate that unrest about Theophilus's acts continued to rumble through Cyril's episcopacy.

It is more difficult to trace Theophilus's legacy during the reign of Dioscorus, who maintained the force of the Alexandrian patriarchate until 451. The archbishop's power came to an abrupt end at the Council of Chalcedon, when his mistreatment of Constantinopolitan clergy and his adherence to Cyrillian Christology found him on the wrong side of the pope in Rome. Imperial pressure to maintain peace with the western half of the empire, and therefore the pope, brought an end to Alexandrian power at either imperial court. While Theophilus's name is not explicitly invoked, it is not hard to see Theophilus as the precursor for Dioscorus's actions, including continued hostility against the Constantinopolitan patriarchate. When Dioscorus sought to excommunicate first Flavian, archbishop of Constantinople, and later Pope Leo, he was merely embodying the recent practice of the Alexandrian ecclesial throne. Dioscorus was no doubt assured that, given imperial support, he would be successful. That some might view this struggle between two holy bishops as unseemly was possible, but certainly Dioscorus did not anticipate losing his position over it. With Dioscorus's deposition and the staunch opposition of the Egyptian clergy to the Definition of Faith produced at the Council of Chalcedon, the era of the Alexandrian archbishop as major power broker—Theophilus's violent legacy—came to a close.

The Rise of Gaza and a Portable Desert

By later in the fifth and into the sixth century (when sources like the *Life of Peter the Iberian* and the *Sayings* emerged), it was a far different world for Christians in the Roman Empire. Non-Chalcedonian Christians would spend almost the entire next century struggling against a pro-Chalcedonian church often supported by the imperial ruling class. It is in this fraught ecclesial context that most of Evelyn-White's sources for a barbarian raid were composed. Non-Chalcedonian sources, like the *Life of Peter the Iberian*, certainly would not have wished to retain the insalubrious memory of Theophilus's mistreatment of the Nitrian monks. Theophilus was the uncle of the deeply revered Cyril, whose Christology non-Chalcedonian Christians felt had been betrayed in 451.

The final source that Evelyn-White heavily relied on for his reconstruction of a barbarian sack of the desert in the early fifth century is the *Sayings*. This major source for the Golden Age of the desert comes from almost a century after the age's close, as our earliest collections were written in the late fifth century. There were already smaller groupings of gathered sayings in the late fourth century, such as those preserved in a section of Evagrius's *On Prayer* and perhaps the seven instructions that Abba Moses sent to Abba Poemen that remain gathered under the former's extant apothegms in the *Sayings*.[68] But it was the violent loss of the desert as an imagined *eschatia* that triggered the fracturing and restructuring of monastic community inside and outside of the northwestern desert. As noted above, the Tall Brothers and those around them fled from Egypt to Palestine in the wake of the violent altercation with Theophilus. While the Tall Brothers would end up in Constantinople with John Chrysostom, pleading their case, many of the other brethren stayed in Palestine. While she would end up at odds with John Chrysostom, the empress Eudoxia seems to have continued to offer the Tall Brothers support.[69] Given that Eudoxia held an estate in Gaza (and also had a church building underway there), it is not difficult to imagine that Gaza would become a gathering place for many of the exiled abbas in Palestine. Since Lucien Regnault's argument was published in 1981, most recent scholars agree that Palestine also was where the *Sayings* were gathered.[70] The presence of wisdom from both Egyptian and Palestinian abbas in the collection, as well as deep awareness of Egyptian monasticism among the Palestianian abbas of later generations, support a Palestinian gathering location. More precisely, it has been argued that the sayings were collected in Gaza, where education and textual production seem to have been especially valued. The *Sayings* was a memorialization of the lost Egyptian desert produced by a new ascetic community in Gaza, one that included the ascetic progeny of the Egyptian refugees. The *Sayings* are not a historical window back into the Golden Age of the later fourth century but rather a nostalgic remembering of that past by a new monastic community at the end of the fifth century.

Scholarly interest during the past two decades has increasingly turned to explore the monastic communities that emerged in and around Gaza. As Brouria Bitton-Ashkelony and Aryeh Kofsky have noted in their volume on the development of the Gazan monastic school, an influx of monks from Egypt played a crucial role in the growth of monasticism at Gaza.[71] That several Egyptian refugee monks settled at Gaza is worth pausing to consider, as it points to some of the complex dynamics within fifth-century Christianity, especially in the wake of the first Origenist controversy. The founder of Gazan monasticism was purported to be a certain Hilarion. He is important to our study for two reasons: A prominent *Life of Hilarion* was written by Jerome, and Hilarion may have mentored Epiphanius of Cyprus in monastic practice.[72] The close relationship of Epiphanius to Gazan monasticism (regardless of whether Hilarion mentored him) is evidenced in a lost letter Epiphanius wrote celebrating Hilarion. This lost text that Jerome tells us about, along with Jerome's own attempts to claim Hilarion's legacy, suggest that the Gazan monastic community should have been a stronghold for anti-Origenism. But that the so-called Origenist monks who fled with the Tall

Brothers were able to establish themselves in Gaza indicates that the situation at Gaza was not so simple.

As noted in the Introduction, James Goehring rightly cautions us against imagining well-delineated boundaries between monks around theological stances. In particular, his discussion of the continued interactions between Melitian and non-Melitian monks at Labla should give pause, as it indicates that, across the fifth and into the sixth century, monks of opposing theological positions could and did continue to live in relationship with one another.[73] The arguments that felt so intense to bishops (and the handful of monks closely affiliated with them) across the fourth and fifth centuries did not preclude other monks from living peaceably together. As Goehring asserts, "ascetic ideology" mattered more to many of these monks than theological positions.[74] Such an explanation makes legible the situation between the existing Gazan monks and the new Egyptian influx. The distaste that our sources indicate many Christians felt about Theophilus's aggression in Nitria may have spurred the monks consciously to live in community alongside one another in peace, focusing on their shared ascetic practice.

And yet, a few decades later, the mixture of monks at Gaza was perhaps still perceived as odd, as may be indicated in Sozomen's desire to smooth over the disagreement between Epiphanius and the Tall Brothers. Sozomen himself was a son of Gaza, and in his *Church History* he offers a detailed description of Gazan monasticism and Hilarion's influence in the region (including on Sozomen's own family).[75] His extended description of Gaza indicates his continued concern for and desire to highlight his homeland. As part of his text, Sozomen presents a retelling of the struggles among Theophilus, the Tall Brothers, Epiphanius, and John Chrysostom. In his version, Sozomen recounts an otherwise unknown encounter between the Tall Brothers and Epiphanius in Constantinople after Theophilus's sack of Nitria.[76] The scene begins with the empress Eudoxia's young son falling ill. Sozomen asserts that Epiphanius refused Eudoxia's request that he pray for the child because of her engagements with the "heretical" Tall Brothers. In response, the monks (with Eudoxia's permission) sought an audience with Epiphanius. They confronted him about his denunciation of them as heretics, querying whether he had actually read any of their writings. When he admitted that he had not, they countered that they had read his *Well-Anchored Man* and had in fact defended him when they heard accusations of heresy against his name. Sozomen claims that Epiphanius was "measurably convinced" after their conversation and soon after left Constantinople for Cyprus. With this peaceful engagement with the

Tall Brothers and his subsequent departure, Epiphanius's involvement in the first Origenist controversy came to a close.

As Andrew Jacobs notes, while the historical Epiphanius may be unavailable to modern historians, late ancient authors could include his famous persona to help retell important events.[77] It is impossible to know whether peace between Epiphanius and the Tall Brothers actually ever occurred. Rather, Sozomen uses Epiphanius's celebrity to re-narrate an embarrassing moment in the Christian past, smoothing over the uncomfortable realities of a well-known bishop and several prominent holy men fighting one another. The disagreement was especially unpalatable for a local Christian like Sozomen because both Epiphanius and the monks who fled with the Tall Brothers had become prominent figures in the larger Gazan monastic movement. And while the monks at Gaza may have been able to ignore theological differences between their abbas, a politically savvy Christian like Sozomen, who found himself in the imperial city of Constantinople, could not. The opposition between Epiphanius and the Tall Brothers required resolution. That Theophilus's actions were already widely questioned made it easy to shift all blame for the fallout away from Epiphanius and on to Theophilus.[78]

The complex Gazan context that Sozomen depicts forms the most plausible context for the development of the *Sayings*. The *Sayings* similarly witness a complex ascetic heritage, containing the stories both of abbas tied to the Tall Brothers and of others linked to Theophilus, as well as traditions attributed to Epiphanius and to several prominent Gazan abbas. The Egyptian refugees and their ascetic progeny have rarely been viewed as the constructors of the *Sayings* because the *Sayings*, in particular the Greek versions, have traditionally been seen as anti-Origenist collections. While scholars have surmised that the brethren accused of Origenism could not have authored the anti-Origenist *Sayings*, we must keep in mind that some of the early collections of the *Sayings* in Syriac and those manuscripts that witness to the oldest Greek alphabetical *Sayings* were gathered alongside portions or full copies of Palladius's *Lausiac History* and the *History of the Monks of Egypt* (which, as noted earlier, was likely written by a monk of Rufinus's acquaintance).[79] That is, many of the earliest witnesses evidence the gathering of texts attributed to Origenists alongside *Sayings* collections. As discussed in the Introduction, a saying attributed to Abba Lot tends to be given much weight in the argument for the *Sayings* as anti-Origenist, and thus is worth reviewing.[80] The saying tells of an older, ill abba who comes to live with Lot. When the sick abba begins quoting Origen, Lot becomes anxious and seeks Abba Arsenius's advice. Arsenius suggests an ultimatum: Stay quiet about Origen or leave. The saying concludes with the elder abba departing rather than abandoning Origen's writings. While one can understand why scholars might tend to read this saying as anti-Origenist, as I showed in the Introduction, such a reading is not the only or the best understanding of the text. My argument about Theophilus's violence against the abbas in this chapter opens an alternative reading. Notably absent in the story is any denunciation of Origen's writings or of the elder abba for quoting them. Rather, the story preserves monastic *anxiety* about the consequences of being caught mentioning Origen. Such distress would have been especially understandable in the aftermath of Theophilus's raid on Nitria and the subsequent fate of John Chrysostom. Abba Arsenius as the source of Lot's advice also should be factored into interpretation of this passage. As argued earlier, the interactions of Arsenius and Theophilus represent the delicate relations between imperial and ecclesial power, Arsenius serving as a cipher for the former because of his purported former role at the imperial court. In the saying, Arsenius does not describe the reading of Origen's texts as heresy or even as error; rather, he merely makes clear that such behavior is not permissible among the abbas of the northwestern desert. Such a prohibition had been forcefully performed by Theophilus at Nitria, and later generations would not forget that.

In support of reading the *Sayings* as anti-Origenist, scholars have also tended to view the extant stories about Evagrius and the Tall Brother, Dioscorus, as having been expunged of their more theologically problematic content. Without the reading of Lot's saying as anti-Origenist and given the ascetic focus of the *Sayings*, such assertions seem unlikely. If the *Sayings* were gathered to memorialize ascetic wisdom from the desert, then a given abba's theological speculation would have been irrelevant regardless of whether they had been readers of Origen.[81] In fact, given how problematic mention of Evagrius would have been, especially after the second Origenist controversy in the mid-sixth century, the fact that anything has remained under his name is an indication of the value assigned to his ascetic wisdom in spite of his Origenist reputation. Rather than seeing Evagrius as expunged of his theology, we ought to read his presence in the *Sayings* as indicating the strength of his legacy.

More problematic are claims that Dioscorus's theology has been expunged. There is no extant theological text of Dioscorus indicating his views on Origen one way or the other. At the same time, his legacy seems to have been important to the earliest gatherers of the *Sayings*. Abba Poemen's community has long been recognized as having preserved the original core of the *Sayings*, as about a quarter of extant Greek narratives (across the Alphabetical, Anonymous, and Systematic traditions) are tied to Poemen's name.[82] Of the three sayings of Dioscorus found in most Greek alphabetical collections, one intimately ties Poemen to Dioscorus's legacy, an indication that the early Poemenian gatherers continued to value Dioscorus as a model.[83] Moreover, the Sahidic Coptic *Sayings* evidences that much more of Dioscorus's wisdom was preserved than our extant Greek or Latin collections belie.[84] One might expect the Coptic version, translated in an Egyptian desert meant to be firmly under Alexandrian ecclesial authority, would have been more inclined to expunge Origenist-inclined abbas. That they retained more than their Greek-speaking counterparts perhaps hints at the mixed success of Theophilus's campaign. Further, the fact that our extant Sahidic Coptic version was once housed in the White Monastery's library, a monastic institution whose most famous archimandrite was the prolific author and defender of orthodoxy Shenoute who wrote the discourse *I Am Amazed* to refute a purported local Origenist, underscores how valued the ascetic legacy of the Tall Brothers continued to be and how complex responses to Theophilus's actions likely remained.[85] All these points make clear that to refer to the *Sayings* as anti-Origenist is neither a particularly accurate nor a helpful designation. The *Sayings*, if anything, in both the Greek Alphabetical and Sahidic Coptic, register the continued mixed legacy of the fight between the Tall Brothers and Theophilus.

But if the *Sayings* are not anti-Origenist, how do we explain their nature and mode of formation in the light of the golden monastic age they memorialize and how it closed? As noted near the beginning of this section, Bitton-Ashkelony and Kofsky recently have written about the monastic school at Gaza. Their use of the word *school* refers not to a single locus but rather to a way of knowing and being among ascetics in the Gaza region. The ascetic school developed and expanded across Gaza as each disciple left his teacher and established his own monastery, gaining in turn his own students. This monastic school seems to have been in dialogue with the rhetorical school that likewise developed in Gaza from the fourth to the sixth centuries. Thus, rhetorical education was well known among Gazan monks.[86] And that at least some were still reading so-called Origenist authors and expected Gazan abbas to be able to evaluate their writings well into the sixth century is evidenced by letters written by Abbas Barsanuphius and John in response to questions about the writings of Origen, Didymus, and Evagrius.[87] Barsanuphius's initial answer was for the questioning monk to instead focus on reading the *Sayings*.[88] The monk then returned with questions about the unorthodox positions of abbas within the *Sayings* tradition, an indication that the *Sayings* was not read by subsequent generations as theologically consistent.[89]

The *Sayings* not only reflects the ascetic-pedagogical context of Gaza but also indicates deep awareness of the sorts of rhetorical practices used in the locale's intellectual environment. As Lillian Larsen has compellingly shown, the *Sayings* are monastic appropriations and adaptations of the Greco-Roman gnomic tradition so central to rhetorical education. The *Sayings* structurally represent a best-of showcase of monastic wisdom that would have easily been memorized and adapted in writing exercises, each apothegm being slightly expanded or truncated as the learner repeated it.[90] And that some of the extant stories seem to have originally been extracted from longer hagiographies only bolsters the comparison to Greco-Roman literary extracts.[91] Moreover, the *Sayings*, like their traditional counterparts, sought to convey content through apothegms that would inculcate a new monastic ethos in the learner. Attempting to negotiate the pull between earthly life and heavenly hope, the *Sayings* "may be characterized as both nostalgic and forward-looking in their reconstitution of history."[92] As a monk copied each saying, its moral content was simultaneously inscribed in his person, transforming him not into an angel (as hoped) but rather as a new monastic community member.

As noted in Chapter 1, the northwestern Egyptian desert, palpable with real and imagined possibility, had once been the reservoir for such complex negotiations between the earthly and heavenly. With the perceived loss of the Egyptian desert as the locus of monastic formation, a new textualized practice slowly emerged in the *Sayings*. It seems no accident that by the seventh century some versions of the *Sayings* even circulated under an alternate title: *Paradise of the Fathers*.[93] But the stretch between the "loss" at the opening of the fifth century and the construction of a textual tradition near the end of the fifth century constitutes multiple monastic generations. Certainly, the *Sayings* was not formed in immediate response to Theophilus's attack on Nitria. But that particular moment of violence in the desert began a process that, coupled with the tumultuous struggles leading to and following the Council of Chalcedon, led to a textualized desert, a textualized paradise.

Conclusion

Certainly, the *Sayings* served educational purposes for monastic communities, but as noted earlier the *Sayings* also testifies to the need for smoothing over ecclesial disputes, particularly those at the fifth century's outset. As Sozomen's own imagined encounter between Epiphanius and the Tall Brothers indicates, within a few decades a desire to mask the division between the two holy groups existed. The story about Epiphanius and Hilarion dining together offers a productive contrast to the story in Chapter 3 of Theophilus serving monks veal.[94] During the meal, fowl is served, Epiphanius partaking and offering some to Hilarion. The latter attempts to chastise Epiphanius by refusing a piece, saying that since he has become a monk he has never allowed flesh to touch his lips. Epiphanius then counters that he has never gone to bed holding a grudge against another nor allowed anyone to hold one against him. Hilarion then quickly apologizes. The apparent moral of the story is that Epiphanius is in fact the better, truer monk. Or, perhaps, it is that Hilarion was willing to bow to his episcopal authority because his intention was rightly oriented. While Theophilus was depicted as deceptive, Epiphanius's concern for inner disposition absolves him from the supposed error of eating meat. In this juxtaposition, we perhaps catch glimpses of the *Sayings*'s own attempts at smoothing the jagged edges in its mixed heritage. Only the rightly oriented bishop that acted worldly might still be reconciled with the devout monk.

Theophilus's legacy, by contrast, was more fraught. Certainly, after the Council of Chalcedon, when Palestinian and Egyptian Christians found themselves both staunchly opposed to the Chalcedonian Definition of Faith, such desires to reimagine fractured pasts could only have intensified. To bolster their stance, both pro- and anti-Chalcedonian monks would have sought to lean even more heavily on the legacy of Cyril, and therefore on the legacy of his uncle Theophilus as well. The *Sayings* may well have retrojected actual assaults by non-Roman peoples from the mid-fifth century back onto the late fourth and early fifth centuries. It would have been far easier to do so than to imagine that Theophilus had truly been so destructive to the monastic community. Thus, it is at least plausible that there would have been good reason to erase Theophilus's bad record from the *Sayings*.

In this reading, the act of constructing the *Sayings* was one of memorialization. The stories are not historical truths about monastic life almost a century earlier, but rather they reflect nostalgia for an imagined past. In order to construct this Golden Age of monasticism, memory sanctions were once again required. This violent moment of monastic-episcopal interaction triggered the exile that would lead to the eventual construction of the *Sayings*, even as the content of the text itself remained mostly mute on this event. As argued earlier in this book, the Egyptian monks were well-acquainted with memory sanctions. Moreover, such sanctions were violent acts by nature. In the construction of the *Sayings*, such memory sanctions likely accumulated across a particularly violent fifth century. While the *Sayings* were school exercises, they were also meant to inculcate a particular remembering of the past, one that erased unsavory intra-Christian fights and layered new "barbarian" traumas on top. The *Sayings* was a textual event produced from and for the purpose of writing anew the monastic past. This need and this approach allowed for and ultimately produced the variety of collections. Through memory sanctions and nostalgia, emerging out of and in response to acts of violence, the *Sayings* collections became textualized, portable images of a paradise lost.

Epilogue

Theophilus's violation of the desert traumatized many in the desert ascetic community. The perceived loss of the desert—for them, a locus of proximity to the divine, a space of paradisiacal possibility—rent the legacy of the past abbas from the present brethren, especially for those who fled to Palestine. No longer able to traverse the northwestern Egyptian wilderness for a word from a neighboring abba, the new theo-political reality demanded a new way of being ascetic. Within a century, multiple collections of apothegms had emerged—the textual tradition that came to be referred to as the *Sayings of the Desert Fathers*.

The question remains: What are we to make of the possibility of later violence, after Theophilus's incursion, that may indeed have sent subsequent waves of monks from Scetis to Gaza, leading to the presence of figures like Abba Isaiah and Peter the Iberian's old Scetian monk in Palestine? Even if it seems clear that a barbarian raid on Scetis did not occur in 407–8, perhaps Evelyn-White's narration of multiple raids by barbarians seems more easily defended in the light of violent political realities across the fifth century. And even if non-Roman peoples did later in the fifth century send monks fleeing from the northwestern Egyptian desert, what I hope I have shown is that historians can no longer simply assert that it was solely savage barbarians that caused monks repeatedly to abandon the desert. Such a neat explanation does not properly attend to the richer texture of these historical moments of violence. As my comparison of Evelyn-White's meager evidence for the supposed first raid and of the more ample evidence for Theophilus's own raid on Nitria highlights, telling the history of Egyptian monasticism across the fourth to fifth centuries requires a far more complex theo-political contextualization than has until now been the case.

Just as there was slippage between the real and the imagined desert, so too was there slippage between rhetorical and real violence. The language of violence used to describe the desert and the ideal monk formed monks who both incited and became targets of actual acts of violence. That anger was so pernicious a vice among the abbas underscores how rhetorical violence spilled over into physical altercations. The story of Abba Achilles spitting out blood in order to purge himself of anger is an especially visceral but not surprising ascetic remembrance of such violence. And that the violence was self-inflicted highlights the complex relationship between individual and communal violence that intersected with communal and individual memory practices.

I hope also to have shown that the *Sayings* can be cautiously used in such reconstructions but only with resonant contemporary sources and a deep awareness of their nostalgic function. That is, when a saying echoes a fourth-century witness, what we have is a memory of the fourth-century past being retained by later generations for their own purposes. By the time the text of the *Sayings* was gathered, a mixture of loss, smoothing, and memory sanction had been bound in a rhetorical educational process that sought to narrate a past that was useful to Gazan monks at the turn to the sixth century. This multifaceted explanation helps account for the broad and diverse proliferation of the apothegmatic tradition. The *Sayings* as written text was always meant to be malleable and to speak to a constantly emerging present rather than reflect any historical past. Just as Egyptian monks are portrayed as embodying scripture in the desert, Gazan *Sayings* collectors grafted the previous century's embodiments onto their textualized paradise.

Through the lens of a particular historical moment in late antiquity, I have also explored the complex relations between acts of memory and erasure, engagements of places and spaces, and violence. As my linking of memory sanctions and nostalgia in the last chapter hinted, nostalgia is itself an innately violent activity. Nostalgia is not just longing for a lost past but a violent displacement of historical pasts in favor of a more productive, imagined historical narration. Such nostalgia thus serves the present rememberers in their acts of remembering a new community. Moreover, such nostalgia adheres to objects and places, such that these objects and places themselves come to symbolize and produce violence.

While simple comparisons to the present are notoriously fraught, I believe arguments around Confederate statues in the United States are perhaps a productive contemporary example. There are differences: At stake are competing narratives about a place (the imagined space of the "South") and its history. But the underlying impetus for both the erection of statues and their needed removal is violence, acts of violence in a past marked by enslavement and continued acts of violence in the present. That the statues as physical locations situated at the intersection of memories and erasures have become conduits for violence should not be surprising. Among the answers offered in our own moment are similar attempts at smoothing—"balance" narratives that suggest merely raising black heroes' statues alongside those of confederate generals will resolve the issue. As I hope my book has shown, such attempts indicate that the complex web of remembering and forgetting moments of violence, as well as places and imagined spaces in which violence was enacted, is far stickier and likely to incite more violence than we tend to want to admit. The *Sayings* are often used as sources of religious and spiritual wisdom, and especially of peace, but perhaps the wise warnings they proffer are more about the violence inherent in emplotting our pasts through remembering and forgetting.

Notes

Epigraph: Palladius, *Dialogue on the Life of John Chrysostom* 7.31–34, 37–38, 41–42, ed. and trans. Anne-Marie Malingrey, *Palladios: Dialogue sur la vie de Jean Chrysostome* (SC 341; Paris: Éditions du Cerf, 1988), 144, 146.

1. Palladius, *Dialogue* 7.44 (Malingrey, 146).

2. Several scholars have argued for a historical kernel. Wilhelm Bousset, in particular, argued that the kernel formed around sayings of Abba Poemen (*Apophthegmata: Studien zur Geschichte des* ältesten *Mönchtums* (Tübingen: J. C. B. Mohr/Paul Siebeck, 1923), 76–93); Jean-Claude Guy divided the *Sayings*'s development into three stages, of which the last constitutes most of the extant material (primitive words, general words, and narratives/sermons), though he noted that we only have access to this latest layer ("Remarques sur le texte des *Apophthegmata Patrum*," *Recherches de Science Religieuse* 43.2 (April–June 1955): 252–58). More recently, Graham Gould (*The Desert Fathers on Monastic Community* (New York: Oxford University Press, 1993)); Douglas Burton-Christie (*The Word in the Desert: Scripture and the Quest for Holiness in Early Christian Monasticism* (Oxford: Oxford University Press, 1993)); and William Harmless ("Remembering Poemen Remembering: The Desert Fathers and the Spirituality of Memory," *Church History* 69.3 (2000): 483–518) have all likewise asserted authentic cores in the *Sayings*.

3. Stephen J. Davis offers a compelling assessment of the *Sayings* and the evocation of memory in his "The Category of Memory in Recent Scholarship on the Desert Fathers" (in *From Cairo to the New World: Coptic Studies Presented to Gawdat Gabra on the Occasion of His Sixty-Fifth Birthday*, ed. Y. N. Youssef and S. Moawad (Colloquia Antiqua 9; Leuven: Peeters, 2013) 59–76). Roger S. Bagnall has done a great deal to bring material culture into discussions of Christianity in Egypt more broadly, including desert asceticism. See, for example, *Egypt in the Byzantine World, 300–700* (Cambridge: Cambridge University Press, 2007). For a recent, sophisticated exploration of the relationship between the literary portrayals and archaeological/epistolary evidence of Egyptian desert monasticism, see Darlene Brooks Hedstrom, *The Monastic Landscape of Late Antique Egypt: An Archaeological Reconstruction* (Cambridge: Cambridge University Press, 2017); on the rhetorical tradition, see, especially, 139–79.

4. For discussion of scholarly views of Palladius as biased and another fresh attempt at asserting his historical reliability, see Demetrios S. Katos, *Palladius of Helenopolis: The Origenist Advocate* (Oxford: Oxford University Press, 2011), 62–97. For Cassian's problems trying to translate Egyptian monasticism to a Gaulic audience, see Steven D. Driver, *John Cassian and the Reading of Egyptian Monastic Culture* (New York: Routledge, 2002), 21–64.

5. Elizabeth A. Clark, *The Origenist Controversy: The Cultural Construction of an Early Christian Debate* (Princeton, N.J: Princeton University Press, 1992).

6. Again, I am indebted to Elizabeth Clark's argument; on these issues, see *Origenist Controversy*, 43–158.

7. Claudia Rapp, *Holy Bishops in Late Antiquity: The Nature of Christian Leadership in an Age of Transition* (Transformation of the Classical Heritage 37; Berkeley: University of California Press, 2005), 56–153.

8. In the last several decades, a growing number of scholars have come to reassess Palladius's version of events and have attempted to reconstruct and better understand Theophilus's position. See, for example, Susanna Elm, "The Dog That Did Not Bark: Doctrine and Patriarchal Authority in the Conflict Between Theophilus of Alexandria and John Chrysostom of Constantinople," in *Christian Origins: Theology, Rhetoric and Community*, ed. Lewis Ayres and Gareth Jones (New York: Routledge, 1998), 68–93; Norman Russell, *Theophilus of Alexandria* (ECF; New York: Routledge, 2007); Krastu Banev, *Theophilus of Alexandria and the First Origenist Controversy: Rhetoric and Power* (OECS; Oxford: Oxford University Press, 2015).

9. Theophilus, *Second Synodal Letter to the Bishops of Palestine and Cyprus* (=Jerome, *Letter* 92; Hilberg, *Sancti Eusebii Hieronymi: Epistulae* (CSEL 55), 147–55).

10. Theophilus, *Letter to Anastasius* is no longer extant, but it is referred to in Anastasius, *Letter to Simplician of Milan* (=Jerome, *Letter* 95; Hilberg (CSEL 55) 157-8); Theophilus, *Letters to Jerome* (=Jerome, *Letters* 87 and 89; Hilberg (CSEL 55) 140, 142–43).

11. Theophilus, *Letter to the Saints in Scetis* (PG 86.967C–D).

12. Theophilus, *Letter to Origenist Monks* (PG 86.967B–C).

13. *The Funerary Speech for John Chrysostom*, ed. and trans. Timothy D. Barnes and George Bevan (Liverpool: Liverpool University Press, 2013), 6–9.

14. Sulpicius Severus, *Dialogues* 1.7. (*Sulpicii Severi: Libri Qui Supersunt*, edited by Carolus Halm (CSEL 1; Vindobonae: Apud Geroldi Filium Bibliopolam Academiae, 1866), 158–59).

15. Evagrius, *On Prayer* 106–12 (*Évagre le Pontique, Chapitres sur la Prière: Édition du texte grec, introduction, traduction, notes et index*, ed. and trans. Paul Géhin (SC 589; Paris: Éditions du Cerf, 2017), 322, 324, 326, 328, 330).

16. Derwas J. Chitty, "The Books of the Old Men," *Eastern Churches Review* 6 (1974): 16–17; Lucien Regnault, "Les Apophtegmes en Palestine aux Ve–Vie siècles," *Irénikon* 54 (1981): 320–30; Graham Gould, *The Desert Fathers*, 1–25.

17. James E. Goehring, *Ascetics, Society, and the Desert: Studies in Early Egyptian Monasticism* (Harrisburg, Pa.: Trinity International Press, 1999), 208–9.

18. *Sayings* (Greek, Alphabetical) Lot 1 (PG 65: 253, 256).

19. *Sayings* (Greek, Alphabetical) Arsenius 42 (PG 65: 105, 108).

20. *Sayings* (Greek, Alphabetical) Arsenius 7, 8, 28 (PG 65: 89, 96–97); Arsenius 7 = *Sayings* (Syriac) Ms. Sin. syr. 46 2vb.23–3ra.7; Arsenius 8 = *Sayings* (Syriac) Ms. Sin. syr. 46 3ra.7–24. Note that Arsenius once also refused the initial visit of Theophilus's predecessor, Archbishop Timothy. Whereas Arsenius seems to express no regret for denying Theophilus's visits, Arsenius expressed remorse and received Timothy the next time Timothy attempted a visit (*Sayings* (Greek, Alphabetical) Arsenius 34 (PG 65: 101)).

21. *Sayings* (Greek, Alphabetical) Arsenius 8 (PG 65: 89); *Sayings* (Syriac) Ms. Sin. syr. 46 3ra.7–24.

22. *Sayings* (Greek, Alphabetical) Theophilus 5 (PG 65: 201); *Sayings* (Syriac) Ms. Sin. syr. 46 19vb.29–20ra.4.

23. The Latin reads *Arsetes*. Jerome, *Letter* 108.14 (Hilberg (CSEL 55) 324).

24. Palladius, *Lausiac History* 7; 46.2 (*The Lausiac History of Palladius: A Critical Discussion, Together with Notes on Early Monachism*, ed. Cuthbert Butler (Texts and Studies 6, 1–2; Cambridge: Cambridge University Press, 1898–1904), 24–25, 134.

25. Sozomen, *Church History* 6.30 (*Sozomène: Histoire Ecclésiastique, livres VII–IX*, ed. Joseph Bidez and Günther Christian Hansen (SC 516; Paris: Éditions du Cerf, 2008), 418.

26. John Rufus, *Life of Peter the Iberian*, 150 (*John Rufus: The Lives of Peter the Iberian, Theodosius of Jerusalem and the Monk Romanus*, ed. and trans. Cornelia B. Horn and Robert R. Phenix Jr. (Atlanta, Ga.: Society of Biblical Literature, 2008), 222; =Raabe 113.

27. Gérard Garitte, "Une lettre de S. Arsène en géorgien," *Le Muséon* 68 (1955): 259–78.

28. For a good discussion of the find and speculation of Arsenius's potential role in the arrival of the texts in the desert, see Blossom Stefaniw, "The School of Didymus the Blind in Light of the Tura Find," in *Monastic Education in Late Antiquity: The Transformation of Classical Paideia*, ed. Lillian I. Larsen and Samuel Rubenson (Cambridge: Cambridge University Press, 2018), 155.

29. *Sayings* (Greek, Alphabetical) Theophilus 3 (PG 65: 200); *Sayings* (Syriac) Ms. Sin. syr. 46 54vb.2–24.

30. *Sayings* (Greek, Alphabetical) Theophilus 1 (PG 65: 197); *Sayings* (Syriac) Ms. Sin. syr. 46 3va.29–3vb.14.

31. *Sayings* (Greek, Alphabetical) Theophilus 2 (PG 65: 197); *Sayings* (Coptic) Chaîne 114.

32. *Sayings* (Greek, Alphabetical) Theophilus 4 (PG 65: 200).

33. *Sayings* (Greek, Alphabetical) Evagrius 1 (PG 65: 173).

34. *Sayings* (Greek, Alphabetical) Evagrius 2, 3, 6 (PG 65: 173, 176). Evagrius 3 = *Sayings* (Coptic) Chaîne 79.

35. *Sayings* (Greek, Alphabetical) Evagrius 7 (PG 65: 176); *Sayings* (Syriac) Ms. Sin. syr. 46 11vb.9–27.

36. *Sayings* (Greek, Alphabetical) Euprepius 7 (PG 65: 172); *Sayings* (Coptic) Chaîne 57; *Sayings* (Syriac) Ms. Sin. syr. 46 11va.23–11vb8.

37. For the purposes of this study, Bo Holmberg's table of sayings in Ms. Sin. syr. 46 has been indispensable (Holmberg, "The Syriac Collection of *Apophthegmata Patrum* in MS Sin. syr. 46," *Studia Patristica* 55 (Leuven: Peeters, 2013), 41–57.

38. Brent D. Shaw, *Sacred Violence: African Christians and Sectarian Hatred in the Age of Augustine* (Cambridge: Cambridge University Press, 2011), 1–9, especially 4; Thomas Sizgorich, *Violence and Belief in Late Antiquity: Militant Devotion in Christianity and Islam* (Philadelphia: University of Pennsylvania Press, 2009), especially for Christian ascetics, see 108–43.

39. David Brakke, *Demons and the Making of the Monk: Spiritual Combat in Early Christianity* (Cambridge, Mass.: Harvard University Press, 2006).

40. Roger S. Bagnall, "Official and Private Violence in Roman Egypt," *Bulletin of the American Society of Papyrologists* 26 (1989): 202–3.

41. Ari Z. Bryen, *Violence in Roman Egypt: A Study in Legal Interpretation* (Philadelphia: University of Pennsylvania Press, 2013), 74.

CHAPTER 1

Epigraph: Translated from É. Amélineau, "Vie de Macaire de Scéte," *Histoire des monastères de la Basse-Égypte*, Annales du Musée Guimet, 25 (Paris: Leroux, 1894), 80–81. The date of the manuscript is uncertain. T. Vivian makes a case for a composition date of about 450 C.E.

based on the absence of anti-Chalcedonian language and the presence elsewhere in the *Life of Macarius the Egyptian* of the "intermediate version of the legend of Maximius and Domitius." He acknowledges, however, that the manuscript witnesses date to the tenth century, and A. Guillaumont has tended to date the text to between 623 and 784 C.E. See Tim Vivian, trans., *St. Macarius the Spirit Bearer: Coptic Texts Relating to Saint Macarius the Great* (Crestwood, N.Y.: St. Vladimir's Seminary Press, 2004), 35–43; Antoine Guillaumont, "Christianismes orientaux," *École pratique des hautes études: Section des sciences religieuses*, Annuaire 1968–1969, Tome 76, 182. The more recent work of Satoshi Toda adds greatly to our understanding of the relationships between various translations of the text. Toda warns, however, that the matter of dating remains uncertain, arguing that the only certainty is the *terminus ante quem* of the text, 784 C.E. Satoshi Toda, *Vie de S. Macaire L'egyptien: Edition et traduction des textes copte et syriaque* (Eastern Christian Studies Series, Piscataway, N.J.: Gorgias Press, 2012) 507.

1. Athanasius, *Life of Antony* 13.2 (*Vie d'Antoine*, ed. and trans. G. J. M. Bartelink (SC 400; Paris: Éditions du Cerf, 1994), 170). Note the similarity to Mark 1:24 (and parallels), where a demon asks Jesus a similar question: "What do you have to do with us?"

2. As recent scholarship has shown, there were many other forms of asceticism (e.g., urban, stylite, wandering, communal) in other geographical locales (e.g., Syria, Palestine, Italy) in the early centuries of Christianity. Even in the deserts of Egypt many different modes of ascesis (anchoretic, semi-anchoretic, cenobite) flourished alongside one another. The pivotal argument for the "desertification" of ascetic literary traditions is J. E. Goehring, "The Encroaching Desert: Literary Production and Ascetic Space in Early Christian Egypt," in *Ascetics, Society, and the Desert: Studies in Early Egyptian Monasticism* (Harrisburg, Pa.: Trinity Press International, 1999), 73–88.

3. Walter E. Crum, *A Coptic Dictionary* (Oxford: Oxford University Press, 1939), 609b.

4. H. Cadell and R. Rémondon, "Sens et emplois de τὸ ὄρος dans les documents papyrologiques," *Revue des études grecques* 80 (1967): 343–49.

5. Dag Endsjø, *Primordial Landscapes, Incorruptible Bodies: Desert Asceticism and the Christian Appropriation of Greek Ideas on Geography, Bodies, and Immortality* (New York: Peter Lang, 2008). See also Dag Endsjø, "'The Truth Is Out There': Primordial Lore and Ignorance in the Wilderness of Athanasius' Vita Antonii," in *Wilderness in Mythology and Religion: Approaching Religious Spatialities, Cosmologies, and Ideas of Wild Nature*, ed. Laura Feldt (Religion and Society 55; Oakville, Conn.: Equinox, 2012), 113–30.

6. *Sayings* (Greek, Alphabetical) Macarius the Egyptian 3 (PG 65: 261, 264). Interestingly, in the Coptic translation of this apothegm two different terms for desert are deployed. Macarius's home, the "great desert," is identified as *t.noch n.erēmos*, while the "other desert" belonging to the brethren is rendered as *ke.jaie* (*Sayings* (Coptic) Chaîne 181).

7. On Egypt, demons, and the desert before Christianity, see David Frankfurter, *Religion in Roman Egypt: Assimilation and Resistance* (Princeton, N.J.: Princeton University Press, 1998), 273–84.

8. Roger S. Bagnall, *Egypt in Late Antiquity* (Princeton, N.J.: Princeton University Press, 1993), 144–47. Examining papyrological evidence, Bagnall discusses the western oases and the economic value of resources found in its desert. See also Guy Wagner, *Les oasis d'Égypte à l'époque grecque, romaine, et byzantine d'après les documents grecs: Recherches de papyrologie et d'épigraphie grecques* (Bibliothèque d'études 100; Cairo: Institut Français d'Archéologie Orientale, 1987), 306–9; Frankfurter, *Religion*, 42–46 (on the cult of the Nile), 51–52 (on how pilgrims gouged specific places that were deemed powerful, an act indicating the ability of not only institutions but also popular piety practices to designate the location of sacred power).

9. On Greco-Roman attitudes toward demons, see Frankfurter, *Religion*, 273–74; Frederick E. Brenk, S.J., "In the Light of the Moon: Demonology in the Early Imperial Period," *Aufstieg und Niedergang der römischen Welt* 2: 16.2 (1986): 2008–145.

10. Peter Brown, *The World of Late Antiquity AD 150–750* (London: Thames and Hudson, 1991), 53–55.

11. David Frankfurter, *Evil Incarnate: Rumors of Demonic Conspiracy and Ritual Abuse in History* (Princeton, N.J.: Princeton University Press, 2006), 103, 35.

12. Frankfurter, *Evil*, 34–35.

13. Brakke, *Demons*, 5. On the role of demons in monastic formation, see also R. Valantasis, "Daemons and Perfecting of the Monk's Body: Monastic Anthropology, Daemonology, and Asceticism," *Semeia* 58.2 (1992): 47–49. Averil Cameron, likewise, has noted that demonologies allowed asceticism not only an opposite against which it could construct itself but also an opposite it could defeat repeatedly ("Ascetic Closure and the End of Antiquity," in *Asceticism*, ed. V. L. Wimbush and R. Valantasis (Oxford: Oxford University Press, 1995), 158).

14. Annette Yoshiko Reed, *Fallen Angels and the History of Judaism and Christianity* (Cambridge: Cambridge University Press, 2005), 164–65. Here, Reed points to Justin's *2 Apology 5* as illustrative of his interpretative moves.

15. Reed, *Fallen Angels*, 175.

16. As Reed notes, the Enochic literature continued to be popular in certain monastic circles, as evidenced, for example, at the monastery of Abba Jeremiah at Saqqara (*Fallen Angels*, 229–30).

17. Reed, *Fallen Angels*, 188.

18. Here and in the conversation that follows, I will treat fallen angels and demons as interchangeable, as this seems to be how Origen (and those who followed after him) viewed the relationship between these two terms.

19. Origen, *On First Principles* 2.8.3 (*Origène: Traité des Principes*, ed. Henri Crouzel and Manlio Simonetti (SC 252; Paris: Éditions du Cerf, 1978), 342–48).

20. Origen, *On First Principles* 1.5.4–5 (Crouzel, *Principes* (SC 252), 182–94).

21. Origen, *On First Principles* 1.5.2–3 (Crouzel, *Principes* (SC 252), 176–82).

22. Although no source explicitly asserts this, the ensuing arguments that would occur around Origen's cosmology in both the first and the second Origenist controversies implies that just such an understanding of the irredeemability of demons must have been developing across the fourth to sixth centuries.

23. Goehring, *Ascetics, Society, and the Desert*, 196–218.

24. Origen, *Against Celsus* 3.29 (*Origène: Contre Celse*, ed. Marcel Borret (SC 136; Paris: Éditions du Cerf, 1968), 70).

25. Origen, *Against Celsus* 2.49–51 (*Origène: Contre Celse*, ed. Marcel Borret (SC 132; Paris: Éditions du Cerf, 1967), 394–406); *On First Principles* 3.3.3 (*Origène: Traité des Principes*, ed. Henri Crouzel and Manlio Simonetti (SC 268; Paris: Éditions du Cerf, 1980), 190).

26. Origen, *On First Principles* 3.2.2 (Crouzel, *Principes* (SC 268), 158–62).

27. Origen, *On First Principles* 1.6.3 (Crouzel, *Principes* (SC 252), 200–204).

28. Origen, *On First Principles* 3.2.4 (Crouzel, *Principes* (SC 268), 170).

29. Ellen Muehlberger, *Angels in Late Ancient Christianity* (New York: Oxford University Press, 2013), 30.

30. Origen, *On First Principles* 2.8.3 (Crouzel, *Principes* (SC 252), 342–48). Origen's notion of cooling is based on what he viewed as the intimate linguistic link between *psuchē* ("soul") and *psuchros* ("cold").

31. Origen, *On First Principles* 1.6.4 (Crouzel, *Principes* (SC 252), 204–5).

32. Origen, *On First Principles* 2.8.3 (Crouzel, *Principes* (SC 252), 344, 346). Evagrius, following Origen, also noted that demonic bodies are icy (Evagrius, *On Thoughts* 9; Evagrius, *Sur les pensées*, edited and translated by Paul Géhin, Claire Guillaumont, and Antoine Guillaumont (SC 438; Paris: Éditions du Cerf, 1998), 180–84). In fact, demonic proximity can cause coolness and yawning in an ascetic (Evagrius, *On Thoughts* 33 (Géhin, *Sur les pensées* (SC 438), 266–70).

33. Athanasius, *Life of Antony* 33.1 (Bartelink, *Vie d'Antoine* (SC 400), 224, 226, 228). See also Brakke, *Demons*, 43–44.

34. Frankfurter, *Religion*, 273–74.

35. Evagrius, *On Thoughts* 20 (Géhin, *Sur les pensées* (SC 438), 224).

36. Athanasius, *Life of Antony* 13, 40, 51 (Bartelink, *Vie d'Antoine* (SC 400), 168–72, 242–44, 272–74).

37. Origen, *On First Principles* 3.1.4, 3.2.2–3 (Crouzel, *Principes* (SC 268) 26–28, 158–68). For a fuller discussion of Origen's view of the body, see P. Brown, *The Body and Society: Men, Women, and Sexual Renunciation in Early Christianity*, 2nd ed. (New York: Columbia University Press, 2008), 160–77; Lynda L. Coon, "Somatic Styles of the Early Middle Ages," *Gender and History* 20.3 (November 2008): 463–86.

38. Antony, *Letter* 1 (François Nau, "La version syriaque de la première lettre de saint Antoine," *Revue de l'Orient Chrétien* 14 (1909), 289–97). Samuel Rubenson, while arguing for the authenticity of the letters, notes the inadequacies of Nau's edition (*The Letters of St. Antony: Monasticism and the Making of a Saint* (Minneapolis, Minn.: Fortress Press, 1995), 17). It nonetheless remains the standard. See also Brown, *Body and Society*, 218–24.

39. Evagrius describes the soul as tripartite (*Praktikos* 89 (*Évagre: Traité pratique ou le Moine*, ed. Antoine Guillaumont and Claire Guillaumont (SC 171; Paris: Éditions du Cerf, 1971), 680–88). In his *Great Letter*, Evagrius describes the fall of the intellect into a soul and then a body (26; (*Euagrius Ponticus*, edited and translated by Wilhelm Frankenberg (Abhandlungen der Königlichen Gesellschaft der Wissenschaften zu Göttingen. Philologisch-historische klasse, bd. 13.2; Berlin: Weidmannsche buchhandlung, 1912), 616, 618). In his *Praktikos*, Evagrius explains that asceticism serves as a catharsis from passions, taming the impassioned body (78, 80, 84, 85, 86 (Guillaumont, *Traité pratique* (SC 171), 666, 668, 674, 676).

40. Evagrius, *Talking Back* (Frankenberg, *Euagrios Ponticus*, 472–545).

41. Evagrius, *Praktikos* 24 (Guillaumont, *Traité pratique* (SC 171), 556).

42. *Sayings* (Greek, Alphabetical) Achilles 4 (PG 65: 125).

43. Although how deprived many ascetics were has rightly been called into question by scholars. See, for example, Ewa Wipszycka, *Les ressources et les activités économiques des églises en Égypte du IVe au VIIIe siècle* (Papyrologica Bruxellensia 10; Brussels: Fondation Égyptologique Reine Élisabeth, 1972); James E. Goehring, "The World Engaged: The Social and Economic World of Early Egyptian Monasticism," in *Ascetics, Society, and the Desert*, 39–52.

44. Although note the case of the monastic cells at Esna (roughly 850 km to the south of the northwestern desert, where its ascetic inhabitants constructed their cells in such a way as to limit exposure to sun and yet still receive cooling breezes (Serge Sauneron and Jean Jacquet, *Les Ermitages chrétiens du desert d'Esna*, 2 vols. (Cairo: Institut français d'archéologie orientale du Caire, 1972). While comparable evidence does not exist for cells located in the northwestern desert, we should still be wary of too completely succumbing to rhetorical portrayals of destitute, suffering monks.

45. *Sayings* (Greek, Alphabetical) Zacharias 1 (PG 65: 177, 180); *Sayings* (Syriac) Ms. Sin. syr. 46 35va.10–21.

46. *Sayings* (Greek, Alphabetical) Theodora 3 (PG 65: 201).

47. *Sayings* (Greek, Alphabetical) John the Little 18 (PG 65: 209, 212).

48. *Sayings* (Greek, Alphabetical) Macarius the Egyptian 2 (PG 65: 260–61); *Sayings* (Coptic) Chaîne 242; *Sayings* (Syriac) Ms. Sin. syr. 46 42va6–43ra.27.

49. Scetis is the Latin version of the region's name. In late antiquity, it carried at least two other names: in Greek, it was probably known as *Skētēs*; in Bohairic Coptic, it was most often referred to as *Shiēt*. For a discussion of and references to the uses of this variety of names and those of Nitria and Kellia, see Hugh G. Evelyn-White, *The Monasteries of the Wadi 'n Natrun: New York, Metropolitan Museum of Art, Egyptian Expedition, 1926–1933*, 3 vols. (New York: Arno Press, 1973), 2:27–36. While what precisely the name means remains unclear, popular etymology asserts that *Shiēt* means "the weighing of hearts," therefore serving as a descriptive appellation of the asceticism carried out there. This interpretation of the name is found in later Syriac texts and should be contextualized in the long history of Coptic-Syriac Christian interaction (for more on which, see Lucas Van Rompay, "Coptic Christianity, Syriac contacts with," in *The Gorgias Encyclopedic Dictionary on the Syriac Heritage (GEDSH)*, ed. Sebastian Brock, Aaron Butts, George Kiraz, and Lucas Van Rompay (Piscataway, N.J.: Gorgias Press, 2011), 103–6). In the thirteenth-century manuscript, Ms. Vat. Sir. 26, a particular region in the Egyptian desert, Ēsqete (a Syriac transliteration of *Scetis*), is equated with Shehit (a Syriac rendering of *Shiēt*), both being given the etymology "weighing the heart, scales for (weighing) thoughts." This etymology is referenced in four other manuscripts (thirteenth through fifteenth centuries): *British Library (B.L.) Add.* 17, 256, *B.L. Add.* 14, 715; *B.L. Add.* 14, 735; *B.L. Add.* 17, 231 (William Wright, *Catalogue of Syriac Manuscripts in the British Museum, Acquired Since the Year 1838*, Vols. 1 and 3 (London: British Museum, 1870–72).

50. For the traditional description of the emergence of the four communities, see H. G. Evelyn-White's chapter on the issue in his *Wadi 'n Natrun*, 2:95–124. Both the original community of Baramus and that of John the Little have undergone excavation in recent years. For Baramus, see Karel Innemée, "Excavations at Deir al-Baramus 2002–2005," *Bulletin de la Société d'archéologie copte* 45 (2006): 50–78. For John the Little, see Stephen Davis, Darlene Brooks Hedstrom, et al., "Yale Monastic Archaeology Project: John the Little, Season 1 (June 7–June 27, 2006)," *Mishkah: The Egyptian Journal of Islamic Archeology* 3 (2009): 47–52; Stephen Davis, Darlene Brooks Hedstrom, et al., "Yale Monastic Archaeology Project: John the Little, Season 2 (May 14–June 17, 2007)," *Mishkah: The Egyptian Journal of Islamic Archeology* 3 (2009): 59–64; Darlene Brooks Hedstrom, Stephen J. Davis, et al., "New Archaeology at Ancient Scetis: Surveys and Initial Excavations at the Monastery of St. John the Little in Wādī al-Naṭrūn (Yale Monastic Archaeology Project)," *Dumbarton Oaks Papers* 64 (2011): 217–27; Stephen J. Davis, "Life and Death in Lower and Upper Egypt: A Brief Survey of Recent Monastic Archaeology at Yale," *Journal of Canadian Society for Coptic Studies* 3 (2012): 9–26; Gillian Pyke and Darlene Brooks Hedstrom, "The Afterlife of Sherds: Architectural Re-Use Strategies at the Monastery of John the Little, Wadi Natrun," in *Functional Aspects of Egyptian Ceramics in Their Archaeological Context*, ed. Bettina Bader and Mary F. Ownby (Orientalia Lovaniensia Analecta 217; Leuven: Peeters, 2013) 307–25.

51. John Cassian, *Conferences* 10.2.3 (*Conlationes*, ed. and trans. Michael Petschenig (CSEL 13; Vienna: Gerold, 1886), 287).

52. Nitria, used here and throughout, is based on the Latin version of the name, as it is the most commonly used name in scholarship on this region. In late antiquity, it carried at least two other names: in Greek, *to oros tēs nitrias* (the mountain of Nitria), and in Bohairic Coptic, *ptou m-pernoudj* (the mountain of Pernoudj). It also is referenced in Sahidic Coptic as

ptoou m-phosm (the Mountain of Natron). Again, see H. G. Evelyn-White, *Wadi 'n Natrun*, 2:17–24, for further discussion. Palladius asserts that it took him a day and a half to travel from Alexandria across Lake Mareotis to Nitria, *Lausiac History* 7 (Butler, *Lausiac History*, 24–25).

53. Palladius, *LH* 8.5 (Butler, *Lausiac History*, 28). Note that in Rufinus's Latin recension of the *HME* (more on which below) the description of Nitria is followed by an independent section about Kellia (Rufinus, *HME* 22; *Tyrannis Rufinus: Historia monachorum, sive, De Vita sanctorum patrum*, ed. Eva Schulz-Flügel (Patristische Texte und Studien 34; New York: De Gruyter, 1990), 358–59).

54. Palladius, *LH* 7.1 (Butler, *Lausiac History*, 24).

55. For a good discussion of how natron was used in burials, see Françoise Dunand, "Between Tradition and Innovation: Egyptian Funerary Practices in Late Antiquity" in *Egypt in the Byzantine World, 300–700*, ed. Roger S. Bagnall (Cambridge: Cambridge University Press, 2007), 169–72.

56. Palladius, *LH* 18.1 (Butler, *Lausiac History*, 47).

57. *Sayings* (Greek, Alphabetical) Antony 34 (PG 65: 35, 38), which states that Antony and Amoun specified the location for more remote cells roughly twelve miles from Nitria.

58. Evelyn-White, *Wadi 'n Natrun*, 2:24–27; Catherine Thirard, "Des Kellia au Wadi Natrun ou les Facteurs de pérennisation d'une colonie ascétique," in *Actes du Huitième Congrès International d'Études Coptes, 28 juin–3 juillet 2004*, ed. Nathalie Bosson and Anne Bouvarel-Boud'hors (Leuven: Peeters, 2007), 369.

59. Palladius, *LH* 20 (Butler, *Lausiac History*, 62–63). The later *Sayings* also preserves stories of a certain Theodore who purportedly lived at Pherme. *Sayings* (Greek, Alphabetical) Theodore of Pherme 1–29 (PG 65: 188, 189, 192, 193, 196); Theodore of Pherme 2 = *Sayings* (Coptic) Chaîne 35; Theodore of Pherme 24 = *Sayings* (Coptic) Chaîne 36; Theodore of Pherme 8 = *Sayings* (Syriac) Ms. Sin. syr. 46 16va.17–29; Theodore of Pherme 13 = *Sayings* (Syriac) Ms. Sin. syr. 46 37ra.12–16; Theodore of Pherme 16 = *Sayings* (Syriac) Ms. Sin. syr. 46 36ra.21–25; Theodore of Pherme 20 = *Sayings* (Syriac) Ms. Sin. syr. 46 20va.8–16; Theodore of Pherme 21 = *Sayings* (Syriac) Ms. Sin. syr. 46 54vb.25–55ra.20; Theodore of Pherme 24 = *Sayings* (Syriac) Ms. Sin. syr. 46 7rb.18–31; Theodore of Pherme 25 = *Sayings* (Syriac) Ms. Sin. syr. 46 7rb.32–7vb.10; Theodore of Pherme 27 = *Sayings* (Syriac) Ms. Sin. syr. 46 65vb.5–66ra.7; Theodore of Pherme 29 = *Sayings* (Syriac) Ms. Sin. syr. 46 66rb.15–66va.6.

60. Palladius, *LH* 20.1 (Butler, *Lausiac History*, 62).

61. Pherme has been identified as the offshoot community found southeast of Kellia, that is Qusur Hégeila and 'Érayma. See Philippe Bridel et al., eds., *Explorations aux Qouçoûr Hégeila and 'Éreima lors des campagnes 1987, 1988 et 1989*, EK 8184, Vol. 4 (Louvain: Peeters, 2003). And, more recently, Tomasz Herbich, Darlene Brooks Hedstrom, and Stephen J. Davis, "A Geophysical Survey of Ancient Pherme: Magnetic Prospection at an Early Christian Monastic Site in the Egyptian Delta," *Journal of the American Research Center in Egypt* 44 (2007), 129–37; Darlene Brooks Hedstrom, Stephen J. Davis, et al., "Yale Monastic Archaeology Project: Pherme (Qusur Higayla and Qusur 'Erayma), Season 1 (May 29–June 8, 2006)," in *Mishkah: The Egyptian Journal of Islamic Archeology* 3 (2009), 53–57.

62. In the *History of the Monks of Egypt* (hereafter, in the notes, *HME*) 23 (*Historia Monachorum in Aegypto: Édition critique du text grec et traduction annotée*, ed. André-Jean Festugière (Subsidia Hagiographica 34; Brussels: Société des Bollandistes, 1971), 130–31), the author claims that the distance between Scetis and Nitria is "a day and a night's journey."

63. Palladius, *LH* 18.10 (Butler, *Lausiac History*, 51).

64. *Sayings* (Greek, Alphabetical) Achilles 5 (PG 65: 125).

65. *Sayings* (Greek, Alphabetical) Macarius the Egyptian 39 (PG 65: 280–81).

66. Palladius, *LH* 18.10 (Butler, *Lausiac History*, 51).

67. P. Bridel, "Répartition géographique de ri d'après la chronologie," *Le site monastique copte des Kellia: Sources historiques et explorations archéologiques,* in *Actes du Colloque de Genève, 13 au 15 août 1984* (Geneva: Mission suisse d'archéologie copte de l'Université de Genève, 1986), 55–61.

68. Tim Vivian, "The Peaceable Kingdom: Animals as Parables in the *Virtues of Saint Macarius,*" *Anglican Theological Review* 85.3 (2003): 477–91.

69. Anton Voytenko, "Paradise Regained or Paradise Lost: The Coptic (Sahidic) Life of St. Onnophrius and Egyptian Monasticism at the End of the Fourth Century," in *Actes du huitième Congrès international d'études coptes: Paris, 28 juin–3 juillet 2004,* ed. Nathalie Bosson and Anne Boud'hors, 2 vols. (Orientalia Lovaniensia Analecta 163; Leuven: Peeters, 2007), 639.

70. For a thorough examination of traditions surrounding the garden of Jannes and Jambres, see Albert Pietersma, ed., *The Apocryphon of Jannes and Jambres the Magicians: P. Chester Beatty XVI (with New Editions of Papyrus Vindobonensis Greek inv. 29456 + 29828 and British Library Cotton Tiberius B. v f. 87)* (Leiden: Brill, 1994), 117–18.

71. *Sayings* (Greek, Alphabetical) Macarius the Egyptian 2 (PG 65: 260–61), *Sayings* (Coptic) Chaîne 242, *Sayings* (Syriac) Ms. Sin. syr. 46 42va.6–43ra.27; Evagrius, *Talking Back* 4.23 (Frankenberg, *Euagrios Ponticus,* 504, 506); *HME* 21.5–12 (Festugière, *Historia Monachorum,* 125–26); Rufinus, *HME* 29.1.2–5 (Schulz-Flügel, *Historia monachorum,* 369–70); Palladius, *LH* 18.5–9 (Butler, *Lausiac History,* 50–51).

72. Marcus Plested notes the "thorny" issue of the Macarii in his discussion of the writings attributed to one or the other Macarius in *The Macarian Legacy: The Place of Macarius-Symeon in the Eastern Christian Tradition* (Oxford: Oxford University Press, 2004), 12–13. For a thorough discussion, see Gabriel Bunge, "Évagre le Pontique et les deux Macaire," *Irénikon* 56 (1983): 215–28, 323–360. D. Brakke offers a good discussion of these particular stories in "Macarius's Quest and Ours: Literary Sources for Early Monasticism," *Catholic Studies Quarterly* 48 (2013): 239–51.

73. Samuel Rubenson, "Textual Fluidity in Early Monasticism: Sayings, Sermons and Stories," in *Snapshots of Evolving Traditions: Jewish and Christian Manuscript Culture, Textual Fluidity, and New Philology,* ed. Liv Ingeborg Lied and Hugo Lundhaug (Berlin: De Gruyter, 2017), 178–200. Given the later gathering of the *Sayings* in Palestine, alongside rabbinical schools, it is worth noting that there was midrash about Jannes and Jambres as well (K. Osawa, "Jannes and Jambres: The Role and Meaning of Their Traditions in Judaism," *Sonderdruck Frankfurter Judaistische Beiträge* 37 (2011–12): 55–73).

74. Evagrius, *Talking Back* 4.23 (Frankenberg, *Euagrios Ponticus,* 504, 506).

75. Evagrius, *On the Eight Thoughts* 5.6 (PG 79: 1149).

76. *HME* 21.5–12 (Festugière, *Historia Monachorum,* 125–26).

77. *HME* 21.7 (Festugière, *Historia Monachorum,* 125–26).

78. *HME* 21.9 (Festugière, *Historia Monachorum,* 126).

79. *HME* 8.40; 10.2–22; 17.1 (Festugière, *Historia Monachorum,* 62, 75–84, 113).

80. *HME* 21.5 (Festugière, *Historia Monachorum,* 125).

81. *HME* 10.20 (Festugière, *Historia Monachorum,* 84).

82. *HME* 10.21 (Festugière, *Historia Monachorum,* 84).

83. Rufinus, *HME* (Latin) 29.1.2 (Schulz-Flügel, *Historia monachorum,* 369).

84. Vivian, "The Peaceable Kingdom," 477–91.

85. Palladius, *LH* 1.3, 7.5, 14.6, 21.17, 25.6 (Butler, *Lausiac History,* 15–16, 26, 39, 69, 80).

86. Palladius, *LH* 7.5 (Butler, *Lausiac History,* 26).

87. Palladius, *LH* 1.3 (Butler, *Lausiac History*, 15–16).

88. Palladius, *LH* 21.17 (Butler, *Lausiac History*, 69).

89. Palladius, *LH* 14.6 (Butler, *Lausiac History*, 39).

90. Palladius, *LH* 21.16 (Butler, *Lausiac History*, 69).

91. Palladius, *LH* 21.17 (Butler, *Lausiac History*, 69).

92. Palladius, *LH* 21.16–17 (Butler, *Lausiac History*, 69).

93. Epiphanius, *Letter to John of Jerusalem* (= Jerome, *Letter* 51; Hilberg. *Sancti Eusebii Hieronymi: Epistulae* (CSEL 54): 395–412). Jerome, *Against John* 11 (Critical edition: *S. Hieronymus Presbyteri Opera. Opera III, Opera Polemica 3: Contra Iohannem*, ed. Jean Louis Feiertag (CCSL 79A; Turnhout: Brepols, 1999)). Theophilus takes umbrage with Origen's claim, in *On First Principles*, that resurrected bodies dissolved entirely. He counters that if this is true, then the Lord defeated the Devil for no reason (Theophilus, *Second Synodal Letter to the Bishops of Palestine and Cyprus* 2 (preserved in Jerome, *Letter* 92; Hilberg (CSEL 55), 149).

94. Translated from *PG* 34: 255, which reflects Vienna, hist. graec. 9, and Vienna, hist. graec. 84. These two manuscripts are grouped by Butler under his B family of witnesses to the *LH*.

95. Theophilus, *Sixteenth Festal Letter* 16 (= Jerome, *Letter* 96; Hilberg (CSEL 55), 175–76).

CHAPTER 2

Epigraph: Evagrius, *To Eulogios* 23 (*Évagre le Pontique: À Euloge, Les Vices opposes aux vertus*, ed. and trans. Charles-Antoine Fogielman (SC 591; Paris: Éditions du Cerf, 2017), 366.

1. As the title of this chapter indicates, I am deeply indebted to the language and previous scholarship of Luke Dysinger on Evagrius's views of prayer and psalmody. In particular, I am building on his portrayal of psalmody as weapon in his chapter "The Psalter as Spiritual Weapon," in *Psalmody and Prayer in the Writings of Evagrius Ponticus* (Oxford: Oxford University Press, 2005), 131–49.

2. Here I cite the psalms according to the numbering of the Septuagint, with the Masoretic numbers in square brackets.

3. *Life of Macarius the Egyptian* 18 (Amélineau, *Histoire des monastères*), 80–81.

4. Pierre Corboud, "L'oratoire et les niches-oratoires: Les lieux de la prière," in *Le site monastique copte des Kellia: Sources historiques et explorations archéologiques*, ed. Philippe Bridel, *Actes du Colloque de Genève, 13 au 15 août 1984* (Geneva: Mission Suisse d'archéologie copte de l'Université de Genève, 1986), 85–92.

5. Darlene Brooks Hedstrom, "The Geography of the Monastic Cell in Early Egyptian Monastic Literature," *Church History* 78.4 (Dec. 2009): 756–91.

6. Although some discrepancy in orientation exists, it tended to be minimal. As R. Kasser argues, it is possible to account for such discrepancy if one assumes that eastern orientation was being calculated by seeking the point of the rising sun on the horizon. If east was discerned in this manner, then the seasonal shifting of the sun's rising point explains the slight variations in building orientation. (Rodolphe Kasser, "Sortir du monde, réflexions sur la situation et le développement des établissements monastiques des Kellia," *Revue de théologie et de philosophie* 26.2 (1976): 111–24.)

7. *Sayings* (Greek, Alphabetical) Arsenius 30 (PG 65: 97).

8. Corboud, "L'Oratoire," 85–92.

9. The art historian who has preserved and recorded these crosses is Marguerite Rassart-Debergh. For discussion of the crosses at Kellia, see her "Le Thème de la croix sur les peintures

murals des Kellia, entre l'Égypte et la Nubie chrétiennes," in *Nubische Studien: Tagungsakten der 5. Internationalen Konferenz der International Society for Nubian Studies*, ed. Martin Krause (Mainz am Rhein: Philip von Zabern, 1986), 363–66; "Quelques croix kelliotes" in *Nubia et Oriens Christianus*, ed. Piotr O. Scholz and Reinhard Stempel (Cologne: J. Dinter, 1988), 373–85; "Les Peintures" in *Les Kellia, ermitages coptes en Basse-Egypte*, ed. Yvette Mottier and Nathalie Bosson (Geneva: Éditions du Tricorne, 1989), 57–77; "L'ermitage QIz 19/20: Choix de peintures" in *EK 8184 III: Explorations aux Quoçoûr el-Izeila lors des campagnes 1981, 1982, 1984, 1985, 1986, 1989 et 1990*, ed. Philippe Bridel, Nathalie Bosson, and Daniel Sierro (Leuven: Mission suisse d'archéologie copte de l'Université de Genève, 1999), 122–51; "Les décors" in *Kellia: L'Ermitage copte QR 195* II, ed. Pascale Ballet, Nathalie Bosson, and Marguerite Rassart-Debergh (Cairo: FIFAO, 2003), 331–489; "Peintures Kelliotes, 1999" in *Coptic Studies on the Threshold of a New Millennium* 2, ed. Mat Immerzeel and Jacques van der Vliet (Leuven: Peeters, 2004) 1471–77.

10. Rassart-Debergh has drawn the crosses found on the four walls of an excavated cell, portraying at least seventeen different crosses on the eastern, western, and northern walls of the room. It seems likely that this painting program continued on the southern wall as well, but most of the painted plaster on that wall is no longer extant. The original images can be found in "L'ermitage QIz 19/20: Choix de peintures" in *EK 8184 III*, folding pl. II, figures 134–37. Reproductions of the images have been more recently published in Elizabeth Bolman, "Depicting the Kingdom of Heaven: Paintings and Monastic Practice in Early Byzantine Egypt," in *Egypt in the Byzantine World 300–700*, ed. Roger Bagnall (Cambridge: Cambridge University Press, 2007), 412–14.

11. Bolman, "Depicting the Kingdom of Heaven," 412, 415.

12. Evagrius, *Vices* 3 (Fogielman, *À Euloge* (SC 591), 420).

13. Evagrius, *Praktikos* Prologue 4 (*Traité pratique ou le moine*, ed. Antoine Guillaumont and Claire Guillaumont (SC 171; Éditions du Cerf, 1971), 488).

14. *Sayings* (Greek, Alphabetical) Syncletica 9 (PG 65: 425); *Sayings* (Coptic) Chaîne 41.

15. Evagrius, *Vices* 6 (Fogielman, *À Euloge* (SC 591), 426).

16. Evagrius, *On Thoughts* 33 (Géhin, *Sur les pensées* (SC 438), 266–70).

17. Evagrius, *On Thoughts* 33 (Géhin, *Sur les pensées* (SC 438), 268). In Rufinus's additions to *HME*, he notes a similar tradition surrounding Macarius of Alexandria, in which Macarius is able to see demons imaged as Ethiopian boys who would distract brethren in church and "if they [the demons] could put their fingers into their [brethren's] mouths, they made them yawn" (Rufinus, *HME* 29.4.7 (Schulz-Flügel, *Historia monachorum*, 372).

18. For a good examination of the dynamics between illness and demons among ascetics, see Andrew Crislip, *Thorns in the Flesh: Illness and Sanctity in Late Ancient Christianity* (Philadelphia: University of Pennsylvania Press, 2013).

19. *Sayings* (Greek, Alphabetical) Longinus 3 (parallel in *Sayings* (Coptic) Chaîne 221); *Sayings* (Greek, Alphabetical) Poemen 7 (parallels in *Sayings* (Coptic) Chaîne 229 and *Sayings* (Syriac) Ms. Sin. syr. 46 53ra.23–53bv.8); Evagrius, *Eulogios* 26 (Fogielman, *À Euloge* (SC 591), 380).

20. Evagrius, *Eulogios* 18 (Fogielman, *À Euloge* (SC 591), 346).

21. *Sayings* (Greek, Alphabetical) Ammonas 8 (PG 65: 121).

22. *Sayings* (Greek, Alphabetical) John the Little 40 (PG 65: 217, 220).

23. Evagrius, *A Word About Prayer* 2 (*De doctrina spirituali Christianorum orientalium. Quaestiones et scripta I*, edited and translated by Irénée Hausherr (OC 30.3; Rome: PIOS, 1933), 149–50).

24. Evagrius, *Gnostic Chapters* 5.28, 5.31 (*Les six centuries des "Kephalaia gnostica,"* ed. Antoine Guillaumont (PO 134 (28.1); Paris: Firmin-Didot, 1958), 187, 189).

25. Evagrius, *A Word About Prayer* 2 (Hausherr, *De doctrina spirituali* (OC 30.3), 149–50).

26. As Robert Sinkewicz notes, Evagrius's *Eulogios* seems to represent an early example of gathering and recording apothegms (*Evagrius of Pontus: The Greek Ascetic Corpus*, trans. Robert E. Sinkewicz (Repr. Oxford: Oxford University Press, 2010), 20). See Evagrius, *Eulogios* 4, 6, 19, 26, 29 (Fogielman, *À Euloge* (SC 591), 286, 294, 350, 352, 378, 380, 388). Such a kernel also sits at the end of Evagrius's *On Prayer* 106–12 (Géhin, *Chapitres sur la Prière* (SC 589), 322, 324, 326, 328, 330).

27. This story seems to be an allusion to the story of the slave girl possessed by a Pythian demon in Acts 16, though here the child is male.

28. Evagrius, *Eulogios* 26 (Fogielman, *À Euloge* (SC 591) 380.

29. For a good discussion of the wide array of approaches to the ascetic life, see Daniel Caner, *Wandering, Begging Monks: Spiritual Authority and the Promotion of Monasticism in Late Antiquity*, Transformation of Classical Heritage 33 (Berkeley: University of California Press, 2002).

30. Palladius, *LH* 7.5 (Butler, *Lausiac History*, 26).

31. Robert Taft, *Liturgy of the Hours in East and West: The Origins of the Divine Office and Its Meaning for Today* (2nd ed.; Collegeville, Minn.: Liturgical Press, 1993) 58–62; Luke Dysinger, *Psalmody and Prayer*, 53–61.

32. Palladius, *LH* 17.10 (Butler, *Lausiac History*, 46).

33. Cassian, *Institutes* 2.5.5 (*De institutis coenobiorum et de octo principalium vitiorum remediis, De incarnatione Domini contra Nestorium*, edited and translated by Michael Petschenig (CSEL 17; Vienna: Gerold, 1888, 22).

34. Palladius, *LH* 22.6–8 (Butler, *Lausiac History*, 71–73).

35. *Sayings* (Greek, Alphabetical) Poemen 168 (PG 65: 361); *Sayings* (Syriac) Ms. Sin. syr. 46 1ra.19–1rb.20.

36. Robert F. Taft sees an early structured rule among the Egyptian ascetics (*Liturgy of the Hours*, 58–62). In his reconstruction, he relies heavily on the witness of Cassian. While he acknowledges that some of what Cassian describes seems like later additions, he is probably correct to imagine that two offices comparable to those held in cathedral settings may have been practiced by some ascetics of the northwestern desert.

37. *Sayings* (Greek, Alphabetical) Serapion 1 (PG 65: 413, 416); *Sayings* (Coptic) Chaîne 240.

38. *Sayings* (Greek, Alphabetical) Abba of Rome 1 (PG 65: 388–89).

39. *Sayings* (Greek, Alphabetical) Macarius the Egyptian 33 (PG 65: 276–77); *Sayings* (Coptic) Chaîne 239.

40. Dysinger, *Psalmody and Prayer*, 48.

41. Evagrius, *On Prayer* 85 (Géhin, *Chapitres sur la Prière* (SC 589), 300). There are many instances, but I offer only a handful here. Other examples of Evagrius distinguishing prayer from psalmody can be found in *On Prayer* 82, 83, 87 (Géhin, *Chapitres sur la Prière* (SC 589), 298, 302) and *Eulogios* 7–8 (Fogielman, *À Euloge* (SC 591), 302, 304).

42. Evagrius, *Talking Back* 4.31 (Frankenberg, *Euagrios Ponticus*, 506).

43. Paul R. Kolbet, "Athanasius, the Psalms, and the Reformation of the Self," *Harvard Theological Review* 99 (2006): 89, 93. See also David Brakke, who briefly discusses how the letter is meant to promote a use of the Psalter for self-formation (*Athanasius and the Politics of Asceticism* (Oxford: Oxford University Press, 2005), 194–96).

44. Derek Krueger, "The Old Testament in Monasticism" in *The Old Testament in Byzantium*, ed. Paul Magdalino and Robert Nelson (Washington, D.C.: Dumbarton Oaks, 2010), 218.

See also his *Liturgical Subjects: Christian Ritual, Biblical Narrative, and the Formation of the Self in Byzantium* (Philadelphia: University of Pennsylvania Press, 2014), 18–19.

45. Georgia Frank, "The Memory Palace of Marcellinus" in *Ascetic Culture: Essays in Honor of Philip Rousseau*, ed. Blake Leyerle and Robin Darling Young (Notre Dame, Ind.: University of Notre Dame Press, 2013), 116.

46. *Sayings* (Greek, Systematic) 2.33 Jean-Claude Guy, *Les apophtegmes* (SC 387), 142).

47. Evagrius, *On Prayer* 98 (Géhin, *Chapitres sur la Prière* (SC 589) 314).

48. *Sayings* (Greek, Alphabetical) John the Little 34 (PG 65: 216); *Sayings* (Syriac). The short, frequent prayers John the Little recommends perhaps witness to the roots of what will later be termed "monologic prayers," single-word or short-phrased prayers that one repeated, a practice often considered in relation to the Jesus Prayer.

49. *Sayings* (Greek, Alphabetical) Macarius 19 (PG 65: 269); *Sayings* (Syriac) Ms. Sin. syr. 46 18vb.19–19ra.4.

50. Antoine Guillaumont, "The Jesus Prayer Among the Monks of Egypt," *Eastern Churches Review* 6 (1974): 66–71. While the Jesus Prayer proper may not yet have been used in the northwestern desert, disputes over whether to pray to the Son emerged in the midst of the Origenist controversy. Archbishop Theophilus in his criticism of the so-called Origenist monks claimed that, among other offenses, these brethren disavowed praying to the Son, even in conjunction with prayer to the Father (Theophilus, *Second Synodal Letter* (Jerome, *Letter* 92; Hilberg (CSEL 55) 149)).

51. Dysinger, in his discussion of *Talking Back*, distinguishes between several varieties of *antirrhetic* foci. He asserts that "verses intended to exhort, encourage, or inform the tempted soul constitute the majority of the *Antirrhetikos*" (*Psalmody and Prayer*, 139). While it is true that many of the statements are not focused directly at the demons, I would argue that even such self-inflicted policing was meant to better hone the ascetic as an agent of divine wrath.

52. Evagrius, *On Prayer* 94 (Géhin, *Chapitres sur la Prière* (SC 589), 308).

53. For specific reference to Evagrius, see Dysinger, *Psalmody and Prayer*, 98–99; for more general reference to views of prayer, see Columba Stewart, *Cassian the Monk* (Oxford: Oxford University Press, 1998), 100–104.

54. Columba Stewart, "Imageless Prayer and the Theological Vision of Evagrius Ponticus," in *A History of Prayer: The First to the Fifteenth Century*, ed. Roy Hammerling (Leiden: Brill, 2008), 146.

55. Evagrius, *On Prayer* 3 (Géhin, *Chapitres sur la Prière* (SC 589), 220).

56. Evagrius, *On Prayer* 4 (Géhin, *Chapitres sur la Prière* (SC 589), 222).

57. Stewart, "Imageless Prayer," 137.

58. Gregory of Nyssa, *Life of Moses* (*Gregorii Nysseni De Vita Moysis*, ed. Herbert Musurillo (*Gregorii Nysseni Opera* vol. 7.1; Leiden: Brill, 1964)). For a good discussion of Gregory and Evagrius, see Kevin Corrigan, *Evagrius and Gregory: Mind, Soul, and Body in the Fourth Century* (New York: Routledge, 2016), 1–20 (their relationship), 53–73 (impassibility); Brian E. Daley, S.J., "Evagrius and Cappadocian Orthodoxy" in *Evagrius and His Legacy*, ed. Joel Kalvesmaki and Robin Darling Young (Notre Dame, Ind.: Notre Dame University Press, 2016), 14–48.

59. Stewart, "Imageless Prayer," 156–62.

60. Evagrius, *On Thoughts* 15, 42, 43 (Géhin, *Sur les pensées* (SC 438), 204, 296, 298); *Gnostic Chapters* 1.74, 1.81 (*Les six centuries des "Kephalaia gnostica*," ed. and trans. Antoine Guillaumont (PO 28.1; Paris: Firmin-Didot, 1958), 53, 55); *Psalms* 4.7, 12.4, 33.6 (PG 12: 1164–65, 1204, 1308). For more detail about these texts, see Stewart, "Imageless Prayer," 156–57, especially footnotes 95 and 97.

61. Evagrius, *Talking Back* 6.16 (Frankenberg, *Euagrios Ponticus,* 524). Note that one of the Tall Brothers from Nitria, Ammonius, is said to have joined Evagrius on the trip. For a fuller discussion of this visit, see Stewart, "Imageless Prayer," 157.

62. Evagrius, *On Thoughts* 39 (Géhin, *Sur les pensées* (SC 438), 286).

63. Stewart, "Imageless Prayer," 159.

64. Evagrius, *Exhortation* 2.20 (PG 79: 1236) (numeration follows that of Sinkewicz).

65. Evagrius, *Eulogios* 8 (Fogielman, *À Euloge* (SC 591), 304).

66. Stewart, "Imageless Prayer," 157.

67. *HME* 11.6 (Festugière, *Historia Monachorum in Aegypto,* 91). Here the description is written by an outsider to the Egyptian ascetic community, recording their recollection of Anouph's words.

68. *HME* 11.7 (Festugière, *Historia Monachorum in Aegypto,* 91).

69. *HME* 11.7 (Festugière, *Historia Monachorum in Aegypto,* 91–92).

70. Cassian, *Conferences* 10.6.4 (Petschenig, *Conlationes* (CSEL 13), 292).

71. Cassian, *Conferences* 12.11.5 (Petschenig, *Conlationes* (CSEL 13), 353).

72. *HME* 20.16 (Festugière, *Historia Monachorum,* 123). A fuller account of Evagrius's limited intake of water is found in Rufinus's replacements for this passage (Rufinus, *HME* 27; Schulz-Flügel, *Historia monachorum,* 364).

73. Cassian, *Conferences* 12.11.5 (Petschenig, *Conlationes* (CSEL 13), 353).

74. Stewart, *Cassian the Monk,* 115.

75. Cassian, *Conferences* 9.26 (Petschenig, *Conlationes* (CSEL 13), 273).

76. Cassian, *Conferences* 9.25 (Petschenig, *Conlationes* (CSEL 13), 272).

77. For prayer as ardent: Cassian, *Conferences* 9.25, 9.26 (Petschenig, *Conlationes* (CSEL 13), 272–73). For prayer as all-devouring flame: Cassian, *Conferences* 9.15.2 (Petschenig, *Conlationes* (CSEL 13), 263).

78. Cassian, *Conferences* 9.26 (Petschenig, *Conlationes* (CSEL 13), 273).

79. Stewart, *Cassian,* 114–16.

80. Evagrius, *On Prayer* 115 (Géhin, *Chapitres sur la Prière* (SC 589), 334).

81. Evagrius, *Gnostic Chapters* 1.68 (Guillaumont, *Kephalaia gnostica,* 49).

82. Evagrius, *Gnostic Chapters* 1.30 (Guillaumont, *Kephalaia gnostica,* 31).

83. Evagrius, *Gnostic Chapters* 2.29, 2.51 (Guillaumont, *Kephalaia gnostica,* 73, 81).

84. Evagrius, *Gnostic Chapters* 3.5 (Guillaumont, *Kephalaia gnostica,* 99).

85. Evagrius, *Gnostic Chapters* 1.74 (Guillaumont, *Kephalaia gnostica,* 53).

86. Evagrius, *Gnostic Chapters* 4.29 (Guillaumont, *Kephalaia gnostica,* 149).

87. Evagrius, *Gnostic Chapters* 3.39 (Guillaumont, *Kephalaia gnostica,* 113).

88. Muehlberger, *Angels,* 89–118.

89. Evagrius, *Gnostic Chapters* 3.62, 3.65 (Guillaumont, *Kephalaia gnostica,* 123, 125).

90. Evagrius, *Gnostic Chapters* 2.30, 6.35 (Guillaumont, *Kephalaia gnostica,* 73, 231).

91. Evagrius, *Gnostic Chapters* 6.86 (Guillaumont, *Kephalaia gnostica,* 253).

92. Ammonas, *Letter* 2.1 (*Ammonas, Successeur de Saint Antoine,* ed. and trans. François Nau (Paris: Firmon-Didot, 1915); PO 11), 435–36). Here I follow Muehlberger's reading of this section and the next as indicating "a natural progression, from the labor required, to the promise" of an angel (Muehlberger, *Angels* 234 n. 78).

93. Macarius of Egypt, *Letter* 1.10 (*Die syrische Überlieferung der Schriften des Makarios, Teil 2: Übersetzung,* ed. Werner Strothmann (Wiesbaden: Harrassowitz, 1981), xx). Again, I am deeply indebted to Muehlberger's work, though I am inclined to draw a sharper distinction

between labor leading to a guardian angel and suffering allowing God's mercy in the form of a guardian angel (Muehlberger, *Angels*, 110–11).

94. Evagrius, *Scholia on Proverbs* 189 (*Évagre le Pontique: Scholies aux Proverbes*, ed. Paul Géhin (SC 340; Paris: Éditions du Cerf, 1987), 282, 284).

95. Evagrius, *Talking Back* 4.26 (Frankenberg, *Euagrios Ponticus*, 506).

96. Muehlberger, *Angels*, 96–97.

97. *Sayings* (Greek, Alphabetical) Macarius the Egyptian 33 (PG 65: 276–77); *Sayings* (Coptic) Chaîne 239.

98. *HME* Prologue 5 (Festugière, *Historia Monachorum in Aegypto*, 7).

99. Rufinus, *HME* Prologue 5 (Schulz-Flügel, *Historia monachorum*, 244).

100. *HME* 2.1–2, 4.1, 6.1, 8.18, 8.38 (Festugière, *Historia Monachorum in Aegypto*, 35–36, 40, 43–44, 53–54, 62).

101. Georgia Frank, *The Memory of the Eyes: Pilgrims to Living Saints in Christian Late Antiquity* (Berkeley: University of California Press, 2000), 134–70.

102. Frank, *Memory of the Eyes*, 162.

103. Krueger, "The Old Testament in Monasticism," 218; *Liturgical Subjects*, 18–19.

104. Frank, *Memory*, 160–63.

105. *Sayings* (Greek, Alphabetical) Arsenius 38 (PG 65: 104–5); *Sayings* (Syriac) Ms. Sin. syr. 46 14vb.24–15va.3.

106. Evagrius, *Gnostic Chapters* 3.48, 3.51 (Guillaumont, *Kephalaia gnostica*, 117, 119).

107. Evagrius, *Gnostic Chapters* 4.74 (Guillaumont, *Kephalaia gnostica*, 169).

108. *Sayings* (Greek, Alphabetical) John the Little 2 (PG 65: 204–5) (parallel: *Sayings* (Syriac) Ms. Sin. syr. 46 63va.28–63vb.29); Muehlberger, *Angels*, 170.

109. *Sayings* (Greek, Alphabetical) Ammoes 2 (PG 65: 125); *Sayings* (Coptic) Chaîne 74. Muehlberger, *Angels* 174–75.

110. Palladius, *LH* 7.5 (Butler, *Lausiac History*, 26).

111. *Gospel of Thomas* 82. For up-to-date Coptic and Greek, see *The Apocryphal Gospels: Texts and Translations*, ed. and trans. Bart D. Ehrman and Zlatko Pleše (Oxford: Oxford University Press, 2011), 303–50.

112. *Sayings* (Greek, Alphabetical) Syncletica 1 (PG 65: 421).

113. *Sayings* (Greek, Alphabetical) Joseph of Panephysis 6 (PG 65: 229); *Sayings* (Syriac) Ms. Sin. syr. 46 36va.18–23.

114. *Sayings* (Greek, Alphabetical) Joseph of Panephysis 7 (PG 65: 229); *Sayings* (Syriac) Ms. Sin. syr. 46 26vb.11–28.

115. *Sayings* (Greek, Alphabetical) Arsenius 27 (PG 65: 96).

116. Even Dysinger, who devotes a whole chapter to the nature of prayer as a weapon in Evagrius's thought, does not trace the implications for such an understanding of prayer beyond the basic view that ascetics were battling demons (*Psalmody and Prayer*, 131–49).

117. *Sayings* (Greek, Alphabetical) Macarius the Egyptian 33 (PG 65: 276–77); *Sayings* (Coptic) Chaîne 239.

CHAPTER 3

Epigraph: *Sayings* (Greek, Alphabetical) John the Little 18 (PG 65: 209); *Sayings* (Coptic) Chaîne 86.

1. For a full discussion of each of these types of damning, see Charles W. Hedrick Jr., *History and Silence: Purge and Rehabilitation of Memory in Late Antiquity* (Austin: University of Texas Press, 2000), 89–130.

2. Hedrick, *History and Silence*, 93. He likewise mentions this point about dishonoring and confirming memory in his Introduction (xii, xxi).

3. Hedrick, *History and Silence*, 97.

4. Hedrick, *History and Silence*, 99.

5. Lauren Hackworth Petersen, "The Presence of '*Damnatio Memoriae*' in Roman Art," *Source: Notes in the History of Art* 30.2 (Winter 2011): 2.

6. Petersen, "Presence," 3.

7. Petersen, "Presence," 6.

8. Petersen, "Presence," 7.

9. See, for example, Michelle R. Salzmann, *The Making of a Christian Aristocracy: Social and Religious Change in the Western Roman Empire* (Cambridge, Mass.: Harvard University Press, 2004).

10. Peter Stewart, "The Destruction of Statues in Late Antiquity" in *Constructing Identities in Late Antiquity*, ed. Richard Miles (Repr.; New York: Routledge, 2014), 173.

11. Stewart, "Destruction," 177.

12. For more detail on the stages described see Stewart, "Destruction," 164–66.

13. Stewart, "Destruction," 166, where he points, among other examples, to the statue base of Diadumenianus found in a latrine at Ostia. On which, further, see Thomas Pekáry, *Das römische Kaiserbildnis in Staat, Kult, und Gesellschaft: Dargestellt anhand der Schriftquellen* (Berlin: Gebr. Mann Verlag, 1985), 134.

14. *Sayings* (Greek, Alphabetical) Theophilus 3 (PG 65: 200); *Sayings* (Greek, Anonymous) N162 (François Nau, "Histoires des solitaires égyptiens," *Revue de l'Orient Chrétien* 13 (Paris: Librairie A. Picard: 1908), 53); *Sayings* (Syriac) Ms. Sin. syr. 46 54vb.2–24.

15. David Brakke, "From Temple to Cell, From Gods to Demons," in *From Temple to Church*, ed. Stephen Emmel et al. (Leiden: Brill, 2008), 102.

16. Eunapius, *Lives of the Philosophers and Sophists* 472 (*Lives of the Philosophers. Philostratus and Eunapius, Lives of the Sophists*, ed. and trans. W. C. Wright (LCL 134; Cambridge, Mass.: Harvard University Press, 1921), 422–23).

17. Rufinus, *Church History* 11.22 (*Eusebius Werke 2.2: Die Kirchengeschichte*, ed. Theodor Mommsen (Die Griechischen Christlichen Schriftsteller; Leipzig: J. C. Hinrichs, 1908), 1026).

18. Rufinus, *CH* 11.23 (Mommsen, *Die Kirchengeschichte*, 1026–29).

19. Rufinus, *CH* 11.23 (Mommsen, *Die Kirchengeschichte*, 1029).

20. Rufinus, *CH* 11.24 (Mommsen, *Die Kirchengeschichte*, 1030).

21. Rufinus, *CH* 11.27 (Mommsen, *Die Kirchengeschichte*, 1033).

22. Although it was a different community of monks, it is worth noting that Rufinus unproblematically depicts the monks of Sebaste as having participated in violence to protect John's bones. So at least Rufinus seems untroubled by violent monks.

23. Christine Shepardson offers a similar reading of the temple's destruction: "There can be little doubt that the monumental temple's destruction, the attribution of the destruction to Christians, and the location of a Christian church in the temple precinct would all reinforce a message of the superior power of Christianity over the gods, a message that is hard to imagine Bishop Theophilus not pressing to its fullest advantage in coaxing the landscape of Alexandria to reflect the success of his Christian community, and encourage its continued growth."

(Christine Shepardson, *Controlling Contested Places: Late Antique Antioch and the Spatial Politics of Religious Controversy* (Berkeley: University of California Press, 2014), 236.)

The last folio of the *Alexandrian World Chronicle* (*AWC*), folio VI verso, contains a depiction of Theophilus standing on top of a temple containing a statue of Serapis. To the left of this image are two figures, one with his right arm raised and the other with both its arms raised, near a second image of the temple of Serapis. Whether the figures are monks felling the temple has been a topic of some speculation. I accept Burgess and Dijkstra's dating of the *AWC* to the second half of the sixth century, meaning that this portrayal of the Serapeum's destruction postdates the event by about two centuries. However, a parallel depiction of statue destruction from the fourth century is much more explicit (R. W. Burgess and Jitse H. F. Dijkstra, "The 'Alexandrian World Chronicle,' Its *Consularia* and the Date of the Destruction of the Serapeum (with an Appendix on the List of the *Praefecti Augustales*)," *Millennium: Jahrbuch zu Kultur und Geschichte des ersten Jahrtausends n. Chr.* 10.1 (Dec. 2013): 39–113, especially 66). In his article, Stewart points to a collection of images found in a Roman hypogeum that includes among numerous biblical passages the toppling of a statue (Stewart, "Destruction," 174–75). Similar to the raised-armed figure of *AWC*, this image shows two figures, one with both arms raised preparing to throw a rock and the other with arm raised holding the end of a rope that is tied around the statue's neck. Taken together, Stewart is right to highlight how they image the destruction and toppling likewise found in rhetorical renderings of *damnatio memoriae*. Whether the figure in the *AWC* is a monk remains unclear, but that said individual is depicted as damning and destroying the statue of Serapis is not given this parallel from two centuries earlier.

24. Judith S. McKenzie, Sheila Gibson, and A. T. Reyes, "Reconstructing the Serapeum in Alexandria from the Archaeological Evidence," *Journal of Roman Studies* 94 (2004): 73–121.

25. McKenzie, "Serapeum" 79, 90.

26. McKenzie, "Serapeum" 100–101.

27. McKenzie, "Serapeum" 91.

28. McKenzie, "Serapeum" 95–96.

29. McKenzie, "Serapeum" 99–100.

30. McKenzie, "Serapeum" 101, 103.

31. Rufinus, *CH* 11.26 (Mommsen, *Die Kirchengeschichte*, 1033).

32. McKenzie, "Serapeum," 109.

33. Eunapius, *Lives of the Philosophers* 472 (Wright, *Philostratus and Eunapius*, 417–23); McKenzie, "Serapeum," 107, 110.

34. Evagrius, *Foundations* 3 (PG 40: 1253). A similar rendering also precedes this passage at *Foundations* 2 (PG 40: 1253).

35. Evagrius, *Talking Back* 1.13, 21, 22, 26, 28, 35, 47, 58, 60, 61, 62, 67; 2.1, 4, 5, 9, 12, 15, 23, 25, 32; 3.36, 53; 5.15, 21, 22, 30 (Frankenberg, *Euagrios Ponticus*, 476, 478, 480, 482, 484, 486, 488, 498, 500, 514, 516); *Foundations* 3, 4, 8 (PG 40: 1253, 1256, 1260–61).

36. For the argument that *Talking Back* is based on Evagrius dialoguing with other ascetics, see David Brakke's introduction and translation (David Brakke, ed., *Talking Back: A Monastic Handbook for Combating Demons* (Cistercian Studies 229; Collegeville, Minn.: Cistercian Publications, 2009), 36).

37. Evagrius, *Talking Back* 1.39 (Frankenberg, *Euagrios Ponticus*, 478).

38. Evagrius, *Talking Back* 2.49 (Frankenberg, *Euagrios Ponticus*, 490).

39. Evagrius, *Talking Back* 3.1, 3, 16, 17, 18, 21, 46 (Frankenberg, *Euagrios Ponticus*, 494, 496, 500).

40. Evagrius, *Talking Back* 4.42, 60 (Frankenberg, *Euagrios Ponticus*, 508, 510).

41. Evagrius, *Talking Back* 5.34, 56 (Frankenberg, *Euagrios Ponticus*, 516, 520).

42. Evagrius, *Talking Back* 6.7, 23, 39, 43, 44, 45, 46, 53, 57 (Frankenberg, *Euagrios Ponticus*, 522, 524, 526, 528, 530).

43. Evagrius, *Talking Back* 7.39 (Frankenberg, *Euagrios Ponticus*, 536).

44. Evagrius, *Foundations* 5 (PG 40: 1256–57); *Talking Back* 7.39 (Frankenberg, *Euagrios Ponticus*, 536).

45. Evagrius offers counterattacks for thoughts of past wealth (*Talking Back* 3.25, 34, 50 (Frankenberg, *Euagrios Ponticus*, 496, 498, 500)).

46. Evagrius, *Talking Back* 3.23 (Frankenberg, *Euagrios Ponticus*, 496). The demons of fornication, love of money, listlessness, and vainglory all might suggest improper engagement with one's cell (Evagrius, *Talking Back* 2.40; 3.21; 6.26, 33; 7.7 (Frankenberg, *Euagrios Ponticus*, 490, 496, 524, 526, 532)).

47. Evagrius, *Talking Back* 3.13, 28 (Frankenberg, *Euagrios Ponticus*, 496, 498).

48. Evagrius *Talking Back* 3.4, 5, 6, 8, 9, 10, 14, 37, 38, 40, 43, 44, 48, 50, 54, 57, 58 (Frankenberg, *Euagrios Ponticus*, 494, 496, 498, 500, 502).

49. Evagrius, *Foundations* 4 (PG 40: 1256).

50. Evagrius describes fighting recollections of "past feasting and drinking" (*Talking Back* 1.36 (Frankenberg, *Euagrios Ponticus*, 478)). Similar references to past, sumptuous meals are found at *Talking Back* 1.30, 38, 41 (Frankenberg, *Euagrios Ponticus*, 478, 480). For hoarding and fears of deprivation, see *Talking Back* 1.8, 10, 11, 12, 13, 16, 21, 22, 26, 28, 35, 47, 49, 50, 58, 60, 61, 62, 67 (Frankenberg, *Euagrios Ponticus*, 476, 478, 480, 482, 484); *Foundations* 3, 8 (PG 40: 1253, 1260–61).

51. Evagrius, *Foundations* 5 (PG 40: 1256–57).

52. Evagrius, *Talking Back* 2.25, 45, 55, 65 (Frankenberg, *Euagrios Ponticus*, 488, 490, 492, 494).

53. Evagrius, *Talking Back* 2.1, 35 (Frankenberg, *Euagrios Ponticus*, 484, 490).

54. Evagrius, *Talking Back* 2.24 (Frankenberg, *Euagrios Ponticus*, 488). Here I follow Brakke's translation (Brakke, *Talking Back: A Monastic Handbook for Combating Demons*, 74).

55. On the skillful ways in which ascetics rendered scriptural passages relevant to asceticism, see Elizabeth A. Clark, *Reading Renunciation: Asceticism and Scripture in Early Christianity* (Princeton, N.J.: Princeton University Press, 1999), especially 104–52.

56. Although focused on slightly different concerns, Brakke also points to the tension between ascetic desires for unity and the differentiation attributed to demons (*Demons*, 18–22).

57. Evagrius, *Letter 7* (Frankenberg, *Euagrios Ponticus*, 570).

58. Evagrius, *To Eulogios* 15 (Fogielman, *À Euloge* (SC 591), 332).

59. For *hēsychia* as a requisite state, see Evagrius, *Vices* 6 (Fogielman, *À Euloge* (SC 591), 424, 426).

60. Nienke Vos, "Seeing *Hēsychia*: Appeals to the Imagination in the *Apophthegmata Patrum*" *Studia Patristica* 97 (2013): 33–45.

61. Jennifer Barry's monograph represents an important example of scholarly consideration of exile. In particular, her attention to John Chrysostom's dual exiles in the midst of the Origenist controversy is a welcome intervention. (Jennifer Barry, *Bishops in Flight: Exile and Displacement in Late Antiquity* (Berkeley: University of California Press, 2019)).

62. Brouria Bitton-Ashkelony, *Encountering the Sacred: The Debate on Christian Pilgrimage in Late Antiquity* (Berkeley: University of California Press, 2005), 146–59; Gould, *The Desert Fathers*, 165; John McGuckin, "Aliens and Citizens of Elsewhere: *Xeniteia* in East Christian

Monastic Literature" in *Strangers to Themselves: The Byzantine Outsider: Papers from the Thirty-Second Spring Symposium of Byzantine Studies, University of Sussex*, ed. Dion C. Smythe (London: Routledge, 2016), 28, 32.

63. Evagrius, *To Eulogios* 23 (Fogielman, *À Euloge* (SC 591) 366).

64. *Sayings* (Greek, Alphabetical) Isaac the Theban 2 (PG 65: 241).

65. Evagrius, *On Prayer* 107 (Géhin, *Chapitres sur la Prière* (SC 589), 322, 324).

66. Evagrius, *Scholia on Ecclesiastes* 3 (Évagre *le Pontique: Scholies à l'Ecclésiaste*, ed. and trans. Paul Géhin (SC 397; Paris: Éditions du Cerf, 1993), 62).

67. *Sayings* (Greek, Alphabetical) John Little 31 (PG 65: 213).

68. *Sayings* (Greek, Alphabetical) John Little 30 (PG 65: 213); *Sayings* (Syriac) Ms. Sin. syr. 46 11ra.17–11rb.6.

69. *Sayings* (Greek, Alphabetical) John the Little 2 (PG 65: 204–5); *Sayings* (Syriac) Ms. Sin. syr. 46 63va.28–63vb.29.

70. *Sayings* (Greek, Alphabetical) John the Little 25 (PG 65: 213).

71. Evagrius, *On Thoughts* 5 (Géhin, *Sur les pensées* (SC 438), 168). Evagrius makes a similar comment about how an improperly managed memory might recall "the face of one who has hurt you" (*On Prayer* 46 (Géhin, *Chapitres sur la Prière* (SC 589), 258).

72. Evagrius, *On Thoughts* 5 (Géhin, *Sur les pensées* (SC 438), 168).

73. Evagrius, *Scholia on Ecclesiastes* 52 (Géhin, Évagre *le Pontique* (SC 397), 152).

74. Evagrius, *On Thoughts* 23 (Géhin, *Sur les pensées* (SC 438), 234).

75. Evagrius, *To Eulogios* 13 (Fogielman, *À Euloge* (SC 591) 324). Evagrius continues at 14.14 to describe the dangers of forgetting one's past sins (Fogielman, *À Euloge* (SC 591) 324).

76. Evagrius, *On Prayer* 8 (Géhin, *Chapitres sur la Prière* (SC 589), 226).

77. Evagrius, *Foundations* 9 (PG 40: 1261).

78. Evagrius, *Praktikos* 33 (Guillaumont, *Traité pratique* (SC 171), 576).

79. Evagrius, *On Thoughts* 23 (Géhin, *Sur les pensées* (SC 438), 234).

80. Evagrius, *On Thoughts* 23 (Géhin, *Sur les pensées* (SC 438), 234).

CHAPTER 4

Epigraph: *Sayings* (Greek, Alphabetical) Arsenius 21 (PG 65: 93). While the preceding portion of this saying is preserved as *Sayings* (Syriac) Ms. Sin. syr. 46 68ra.18–68rb.17, the section cited here comparing Scetis and Rome is absent.

1. I am building on a point made by Thomas Sizgorich, who offered a brief but compelling portrayal of the potential confusion between monks and monsters through reference to Foucault among other theorists (*Violence and Belief*, 127–31). For Foucault on monsters as, by definition, lawless creatures, see Michel Foucault, *Abnormal: Lectures at the Collège de France 1974–1975*, trans. Graham Burchell (London: Verso, 2003), 55–56.

2. Evagrius, *On Prayer* 107 (Géhin, *Chapitres sur la Prière* (SC 589), 322, 324).

3. Virginia Burrus, "Wyschogrod's Hand: Saints, Animality, and the Labor of Love," *Philosophy Today* 55 (2011): 419.

4. Patricia Cox Miller, "Jerome's Centaur: A Hyper-Icon of the Desert," *Journal of Early Christian Studies* 4 (1996): 218.

5. Peter Mena, *Place and Identity in the Lives of Antony, Paul, and Mary of Egypt: Desert as Borderland* (London: Palgrave Macmillan, 2019), 61–84. See also his joint piece with An Yountae, "Anzaldúa's Animal Abyss: *Mestizaje* and the Late Ancient Imagination" in *Divinanimality:*

Animal Theory, Creaturely Theology, ed. Stephen D. Moore (New York: Fordham University Press, 2014), 161–81.

6. For an example of more nuanced engagement, see Ralph Mathisen and Danuta Shanzer, eds., *Romans, Barbarians, and the Transformation of the Roman World: Cultural Interaction and the Creation of Identity in Late Antiquity* (Burlington, Vt.: Ashgate, 2011).

7. Synesius, *Letters* 125, 130 (the "barbarous people" are presumably the Austuriani based on Synesius's other references), 132 (again, Synesius invokes the "barbarian" attacking the timid, who presumably are the Austuriani), 133. (*Synesii Cyrenensis: Epistolae*, ed. Antonius Garzya (Rome: Typis Officinae polygraphicae, 1979), 213, 222, 228, 230–31). For a recent and helpful discussion of the state of scholarship on the letters, see David Maldonado Rivera, "The Letter Collection of Synesius of Cyrene," in *Late Antique Letter Collections: A Critical Introduction and Reference Guide*, ed. Cristiana Sogno, Bradley K. Storin, and Edward J. Watts (Berkeley: University of California Press, 2017), 205–20.

8. DenisRoques, *Synésios de Cyrène et la Cyrénaïque du Bas-Empire* (Paris: CNRS, 1987). Ana de Francisco Heredero, "Bárbaros en la Cirenaica a través de la obra de Sinesio de Cirene," in *El espejismo del bárbaro: Ciudadanos y extranjeros al final de la Antigüedad*, ed. David Álvarez Jiménez, Rosa Sanz Serrano, and David Hernández de la Fuente (Castelló de la Plana: Publicacions de la Universitat Jaume I, D.L., 2013), 131–60.

9. Yves Modéran, "*Les Maures et l'Afrique romaine (IVe–VIIe siècle)*," Bibliothèque des Écoles françaises d'Athènes et de Rome (Rome: École française de Rome, 2003), 314. David J. Mattingly, "The Laguatan: A Libyan Tribal Confederation in the Late Roman Empire," *Libyan Studies* 14 (1983): 96–108.

10. Here I borrow Gay Byron's terminology to discuss how Ethiopians were deployed in rhetorical writing, the ethnological idea of Ethiopians being situated in a dense network of meaning that served Roman political purposes rather than actual Ethiopian individuals (*Symbolic Blackness and Ethnic Difference in Early Christian Literature* (London: Routledge, 2002), 1–3).

11. Rufinus, *CH* 10.9–10 (Mommsen, *Die Kirchengeschichte*, 971–73). Note that in his retelling, Rufinus refers to 'Ezana's people generically as "barbarians."

12. For a thorough discussion on how this distinction developed alongside and within ascetic literature, see Byron, *Symbolic Blackness*, 77–103.

13. Byron, *Symbolic Blackness*, 30–44.

14. Byron, *Symbolic Blackness*, 85–103.

15. de Francisco Heredero, "Bárbaros," 137–43.

16. Ammianus Marcellinus, *Roman History* 29.5.17 (*Ammiani Marcellini: Rerum gestarum libri qui supersunt*, ed. Wolfgang Seyfarth, Liselotte Jacob-Karau, and Ilse Ulmann. Bibliotheca Scriptorum Graecorum et Romanorum Teubneriana, Vol. 2 (Leipzig: Teubner, 1999), 118).

17. de Francisco Heredero reads the Edict of Anastasius as an indication of peaceable trade (de Francisco Heredero, "Bárbaros," 138, 141).

18. Synesius, *On Kingship* 23C–25A (PG 66: 1092–96). While most scholars have tended to place the date of *On Kingship* to 399–402, Alan Cameron argues that it was written a few years earlier, in 397–400 (Alan Cameron and Jacqueline Long, *Barbarians and Politics at the Court of Arcadius* (Berkeley: University of California Press, 1993), 107–26).

19. Synesius, *Letter* 130 (Garzya, *Synesii Cyrenensis: Epistolae*, 222). He uses the term *mixobarbaros*.

20. Palladius, *Dialogue* 20.42–43 (Malingrey, *Dialogue* (SC 341), 396).

21. For example, Jennifer Barry's *Bishops in Flight*.

22. Palladius, *LH* 7 (Butler, *Lausiac History*, 25).

23. Cassian, *Conférences* 2.6 (Petschenig, *Conlationes* (CSEL 13), 45–46).

24. Cassian, *Conférences* 2.6 (Petschenig, *Conlationes* (CSEL 13), 45–46).

25. Foucault, *Abnormal*, 56.

26. Evagrius, *To Eulogios* 3.3–4 (Fogielman, *À Euloge* (SC 591), 282).

27. Endsjø, *Landscapes*, 33–34.

28. Endsjø, *Landscapes*, 64–65.

29. Endsjø, *Landscapes*, 78.

30. *Sayings* (Greek, Alphabetical) Macarius the Egyptian 2 (PG 65: 260–61); *Sayings* (Coptic) Chaîne 242; *Sayings* (Syriac) Ms. Sin. syr. 46 42va.6–43ra.27.

31. Synesius, *Letter* 154 (Garzya, *Synesii Cyrenensis: Epistolae*, 271 ("dark cloaks"), 271–77 (his entire defense).

32. Synesius, *Dio* 7 (PG 66: 1132–33).

33. Synesius, *Dio* 7 (PG 66: 1133).

34. Eunapius, *Lives of the Philosophers* 472 (LCL 134: 422–23).

35. Brakke, *Demons*, 178–79.

36. *Sayings* (Greek, Alphabetical) Moses 4 (PG 65: 284); *Sayings* (Syriac) Ms. Sin. syr. 46 26va.17–26vb.11.

37. Brakke, *Demons*, 179.

38. *Sayings* (Greek, Alphabetical) Moses 1 (PG 65: 281) (=*Sayings* (Coptic) Chaîne 184) also offers an intriguing intertext to Moses' demonic and barbarian inhumanity in Moses 4. In the saying, demons are associated with the west. Although reference to "blackness" is lacking, the angels (associated with the east) are described, in opposition to the demons, as "shining." Further, not only the demons, but also barbarians were located, among other places, on the western periphery of the ascetic desert.

39. Palladius, *LH* 19 (Butler, *Lausiac History*, 58–59).

40. Evelyn-White, *Wadi 'n Natrûn*, vol. 2, 153.

41. Peter Van Nuffelen, "Palladius and the Johannite Schism," *Journal of Ecclesiastical History* 64.1 (Jan. 2013): 18.

42. Synesius, *Letter* 67 (Garzya, *Synesii Cyrenensis: Epistolae*, 121–24).

43. Palladius, *Dialogue* 11.135–44 (Malingrey, *Dialogue* (SC 341), 226, 228).

44. Evelyn-White, *Wadi 'n Natrûn*, vol. 2, 153.

45. Theophilus, *Letter to the Saints in Scetis* (PG 86: 967). In the letter, he equates Origen to Arius and claims that some brethren have been honoring Origen, thus slipping into heresy. He goes on to rhetorically query, "Is it right to tolerate such people?" The implication is that Theophilus felt he had no other choice but to attack the Origenist brethren.

46. Augustine, *Letter* 111.1. (*Sancti Aureli Augustini: Epistulae 31–123*, ed. and trans. Alois Goldbacher (CSEL 34.2; Vienna: Tempsky, 1898), 643).

47. Philostorgius, *Church History* 11.8 (*Philostorge: Histoire ecclésiastique*, ed. and trans. Joseph Bidez and Édouard Des Places (SC 564; Paris: Éditions du Cerf, 2013), 524).

48. Synesius, *Downfall of Cyrenaica* 2 (PG 66: 1568).

49. Evelyn-White, *Wadi 'n Natrûn*, vol. 2, 160–61.

50. *Sayings* (Greek, Alphabetical) Arsenius 21 (PG 65: 93).

51. *Sayings* (Greek, Alphabetical) Arsenius 42 (PG 65: 105, 108).

52. *Sayings* (Greek, Alphabetical) Arsenius 34 (PG 65: 101).

53. *Sayings* (Greek, Alphabetical) Arsenius 32 (PG 65: 97, 100).

54. *Sayings* (Greek, Alphabetical) Arsenius 7, 8, 13, 21, 26, 28, 31 (PG 65: 89, 92–93, 96–97); *Sayings* (Syriac) Ms. Sin. syr. 46 2vb.23–3ra.24.

55. *Sayings* (Greek, Alphabetical) Daniel 1 (PG 65: 153); *Sayings* (Coptic) Chaîne 55; *Sayings* (Syriac) Ms. Sin. syr. 46 21ra.16–21rb.1.

56. *Sayings* (Greek, Alphabetical) Daniel 8 (PG 65: 160); *Sayings* (Coptic) Chaîne 176.

57. Evelyn-White, *Wadi 'n Natrûn*, vol. 2, 151–52.

58. Rufus, *Life of Peter the Iberian* 118 (Horn and Phenix, *John Rufus*, 174; = Raabe 85).

59. Rufus, *Life of Peter the Iberian* 118 (Horn and Phenix, *John Rufus*, 174; = Raabe 85).

60. *Sayings* (Greek, Alphabetical) Anoub 1 (PG 65: 129).

61. *Sayings* (Coptic) Chaîne 261.

62. *Sayings* (Greek, Alphabetical) Daniel 1 (PG 65: 153); *Sayings* (Coptic) Chaîne 55; *Sayings* (Syriac) Ms. Sin. syr. 46 21ra.16–21rb.1.

63. *Sayings* (Greek, Alphabetical) Macarius 18 (PG 65: 269). And when an abba dared inhibit an act of theft, he might be chastised for it. So, when an anonymous old man yelled out at being robbed, resulting in the robber's arrest, it was the old man who was wrong. Abba Poemen wrote him an admonishing letter and the old man quickly went to get the robber released from prison (*Sayings* (Greek, Alphabetical) Poemen 90 (PG 65: 344)).

64. Evelyn-White, *Wadi 'n Natrûn*, vol. 2, 154–61.

65. *Sayings* (Greek, Alphabetical) Theodore of Pherme 26 (PG 65: 193).

66. *Sayings* (Greek, Alphabetical) Macarius 5 (PG 65: 264); *Sayings* (Coptic) Chaîne 183; *Sayings* (Syriac) Ms. Sin. syr. 46 8ra.16–29.

67. *Sayings* (Greek, Alphabetical) Isaac 5 (PG 65: 225); *Sayings* (Coptic) Chaîne 58.

68. So, for example, Caroline T. Schroeder argues that male monastic identity was constructed, among other things, around interactions with young boys. ("Queer Eye for the Ascetic Guy? Homoeroticism, Children, and the Making of Monks in Late Antique Egypt," *Journal of the American Academy of Religion* 77.2 (June 2009): 333–47).

69. Palladius, *Dialogue* 7.41–44 (Malingrey, *Dialogue* (SC 341), 146).

70. *Sayings* (Greek, Anonymous) N361 (Nau, "Histoires," *ROC* 18 (1913) 137–38); *Sayings* (Coptic) Chaîne 198.

71. Todd Berzon, *Classifying Christians: Ethnography, Heresiology, and the Limits of Knowledge in Late Antiquity* (Berkeley: University of California Press, 2016); Andrew Jacobs, *Epiphanius of Cyprus: A Cultural Biography of Late Antiquity* (Berkeley: University of California Press, 2016); Young Kim, *Epiphanius of Cyprus: Imagining an Orthodox World* (Ann Arbor: University of Michigan Press, 2015).

72. Epiphanius, *Panarion* 2.69.2.1 (*Ancoratus und Panarion Bd. 3: Panarion haer. 65–80*, ed. Karl Holl (Die Griechischen Christlichen Schriftsteller 37; Leipzig: J. C. Hinrichs, 1933), 153).

73. Theophilus, *First Synodal Letter* (PG 86: 969–71).

74. Theophilus, *Second Synodal Letter* (Jerome, *Letter* 92; Hilberg (CSEL 55): 148).

75. Theophilus, *Sixteenth Festal Letter* 17 (Jerome, *Letter* 96; Hilberg (CSEL 55), 176–77).

76. *Virtues of Macarius* 16 (Amélineau, *Histoire des monastères*, 136–37).

77. *Virtues of Macarius* 17 (Amélineau, *Histoire des monastères*, 137–38).

78. *Sayings* (Greek, Alphabetical) Moses 9 (PG 65: 285); *Sayings* (Coptic) Chaîne 185; *Sayings* (Syriac) Ms. Sin. syr.46 10vb.17–25. The *Virtues of Macarius* 70 likewise predicts a martyr's death for Moses and six brethren. Although their deaths are prophesied, no mention is made of barbarians as the culprits. In this version, it is in fact Macarius the Egyptian rather than Moses who predicts their deaths, and Macarius does so in front of some prominent ascetic

figures: Poemen, Pambo, Evagrius, Moses, Chronius, and two others. Note that seven brothers are supposed to have died and seven brothers are also present for the prediction. There may be number symbolism underlying some of this narrative (*Virtues of Macarius* 70 (Amélineau, *Histoire des monastères*, 185–87)).

79. *Sayings* (Greek, Alphabetical) Moses 10 (PG 65: 285); *Sayings* (Coptic) Chaîne 186; *Sayings* (Syriac) Ms. Sin. syr. 46 49ra.12–49rb.18.

80. *Sayings* (Greek, Alphabetical) Arsenius 38 (PG 65: 105) (=*Sayings* (Syriac) Ms. Sin. syr. 46 14vb.24–15va.3; Palladius, *LH* 19 (Butler, *Lausiac History*, 58–59)).

81. *Sayings* (Alphabetical, Greek) Macarius the Egyptian 22 (PG 65: 272). *Sayings* (Greek, Alphabetical) Moses 13 (PG 65: 285); *Sayings* (Syriac) Ms. Sin. syr. 46 65ra.27–65va.9.

82. Cassian, *Conferences* 7.26.2 (Petschenig, *Conlationes* (CSEL 13), 204). For a good correction of Jean-Claude Guy's misunderstanding of Cassian on Moses, see Stewart, *Cassian*, 138–39.

83. Palladius, *LH* 19 (Butler, *Lausiac History*, 60).

84. While the *Alexandrian Synaxarium*, which is extant in Arabic (Paona 24), preserves his murder by barbarians, the *Constantinopolitan Synaxarium* (August 28) has him die naturally like Palladius (*Le Synaxaire Arabe Jacobite*, ed. René Basset (PO 17; Paris: Firmon-Didot, 1923), 591–94; Hippolyte Delehaye, *Synaxarium ecclesiae Constantinopolitanum e codice Sirmondiano nunc Berolinensi* (Brussels: Apud socios Bollandianos,1902), col. 929–32 (Aug. 28.1)).

85. Evelyn-White, *Wadi 'n Natrûn*, vol. 2, 150.

CHAPTER 5

Epigraph: Theophilus, *Second Synodal Letter* 6 (Jerome 92; Hilberg (CSEL 55), 154). Here I follow Norman Russell's translation, as it captures well the violence that Theophilus is attempting to invoke rhetorically (*Theophilus*, 99).

1. Katos, *Palladius of Helenopolis*, 33–61.

2. Banev, *Theophilus of Alexandria*, 107–72; Norman Russell, "Theophilus of Alexandria as a Forensic Practitioner," *Studia Patristica* 50 (2011): 235–43.

3. Palladius notes these roles for Isidore (*Dialogue* 6; Malingrey, *Dialogue* (SC 341), 130).

4. Norman Russell offers a good summary of Isidore's activities on Theophilus's part (*Theophilus*, 15–17).

5. Palladius, *Dialogue* 6 (Malingrey, *Dialogue* (SC 341), 132).

6. Theophilus, *Second Synodal Letter* 3 (Jerome 92; Hilberg (CSEL 55), 151).

7. This is an ironic claim, considering Theophilus will in turn refuse to present himself before a council in Constantinople in the following years of the Origenist controversy.

8. Palladius is the one who shares that Isidore had spent his youth at Nitria learning asceticism (*Dialogue* 6; Malingrey, *Dialogue* (SC 341), 136).

9. Ps.-Martyrius, *Funeral Oration* 42 (Wallraff, *Oratio Funebris*, 94).

10. Ps.-Martyrius, *Funeral Oration* 38 (Wallraff, *Oratio Funebris*, 90).

11. Ps.-Martyrius, *Funeral Oration* 38 (Wallraff, *Oratio Funebris*, 90).

12. Palladius, *Dialogue* 6 (Malingrey, *Dialogue* (SC 341), 138).

13. Theophilus, *Second Synodal Letter* 1 (Nitrian monks and Origen's writings), 2 (Origen's writings), 3 (Nitrian monks again), 4 (Origen's writings), 5–6 (Nitrian monks) (Jerome 92; Hilberg (CSEL 55), 147–55).

14. Theophilus, *Second Synodal Letter* 3 (Jerome 92; Hilberg (CSEL 55), 150).

15. Theophilus, *Second Synodal Letter* 5 (Jerome 92; Hilberg (CSEL 55), 153).

16. Theophilus, *Second Synodal Letter* 3 (Jerome 92; Hilberg (CSEL 55), 150).

17. Theophilus, *Second Synodal Letter* 3 (Jerome 92; Hilberg (CSEL 55), 150).

18. *Sayings* (Greek, Alphabetical) Theophilus 3 (PG 65: 200); *Sayings* (Greek, Anonymous) N162 (Nau, "Histoires," *ROC* 13 (1908): 53); *Sayings* (Syriac) Ms. Sin. syr. 46 54vb.2–24.

19. Theophilus, *Second Synodal Letter* 1 (Jerome 92; Hilberg (CSEL 55), 147).

20. Sulpicius Severus, *Dialogues* 1.6 (Halm, *Sulpicii Severi*, 157).

21. Theophilus, *Second Synodal Letter* 5 (Jerome 92; Hilberg (CSEL 55), 153–54).

22. Theophilus, *Second Synodal Letter* 6 (Jerome 92; Hilberg (CSEL 55), 154).

23. Theophilus, *Second Synodal Letter* 6 (Jerome 92; Hilberg (CSEL 55), 154).

24. Theophilus, *Second Synodal Letter* 6 (Jerome 92; Hilberg (CSEL 55), 154).

25. Theophilus, *Second Synodal Letter* 3 (Jerome 92; Hilberg (CSEL 55), 151). Palladius, *Dialogue* 7 (Malingrey, *Dialogue* (SC 341), 140).

26. Palladius, *Dialogue* 7 (Malingrey, *Dialogue* (SC 341), 140–42).

27. Sulpicius Severus, *Dialogues* 1.7 (Halm, *Sulpicii Severi*, 158–59).

28. Palladius, *Dialogue* 7 (Malingrey, *Dialogue* (SC 341), 144–46).

29. Theophilus, *Sixteenth Festal Letter* 20 (Jerome 92; Hilbert (CSEL 55), 180).

30. Ps.-Martyrius, *Funeral Oration* 42 (Wallraff, *Oratio Funebris*, 94).

31. Sulpicius Severus, *Dialogues* 1.7 (Halm, *Sulpicii Severi*, 159).

32. For the politics and anti-barbarian sentiments preceding Stilicho's death, see Cameron and Long, *Barbarians and Politics at the Court of Arcadius*. On the general communal anxiety of the era, see Ioannis Papadopoulos, "The Enemy Within: The Rise and Influence of Conspiracy Theories in Rome Before the Gothic Sack (410 AD)," *Leeds International Medieval Congress*, 2017.

33. Jerome's recollection of this visit is preserved in *Against John* 11 (Feiertag, *Hieronymus Presbyteri* (CCSL 79A), 19–21). For a recent discussion of the event, see Kim, *Epiphanius*, 211–13.

34. Clark, *Origenist Controversy*, 94–104.

35. Jerome translated Epiphanius's letter to John defending his choice to ordain outside his jurisdiction (Jerome, *Letter* 51.1–7 (Hilberg (CSEL 54) 403–10).

36. Jerome, *Against John* 37 (Feiertag, *Hieronymus Presbyteri*, 71–73) describes how Isidore had already announced victory to John against Epiphanius, thus undermining Isidore's ability to act as a mediator.

37. Theophilus, *Second Synodal Letter* 6 (Jerome 92; Hilberg (CSEL 55), 154).

38. See, especially, Shaw, *Sacred Violence*, 633–37.

39. Ibid., 649.

40. Ibid., 664.

41. Ibid., 673.

42. Theophilus, *Second Synodal Letter* 1 (Jerome 92; Hilberg (CSEL 55), 148).

43. Palladius, *Dialogue* 7 (Malingrey, *Dialogue* (SC 341), 146).

44. Goehring, *Ascetics, Society, and the Desert*, 196–220.

45. Cassian, *Conferences* 10.2.3 (Petschenig, *Conlationes* (CSEL 13), 287).

46. Theophilus, *Letter to the Saints in Scetis* (PG 86: 967).

47. Theophilus, *Letter to the Saints in Scetis* (PG 86: 967).

48. Theophilus, *Second Synodal Letter* 3 (Jerome 92; Hilberg (CSEL 55), 150).

49. Synesius, *Dio* 7 (PG 66: 1133).

50. Banev, *Theophilus of Alexandria*, 170–72, 188–91.

51. Theophilus, *Second Synodal Letter* 5 (Jerome 92; Hilberg (CSEL 55), 154).

52. Banev, *Theophilus of Alexandria*, 43.

53. Ibid., 42.

54. Delehaye, *Synaxarium ecclesiae Constantinopolitanae*, col. 812 (July 10.4).

55. Banev, *Theophilus of Alexandria*, 42.

56. Sulpicius Severus, *Dialogue* 1.7 ("ubi recens fraternae cladis fervebat invidia"; Halm, *Sulpicii Severi*, 159).

57. Ps.-Martyrius, *Funeral Oration* 43 (Wallraff, *Oratio Funebris*, 94).

58. Sozomen claims that Dioscorus was dead and Ammonius fell ill and soon after died, neither therefore being able to attend the Synod of Oak to defend themselves (*Church History* 8.17.5–6; Bidez and Hansen, *Histoire Ecclésiastique*, 306–8).

59. For a nuanced discussion of the charges brought against John, see Peter Van Nuffelen, "Theophilus Against John Chrysostom: The fragments of a lost *liber* and the Reasons for John's Deposition," *Adamantius* 19 (2013): 139–55. On John's subsequent exile, see Barry, *Bishops in Flight*.

60. Basset, *Le Synaxaire Arabe Jacobite* (PO 17), 591–94; *Sayings* (Greek, Alphabetical) Moses 10 (PG 65: 285) (=*Sayings* (Coptic) Chaîne 186; *Sayings* (Syriac) Ms. Sin. syr. 46 49ra.12–49rb.18).

61. For the controversy covering the entire Mediterranean, see Roberto Alciati and Federico Fatti, "La controversia origenista: Un affare mediterraneo," *Adamantius* 19 (2013): 7–9, which introduces an entire volume devoted to the Origenist controversy.

62. Augustine, *Letter 111.1* (Goldbacher, *Epistulae* 31–123 (CSEL 34.2), 643).

63. Susan Wessel notes that Cyril's early rule as archbishop was taken up with resolving the remaining troubles from Theophilus's time (*Cyril of Alexandria and the Nestorian Controversy: The Making of a Saint and of a Heretic* (OECS; Oxford: Oxford University Press, 2004), 23).

64. Edward J. Watts, *Riot in Alexandria: Tradition and Group Dynamics in Late Antique Pagan and Christian Communities* (Berkeley: University of California Press, 2010), 191.

65. Theophilus, *Fifth Festal Letter* (*Acta Conciliorum Oecumenicorum* 1.1.2, ed. Ed Schwartz (Berlin: De Gruyter, 1965), 41). Theophilus, *Sixth Festal Letter* (*Acta Conciliorum Oecumenicorum* 1.1.2, ed. Ed Schwartz (Berlin: De Gruyter, 1965), 41–42). The Greek of both letters is also in PG 65: 60.

66. Isidore of Pelusium, *Letter* 1.370 (PG 78: 392c).

67. Isidore of Pelusium, *Letter* 1.310 (PG 78: 361c).

68. Evagrius, *On Prayer* 106–12 (Géhin, *Chapitres sur la Prière* (SC 589), 322, 324, 326, 328, 330).

69. The barbarian-ascetic complex emerges at this stage of the Origenist argument as well. As Susanna Elm has shown, "barbarian" fashions filled the court and ascetic entourages themselves might likewise function as a fashion statement. Chrysostom, in fact, accuses Eudoxia of desiring to look monstrous with her fashion choices ("What the Bishop Wore to the Synod: John Chrysostom, Origenism, and the Politics of Fashion at Constantinople," *Adamantius* 19 (2013): 156–69; for the comment on Eudoxia as monstrous, 166).

70. Lucien Regnault, "Les Apophtegmes en Palestine aux Ve–VIe siècles," *Irénikon* 54 (1981): 320–30.

71. Brouria Bitton-Ashkelony and Aryeh Kofsky, *The Monastic School of Gaza* (Leiden: Brill, 2006), 6–7.

72. Jerome, *Life of Hilarion* (*Jérôme: Trois Vies de Moines (Paul, Malchus, Hilarion)*, ed. and trans. Edgardo Morales and Pierre Leclerc (SC 508; Paris: Éditions du Cerf, 2007), 212–99. Hilarion and Epiphanius's mentor-mentee relationship can only be speculated. Jerome mentions a letter Epiphanius wrote to honor Hilarion (*Life of Hilarion* 1.5 (Morales and Leclerc, *Trois Vies*, 212), and Sozomen claims that Epiphanius was trained by the "most celebrated ascetics"

(*Church History* 6.32.3 (Bidez and Hansen, *Histoire Ecclésiastique*, 420)). The *Sayings* (Greek, Alphabetical) collection retains a story of Epiphanius and Hilarion dining together (Epiphanius 4; PG 65: 164).

73. Goehring, *Ascetics, Society, and the Desert*, 200–208.

74. Goehring, *Ascetics, Society, and the Desert*, 199–200.

75. Sozomen, *Church History* 5.10.1–14, 5.15.14 (Bidez and Hansen, *Histoire Ecclésiastique*, 134–42, 164–66).

76. Sozomen, *Church History* 8.15 (Bidez and Hansen, *Histoire Ecclésiastique*, 298–300).

77. Jacobs, *Epiphanius of Cyprus*, 31–64.

78. The desire to redeem Epiphanius of his involvement was not limited to Sozomen. Neither Palladius nor Ps.-Martyrius mentions much about Epiphanius's involvement in the struggle that led to their beloved John Chrysostom's death. Socrates depicts Theophilus as tricking Epiphanius into becoming involved in the affair. Likewise, the anonymous *Life of Epiphanius*, written sometime later in the fifth century, places blame at Theophilus and Eudoxia's feet, and Epiphanius is unwittingly drawn in by their deception (Claudia Rapp, "The *Vita* of Epiphanius of Salamis: An Historical and Literary Study," 2 vols. (Oxford: D.Phil. thesis, Oxford University, 1991), 1: 188–212. For a fuller discussion of the *Life*'s depiction of the Origenist controversy, see Jacobs, *Epiphanius of Cyprus*, 232–33).

79. So, for example, Greek: Vat. gr. 2592 (*HME*), Par. gr. 1596 (*HME and HL*); Syriac: Ms. BL Add. 17176 (*HME*), Ms. BL 14648 (*HME*), Ms. BL Add 12173 (*HME and HL*), Ms. Sin. syr. 46 (*HL* and a few stories from *HME*). It is worth noting that at least since Dom Cuthbert Butler there has been recognition of a relationship between passages from the Latin version of *HME* and the longer recension of Palladius's *LH* (Butler, *Lausiac History*, 15–22).

80. *Sayings* (Greek, Alphabetical) Lot 1 (PG 65: 253, 256).

81. The only clear theological position contained in the *Sayings* is concerned with defending Chalcedon; see *Sayings* (Greek, Alphabetical) Phocas 1 (PG 65: 432–33) and *Sayings* (Greek, Alphabetical) Gelasius 4 (PG 65: 149, 152).

82. The argument that the *Sayings* was gathered by Poemen and his community was first argued by Wilhelm Bousset (*Apophthegmata*, 68–71).

83. *Sayings* (Greek, Alphabetical) Dioscorus 2 (PG 65: 160–61).

84. *Sayings* (Coptic) Chaîne 252–63.

85. Shenoute of Atripe, *I Am Amazed* (*Schenute von Atripe: Contra Origenistas Edition des koptischen Textes mit annotierter Übersetzung und Indizes einschließlich einer Übersetzung des 16. Osterfestbriefs des Theophilus in der Fassung des Hieronymus (ep. 96)*, ed. and trans. Hans-Joachim Cristea (Tübingen: Mohr Siebeck, 2011)).

86. Raymond Van Dam, "From Paganism to Christianity at Late Antique Gaza" *Viator* 16 (1985): 1–20.

87. Barsanuphius and John, *Questions and Answers* 600–604 (*Barsanuphe et Jean de Gaza: Correspondance vol. II Aux Cénobites, tome II Lettres*, 399–616, ed. François Neyt and Paula de Angelis-Noah (SC 451; Paris: Éditions du Cerf, 2001), 804–24).

88. Barsanuphius and John, *Questions and Answers* 600 (Neyt and Angelis-Noah, *Correspondance vol. II Aux Cénobites*, 810).

89. Barsanuphius and John, *Questions and Answers* 605 (Neyt and Angelis-Noah, *Correspondance vol. II Aux Cénobites*, 824, 826).

90. Lillian Larsen, "Early Monasticism and the Rhetorical Tradition: Sayings and Stories as School Texts" in *Education and Religion in Late Antique Christianity: Reflections, Social*

Contexts, and Genres, ed. Peter Gemeinhardt, Lieve Van Hoof, and Peter Van Nuffelen (New York: Routledge, 2016), 13–33.

91. Chiara Faraggiana di Sarzana, "*Apophthegmata Patrum*: Some Crucial Points of Their Textual Transmission and the Problem of a Critical Edition," *Studia Patristica* 29 (Leuven: Peeters, 1997), 455–59.

92. Lillian Larsen, "The *Apophthegmata Patrum* and the Classical Rhetorical Tradition" in *Studia Patristica vol. 39: Historica, Biblica, Ascetica et Hagiographica*, ed. Frances Young, Mark Edwards, and Paul Parvis (Leuven: Peeters, 2006), 414.

93. Enanisho, *Paradise of the Fathers (The Book of Paradise, Being the Histories and Sayings of the Monks and Ascetics of the Egyptian Desert*, ed. and trans. E. A. Wallis Budge (London: Drugulin, 1904)).

94. *Sayings* (Greek, Alphabetical) Epiphanius 4 (PG 65: 164); *Sayings* (Greek, Alphabetical) Theophilus 3 (PG 65: 200); *Sayings* (Greek, Anonymous) N162 (Nau, "Histoires" *ROC* 13 (1908), 53; *Sayings* (Syriac) Ms. Sin. syr. 46 54vb.2–24.

Bibliography

PRIMARY SOURCES

Alexandrian Synaxarium. Le Synaxaire Arabe Jacobite. Ed. René Basset. PO 17. Paris: Firmin-Didot, 1923.

Ammianus Marcellinus. *Roman History. Ammiani Marcellini Rerum gestarum libri qui supersunt.* Ed. Wolfgang Seyfarth, Liselotte Jacob-Karau, and Ilse Ulmann. Bibliotheca Scriptorum Graecorum et Romanorum Teubneriana. 2 vols. Leipzig: Teubner, 1978.

Ammonas. Letter 2.1. *Ammonas, Successeur de Saint Antoine.* Ed. and trans. François Nau. PO 11. Paris: Firmin-Didot, 1915. Pp. 435–36.

Anastasius, *Letter to Simplician of Milan.* Preserved in Jerome, *Letters* 95; Hilberg. *Sancti Eusebii Hieronymi: Epistulae.* CSEL 55. Pp. 157–58.

Antony. *Letter* 1. In Nau, François. "La version syriaque de la première lettre de saint Antoine." *Revue de l'orient chrétien* 14 (1909): 282–97.

Athanasius. *Life of Antony.* In *Athanase d'Alexandrie: Vie d'Antoine.* Ed. G. J. M. Bartelink. SC 400. Paris: Éditions du Cerf, 1994.

Augustine. *Letter* 111. *Sancti Aureli Augustini: Epistulae 31–123.* Ed. and trans. Alois Goldbacher. CSEL 34.2. Vienna: Tempsky, 1898. Pp. 642–57.

Barsanuphius and John, *Questions and Answers. Barsanuphe et Jean de Gaza: Correspondance vol. II Aux Cénobites, tome II Lettres 399–616.* Ed. François Neyt and Paula de Angelis-Noah. SC 451. Paris: Éditions du Cerf, 2001.

Cassian, John. *Conferences. Conlationes.* Ed. and trans. Michael Petschenig. CSEL 13. Vienna: Gerold, 1886.

———. *Institutes. De institutis coenobiorum et de octo principalium vitiorum remediis, De incarnatione Domini contra Nestorium.* Ed. and trans. Michael Petschenig. CSEL 17. Vienna: Gerold, 1888.

Constantinopolitan Synaxarium. Synaxarium ecclesiae Constantinopolitanum e codice Sirmondiano nunc Berolinensi. Ed. Hippolyte Delehaye. Brussels: Apud socios Bollandianos, 1902.

Enanisho. *Paradise of the Fathers (The Book of Paradise: Being the Histories and Sayings of the Monks and Ascetics of the Egyptian Desert).* Ed. and trans. E. A. Wallis Budge. London: Drugulin, 1904.

Epiphanius. *Letter to John of Jerusalem.* Preserved in Jerome, Letter 51. Hilberg. *Sancti Eusebii Hieronymi: Epistulae.* CSEL 54: 395–412.

———. *Panarion. Ancoratus und Panarion Bd. 3: Panarion haer. 65–80.* Ed. Karl Holl. Die Griechischen Christlichen Schriftsteller 37. Leipzig: J. C. Hinrichs, 1933.

Eunapius. *Lives of the Philosophers. Philostratus and Eunapius, Lives of the Sophists.* Ed. and trans. W. C. Wright, LCL v. 134. Cambridge, Mass.: Harvard University Press, 1921.

Evagrius. *To Eulogios. Évagre le Pontique: À Euloge, Les Vices opposes aux vertus.* Ed. and trans. Charles-Antoine Fogielman. SC 591. Paris: Éditions du Cerf, 2017.

———. *Excerpts. À travers la tradition manuscrite d'Evagre le Pontique: Essai sur les manuscrits grec conserves à la Bibliothèque nationale de Paris.* Ed. Joseph Muyldermans. Bibliothèque du Muséon 3. Louvain: Muséon, 1932.

———. *Exhortation.* PG 79: 1236–40.

———. *Foundations.* PG 40: 1252–64.

———. *The Gnostic. Évagre Le Pontique: "Le gnostique" ou, À celui qui est devenu digne de la science.* Ed. and trans. Antoine Guillaumont. SC 356. Paris: Éditions du Cerf, 1989.

———. *Gnostic Chapters.* Critical edition of entire text of longer Syriac version (S2) found in *Les six centuries des "Kephalaia gnostica."* Ed. and trans. Antoine Guillaumont. PO 28.1. Paris: Firmin-Didot, 1958.

———. *Great Letter. Euagrius Ponticus.* Ed. and trans. Wilhelm Frankenberg. Abhandlungen der Königlichen Gesellschaft der Wissenschaften zu Göttingen. Philologisch-historische klasse, bd. 13.2. Berlin: Weidmannsche buchhandlung, 1912. Pp. 610–19.

———. *Letters. Euagrius Ponticus.* Ed. Wilhelm Frankenberg. Abhandlungen der Königlichen Gesellschaft der Wissenschaften zu Göttingen. Philologisch-historische klasse, bd. 13.2. Berlin: Weidmannsche buchhandlung, 1912. Pp. 554–634.

———. *Praktikos. Traité pratique, ou, Le moine.* Ed. Antoine Guillaumont and Claire Guillaumont. SC 171. Paris: Éditions du Cerf, 1971.

———. *On the Eight Thoughts.* PG 79: 1145–64.

———. *On Prayer. Évagre le Pontique, Chapitres sur la Prière: Édition du texte grec, introduction, traduction, notes et index.* Ed. Paul Géhin. SC 589. Paris: Les Éditions du Cerf, 2017.

———. *Psalms.* PG 12: 1053–1686.

———. *Reflections. À travers la tradition manuscrite d'Evagre le Pontique: Essai sur les manuscrits grec conserves à la Bibliothèque nationale de Paris.* Ed. Joseph Muyldermans. Bibliothèque du Muséon 3. Louvain: Muséon, 1932.

———. *Scholia on Ecclesiastes. Évagre le Pontique: Scholies à l'Ecclésiaste.* Ed. Paul Géhin. SC 397. Paris: Cerf, 1993.

———. *Scholia on Proverbs. Évagre le Pontique: Scholies aux Proverbes.* Ed. Paul Géhin. SC 340. Paris: Éditions du Cerf, 1987.

———. *Talking Back. Euagrios Ponticus.* Ed. Wilhelm Frankenberg. Abhandlungen der Königlichen Gesellschaft der Wissenschaften zu Göttingen, Philologisch-historische klasse, Neue Folge 13.2. Berlin: Weidmannsche buchhandlung, 1912. Pp. 472–544.

———. *On Thoughts. Sur les pensées.* Ed. Paul Géhin, Claire Guillaumont, and Antoine Guillaumont. SC 438. Paris: Éditions du Cerf, 1998.

———. *Vices. Évagre le Pontique: À Euloge, Les Vices opposes aux vertus.* Ed. Charles-Antoine Fogielman. SC 591. Paris: Éditions du Cerf, 2017.

———. *A Word About Prayer. De doctrina spirituali Christianorum orientalium: Quaestiones et scripta I.* Ed. Irénée Hausherr. Orientalia Christiana 30.3. Rome: PIOS, 1933. Pp. 149–52.

Evagrius of Pontus: The Greek Ascetic Corpus. Trans. Robert E. Sinkewicz. Repr. Oxford: Oxford University Press, 2010.

Gospel of Thomas 82. *The Apocryphal Gospels: Texts and Translations.* Ed. and trans. Bart D. Ehrman and Zlatko Pleše. Oxford: Oxford University Press, 2011. Pp. 303–50.

Gregory of Nyssa, *Life of Moses. Gregorii Nysseni De Vita Moysis. Gregorii Nysseni Opera vol. 7.1.* Ed. Herbert Musurillo. Leiden: Brill, 1964.

Historia Monachorum in Aegypto: Édition critique du text grec et traduction annotée. Ed. André-Jean Festugière. Subsidia Hagiographica 53. Brussels: Société des Bollandistes, 1971.

Isidore of Pelusium. *Letter* 1.310. PG 78: 361.

———. *Letter* 1.370. PG 78: 392.

Jerome. *Against John. S. Hieronymus Presbyteri Opera. Opera III, Opera Polemica 3: Contra Iohannem.* Ed. Jean Louis Feiertag. CCSL 79A. Turnhout: Brepols, 1999.

———. *Letter* 51. Ed. Hilberg. *Sancti Eusebii Hieronymi: Epistulae.* CSEL 54. Pp. 403–10.

———. *Letter* 108. Ed. Hilberg. *Sancti Eusebii Hieronymi: Epistulae.* CSEL 55. Pp. 306–51.

———. *Life of Hilarion. Jérôme: Trois Vies de Moines (Paul, Malchus, Hilarion).* Ed. and trans. Edgardo Morales and Pierre Leclerc. SC 508. Paris: Éditions du Cerf, 2007. Pp. 212–99.

Life of Macarius the Egyptian. "Vie de Macaire de Scéte." Ed. Émile Amélineau. In *Histoire des monastères de la Basse-Égypte.* Annales du Musée Guimet, 25. Paris: Leroux, 1894. Pp. 46–117.

Macarius of Egypt. *Letter* 1.10. *Die syrische Überlieferung der Schriften des Makarios, Teil 2: Übersetzung.* Ed. Werner Strothmann. Wiesbaden: Harrassowitz, 1981. Pp. xvi–xxii.

Origen. *Against Celsus.* In *Origène: Contre Celse*, ed. Marcel Borret. SC 132. Paris: Éditions du Cerf, 1967; and in *Origène: Contre Celse*, ed. Marcel Borret. SC 136. Paris: Éditions du Cerf, 1968.

———. *On First Principles* 1–2. In *Origène: Traité des Principes*, ed. Henri Crouzel and Manlio Simonetti. SC 252. Paris: Éditions du Cerf, 1978.

———. *On First Principles* 3. In *Origène: Traité des Principes*, ed. Henri Crouzel and Manlio Simonetti. SC 268. Paris: Éditions du Cerf, 1980.

Palladius. *Dialogue on the Life of John Chrysostom. Palladios: Dialogue sur la vie de Jean Chrysostome.* Ed. and trans. Anne-Marie Malingrey. SC 341. Paris: Éditions du Cerf, 1988.

———. *Lausiac History. The Lausiac History of Palladius: A Critical Discussion, Together with Notes on Early Monachism.* Ed. Cuthbert Butler. Texts and Studies 6, 1–2. Cambridge: Cambridge University Press, 1898–1904.

Philostorgius, *Church History. Philostorge: Histoire ecclésiastique.* Ed. and trans. Joseph Bidez and Édouard Des Places. SC 564. Paris: Éditions du Cerf, 2013.

Ps.-Martyrius. *Funeral Oration. Oratio Funebris in Laudem Sancti Iohannis Chrysostomi: Epitaffio Attribuito a Martirio di Antiochia.* Ed. Martin Wallraff. Spoleto: Fondazione Centro italiano di studi sull'Alto Medioevo, 2007.

Rufinus. *Church History. Eusebius Werke 2.2: Die Kirchengeschichte.* Ed. Theodor Mommsen. Die Griechischen Christlichen Schriftsteller. Leipzig: J. C. Hinrichs, 1908.

———. *Historia Monachorum. Tyrannis Rufinus: Historia monachorum, sive, De Vita sanctorum partum.* Ed. Eva Schulz-Flügel. Patristische Texte und Studien 34. New York: De Gruyter, 1990.

Rufus, John. *Life of Peter the Iberian. John Rufus: The Lives of Peter the Iberian, Theodosius of Jerusalem and the Monk Romanus.* Ed. and trans. Cornelia B. Horn and Robert R. Phenix Jr. Atlanta: Society of Biblical Literature, 2008.

Sayings of the Desert Fathers (Greek, Alphabetical). PG 65: 71–440.

——— (Greek, Anonymous): François Nau. "Histoires des solitaires égyptiens." *Revue de l'Orient Chrétien* 12 (1907): 48–68, 171–81, 393–404. *ROC* 13 (1908): 47–57, 266–83. *ROC* 14 (1909): 357–79. *ROC* 17 (1912): 204–11, 294–301. *ROC* 18 (1913): 137–46.

——— (Greek, Systematic). *Les apophtegmes des pères.* Ed. Jean-Claude Guy. SC 387. Chapters 1–9. (1993). SC 474. Chapters 10–16. (2003). SC 498. Chapters 17–21 (2005).

———— (Coptic). "Le manuscrit de la version copte en dialect sahidique des "Apophthegmata Patrum." Ed. Marius Chaîne. Bibliothèque d'études coptes VI. Cairo 1960.

———— (Syriac). Ms. Sin. syr. 46.

Shenoute of Atripe. *I Am Amazed. Schenute von Atripe: Contra Origenistas Edition des koptischen Textes mit annotierter Übersetzung und Indizes einschließlich einer Übersetzung des 16. Osterfestbriefs des Theophilus in der Fassung des Hieronymus (ep. 96).* Ed. and trans. Hans-Joachim Cristea. Tübingen: Mohr Siebeck, 2011.

Socrates, *Church History. Socrate de Constantinople: Histoire ecclésiastique.* Tome 3. Ed. Pierre Périchon, S.J., and Pierre Maraval. SC 505. Paris: Éditions du Cerf, 2006.

Sozomen, *Church History. Sozomène: Histoire Ecclésiastique, livres VII–IX.* Ed. Joseph Bidez and Günther Christian Hansen. SC 516. Paris: Éditions du Cerf, 2008.

St. Macarius the Spirit Bearer: Coptic Texts Relating to Saint Macarius the Great. Trans. Tim Vivian. Crestwood. New York: St. Vladimir's Seminary Press, 2004.

Sulpicius Severus. *Dialogues. Sulpicii Severi: Libri Qui Supersunt.* Ed. Carolus Halm. CSEL 1. Vindobonae: Apud Geroldi Filium Bibliopolam Academiae, 1866.

Synesius. *Dio.* PG 66: 1112–1164.

————. *Downfall of Cyrenaica.* PG 66: 1565–68.

————. *Letters. Synesii Cyrenensis: Epistolae.* Ed. Antonius Garzya. Rome: Typis Officinae polygraphicae, 1979.

————. *On Kingship.* PG 66: 1053–108.

Theophilus. *Letters to Jerome.* Preserved in Jerome, *Letters* 87 and 89; Hilberg. *Sancti Eusebii Hieronymi: Epistulae.* CSEL 55. Pp. 140, 142–43.

————. *Letter to Origenist Monks.* PG 86.967B–C.

————. *Letter to the Saints in Scetis.* PG 86: 967C–D.

————. *First Synodal Letter.* PG 86: 969C–971B.

————. *Second Synodal Letter to the Bishops of Palestine and Cyprus.* Preserved in Jerome, *Letter* 92. Hilberg. *Sancti Eusebii Hieronymi: Epistulae.* CSEL 55. Pp. 147–55.

————. *Fifth Festal Letter. Acta Conciliorum Oecumenicorum* 1.1.2. Ed. Ed Schwartz. Berlin: De Gruyter, 1965. P. 41.

————. *Sixth Festal Letter. Acta Conciliorum Oecumenicorum* 1.1.2. Ed. Ed Schwartz. Berlin: De Gruyter, 1965. Pp. 41–42.

————. *Sixteenth Festal Letter.* Preserved in Jerome, *Letter* 96. Hilberg. *Sancti Eusebii Hieronymi: Epistulae.* CSEL 55. Pp. 159–81.

Virtues of Macarius. Histoire des monastères de la Basse-Égypte. Ed. Émile Amélineau. Annales du Musée Guimet 25. Paris: Leroux, 1894. Pp. 118–202.

SECONDARY SOURCES

Alciati, Roberto, and Federico Fatti. "La controversia origenista: Un affare mediterraneo." *Adamantius* 19 (2013): 7–9.

Bagnall, Roger S. *Egypt in the Byzantine World, 300–700.* Cambridge: Cambridge University Press, 2007.

————. *Egypt in Late Antiquity.* Princeton, N.J.: Princeton University Press, 1993.

————. "Official and Private Violence in Roman Egypt." *Bulletin of the American Society of Papyrologists* 26 (1989): 201–16.

Banev, Krastu. *Theophilus of Alexandria and the First Origenist Controversy: Rhetoric and Power.* OECS. Oxford: Oxford University Press, 2015.

Bar-Asher Siegal, Michal. *Early Christian Monastic Literature and the Babylonian Talmud.* Cambridge: Cambridge University Press, 2013.

Barnes, Timothy D. and George Bevan, ed. and trans. *The Funerary Speech for John Chrysostom.* Liverpool: Liverpool University Press, 2013.

Barry, Jennifer. *Bishops in Flight: Exile and Displacement in Late Antiquity.* Berkeley: University of California Press, 2019.

Berzon, Todd. *Classifying Christians: Ethnography, Heresiology, and the Limits of Knowledge in Late Antiquity.* Berkeley: University of California Press, 2016.

Bitton-Ashkelony, Brouria. *Encountering the Sacred: The Debate on Christian Pilgrimage in Late Antiquity.* Berkeley: University of California Press, 2005.

Bitton-Ashkelony, Brouria, and Aryeh Kofsky. *The Monastic School of Gaza.* Leiden: Brill, 2006.

Bolman, Elizabeth. "Depicting the Kingdom of Heaven: Paintings and Monastic Practice in Early Byzantine Egypt." In *Egypt in the Byzantine World 300–700*, ed. Roger Bagnall. Cambridge: Cambridge University Press, 2007. Pp. 408–33.

Bousset, Wilhelm. *Apophthegmata: Studien zur Geschichte des* ältesten *Mönchtums.* Tübingen: J. C. B. Mohr/Paul Siebeck, 1923.

Brakke, David. *Athanasius and the Politics of Asceticism.* Oxford: Oxford University Press, 2005.

———. *Demons and the Making of the Monk: Spiritual Combat in Early Christianity.* Cambridge, Mass.: Harvard University Press, 2006.

———. "From Temple to Cell, From Gods to Demons." In *From Temple to Church*, ed. Stephen Emmel et al. Leiden: Brill, 2008. Pp. 92–113.

———. "Macarius's Quest and Ours: Literary Sources for Early Monasticism." *Catholic Studies Quarterly* 48 (2013): 239–51.

———, ed. *Talking Back: A Monastic Handbook for Combating Demons.* Cistercian Studies 229. Collegeville, Minn.: Cistercian Publications, 2009.

Brenk, Frederick E., S.J. "In the Light of the Moon: Demonology in the Early Imperial Period." *Aufstieg und Niedergang der römischen Welt* 2: 16.2 (1986): 2008–145.

Bridel, Philippe. *Le site monastique copte des Kellia: Sources historiques et explorations archéologiques. Actes du Colloque de Genève, 13 au 15 août 1984.* Geneva: Mission suisse d'archéologie copte de l'Université de Genève, 1986.

Bridel, Philippe, et al., eds. *Explorations aux Qouçoûr Hégeila and `Éreima lors des campagnes 1987, 1988 et 1989.* EK 8184, vol. 4. Louvain: Peeters, 2003.

Brooks Hedstrom, Darlene. "The Geography of the Monastic Cell in Early Egyptian Monastic Literature." *Church History* 78.4 (Dec. 2009): 756–91.

———. *The Monastic Landscape of Late Antique Egypt: An Archaeological Reconstruction.* Cambridge: Cambridge University Press, 2017.

Brooks Hedstrom, Darlene, Stephen J. Davis, et al. "New Archaeology at Ancient Scetis: Surveys and Initial Excavations at the Monastery of St. John the Little in Wādī al-Naṭrūn (Yale Monastic Archaeology Project)," *Dumbarton Oaks Papers* 64 (2011): 217–27.

———. "Yale Monastic Archaeology Project: Pherme (Qusur Higayla and Qusur `Erayma), Season 1 (May 29–June 8, 2006)." *Mishkah: The Egyptian Journal of Islamic Archaeology* 3 (2009): 53–57.

Brown, Peter. *The Body and Society: Men, Women, and Sexual Renunciation in Early Christianity*, 2nd ed. New York: Columbia University Press, 2008.

————. *The World of Late Antiquity AD 150–750*. London: Thames and Hudson, 1991.

Bryen, Ari Z. *Violence in Roman Egypt: A Study in Legal Interpretation*. Philadelphia: University of Pennsylvania Press, 2013.

Bunge, Gabriel. "Évagre le Pontique et les deux Macaire." *Irénikon* 56 (1983): 215–28, 323–60.

Burgess, R. W., and Jitse H. F. Dijkstra. "The 'Alexandrian World Chronicle', Its *Consularia* and the Date of the Destruction of the Serapeum (with an Appendix on the List of the *Praefecti Augustales*)." *Millennium: Jahrbuch zu Kultur und Geschichte des ersten Jahrtausends n. Chr.* 10.1 (Dec. 2013): 39–113.

Burrus, Virginia. "Wyschogrod's Hand: Saints, Animality, and the Labor of Love." *Philosophy Today* 55 (2011): 412–21.

Burton-Christie, Douglas. *The Word in the Desert: Scripture and the Quest for Holiness in Early Christian Monasticism*. Oxford: Oxford University Press, 1993.

Byron, Gay. *Symbolic Blackness and Ethnic Difference in Early Christian Literature*. London: Routledge, 2002.

Cadell, Hélène, and Roger Rémondon. "Sens et emplois de τὸ ὄρος dans les documents papyrologiques." *Revue des études grecques* 80 (1967): 343–49.

Cameron, Alan, and Jacqueline Long. *Barbarians and Politics at the Court of Arcadius*. Berkeley: University of California Press, 1993.

Cameron, Averil. "Ascetic Closure and the End of Antiquity." In *Asceticism*, ed. V. L. Wimbush and R. Valantasis. Oxford: Oxford University Press, 1995. Pp. 147–61.

Caner, Daniel. *Wandering, Begging Monks: Spiritual Authority and the Promotion of Monasticism in Late Antiquity*. Transformation of Classical Heritage 33. Berkeley: University of California Press, 2002.

Chin, C. Michael. *Grammar and Christianity in the Late Roman World*. Philadelphia: University of Pennsylvania Press, 2008.

Chitty, Derwas J. "The Books of the Old Men." *Eastern Churches Review* 6 (1974): 15–21.

Clark, Elizabeth A. *The Origenist Controversy: The Cultural Construction of an Early Christian Debate*. Princeton, N.J.: Princeton University Press, 1992.

————. *Reading Renunciation: Asceticism and Scripture in Early Christianity*. Princeton, N.J.: Princeton University Press, 1999.

Coon, Lynda L. "Somatic Styles of the Early Middle Ages." *Gender and History* 20.3 (Nov. 2008): 463–86.

Corboud, Pierre. "L'oratoire et les niches-oratoires: Les lieux de la prière," In *Le site monastique copte des Kellia: Sources historiques et explorations archéologiques. Actes du Colloque de Genève, 13 au 15 août 1984*, ed. Philippe Bridel. Geneva: Mission suisse d'archéologie copte de l'Université de Genève, 1986. Pp. 85–92.

Corrigan, Kevin. *Evagrius and Gregory: Mind, Soul, and Body in the Fourth Century*. New York: Routledge, 2016.

Crislip, Andrew. *Thorns in the Flesh: Illness and Sanctity in Late Ancient Christianity*. Philadelphia: University of Pennsylvania Press, 2013.

Crum, Walter E. *A Coptic Dictionary*. Oxford: Oxford University Press, 1939.

Daley, Brian E., S.J. "Evagrius and Cappadocian Orthodoxy." In *Evagrius and His Legacy*, ed. Joel Kalvesmaki and Robin Darling Young. Pp. 14–48.

Dam, Raymond Van. "From Paganism to Christianity at Late Antique Gaza." *Viator* 16 (1985): 1–20.

Davis, Stephen J. "The Category of Memory in Recent Scholarship on the Desert Fathers." In *From Cairo to the New World: Coptic Studies Presented to Gawdat Gabra on the Occasion of*

His Sixty-Fifth Birthday, ed. Y. N. Youssef and S. Moawad. Colloquia Antiqua 9. Leuven: Peeters, 2013. Pp. 59–76.

———. "Life and Death in Lower and Upper Egypt: A Brief Survey of Recent Monastic Archaeology at Yale." *Journal of Canadian Society for Coptic Studies* 3 (2012): 9–26.

Davis, Stephen, Darlene Brooks Hedstrom, et al. "Yale Monastic Archaeology Project: John the Little, Season 1 (June 7–June 27, 2006)," *Mishkah: The Egyptian Journal of Islamic Archeology* 3 (2009): 47–52.

———. "Yale Monastic Archaeology Project: John the Little, Season 2 (May 14–June 17, 2007)," *Mishkah: The Egyptian Journal of Islamic Archeology* 3 (2009): 59–64.

de Francisco Heredero, Ana. "Bárbaros en la Cirenaica a través de la obra de Sinesio de Cirene." In *El espejismo del bárbaro: Ciudadanos y extranjeros al final de la Antigüedad*, ed. David Álvarez Jiménez, Rosa Sanz Serrano, and David Hernández de la Fuente. Castelló de la Plana: Publicacions de la Universitat Jaume I, D.L., 2013. Pp. 131–60.

Delehaye, Hippolyte. *Synaxarium ecclesiae Constantinopolitanum e codice Sirmondiano nunc Berolinensi*. Brussels: Apud socios Bollandianos, 1902.

Driver, Steven D. *John Cassian and the Reading of Egyptian Monastic Culture*. New York: Routledge, 2002.

Dunand, Françoise. "Between Tradition and Innovation: Egyptian Funerary Practices in Late Antiquity." In *Egypt in the Byzantine World, 300–700*, ed. Roger S. Bagnall. Cambridge: Cambridge University Press, 2007. Pp. 163–84.

Dysinger, Luke. *Psalmody and Prayer in the Writings of Evagrius Ponticus*. Oxford: Oxford University Press, 2005.

Early Monasticism and Classical Paideia Project. Lund University, http://portal.research.lu.se /portal/en/projects/early-monasticism-and-classical-paideia(7439b4da-a030-4482-a7dd -5c08c4992977).html. Last accessed: Feb. 26, 2018.

Elm, Susanna. "The Dog That Did Not Bark: Doctrine and Patriarchal Authority in the Conflict Between Theophilus of Alexandria and John Chrysostom of Constantinople." In *Christian Origins: Theology, Rhetoric and Community*, ed. Lewis Ayres and Gareth Jones. New York: Routledge, 1998. Pp. 68–93.

———. "What the Bishop Wore to the Synod: John Chrysostom, Origenism, and the Politics of Fashion at Constantinople." *Adamantius* 19 (2013): 156–69.

Endsjø, Dag. "'The Truth Is Out There': Primordial Lore and Ignorance in the Wilderness of Athanasius' Vita Antonii." In *Wilderness in Mythology and Religion: Approaching Religious Spatialities, Cosmologies, and Ideas of Wild Nature*, ed. Laura Feldt. Religion and Society 55. Oakville, Conn.: Equinox Pub., 2012. Pp. 113–30.

———. *Primordial Landscapes, Incorruptible Bodies: Desert Asceticism and the Christian Appropriation of Greek Ideas on Geography, Bodies, and Immortality*. New York: Peter Lang, 2008.

Evelyn-White, Hugh G. *The Monasteries of the Wadi 'n Natrun. New York, Metropolitan Museum of Art, Egyptian Expedition, 1926–1933*. 3 vols. New York: Arno Press, 1973.

Faraggiana di Sarzana, Chiara. "*Apophthegmata Patrum*: Some Crucial Points of Their Textual Transmission and the Problem of a Critical Edition." *Studia Patristica* 29. Leuven: Peeters, 1997. Pp. 455–67.

Foucault, Michel. *Abnormal: Lectures at the Collège de France 1974–1975*. Trans. Graham Burchell. London: Verso, 2003.

Frank, Georgia. *The Memory of the Eyes: Pilgrims to Living Saints in Christian Late Antiquity*. Berkeley: University of California Press, 2000.

———. "The Memory Palace of Marcellinus." In *Ascetic Culture: Essays in Honor of Philip Rousseau*, ed. Blake Leyerle and Robin Darling Young. Notre Dame, Ind.: University of Notre Dame Press, 2013. Pp. 97–124.

Frankfurter, David. *Evil Incarnate: Rumors of Demonic Conspiracy and Ritual Abuse in History.* Princeton, N.J.: Princeton University Press, 2006.

———. *Religion in Roman Egypt: Assimilation and Resistance.* Princeton, N.J.: Princeton University Press, 1998.

Gaddis, Michael. *There Is No Crime for Those Who Have Christ: Religious Violence in the Christian Roman Empire.* Berkeley: University of California Press, 2005.

Garitte, Gérard. "Une lettre de S. Arsène en géorgien." *Le Muséon* 68 (1955): 259–78.

Goehring, James E. *Ascetics, Society, and the Desert: Studies in Early Egyptian Monasticism.* Harrisburg, Pa.: Trinity Press International, 1999.

Gould, Graham. *The Desert Fathers on Monastic Community.* New York: Oxford University Press, 1993.

Guillaumont, Antoine. "Christianismes orientaux." In *École pratique des hautes études, Section des sciences religieuses.* Annuaire 1968–1969. Tome 76. Pp. 180–83.

———. "The Jesus Prayer Among the Monks of Egypt." *Eastern Churches Review* 6 (1974): 66–71.

Guy, Jean-Claude. "Remarques sur le texte des *Apophthegmata Patrum*." *Recherches de Science Religieuse* 43.2 (April–June 1955): 252–58.

Harmless, William. "Remembering Poemen Remembering: The Desert Fathers and the Spirituality of Memory." *Church History* 69.3 (2000): 483–518.

Hedrick, Charles W., Jr. *History and Silence: Purge and Rehabilitation of Memory in Late Antiquity.* Austin: University of Texas Press, 2000.

Herbich, Tomasz, Darlene Brooks Hedstrom, and Stephen J. Davis. "A Geophysical Survey of Ancient Pherme: Magnetic Prospection at an Early Christian Monastic Site in the Egyptian Delta." *Journal of the American Research Center in Egypt* 44 (2007): 129–37.

Holmberg, Bo. "The Syriac Collection of *Apophthegmata Patrum* in MS Sin. syr. 46." *Studia Patristica* 55. Leuven: Peeters, 2013. Pp. 41–57.

Innemée, Karel. "Excavations at Deir al-Baramus 2002–2005." *Bulletin de la Société d'archéologie copte* 45 (2006): 50–78.

Jacobs, Andrew. *Epiphanius of Cyprus: A Cultural Biography of Late Antiquity.* Berkeley: University of California Press, 2016.

Kasser, Rodolphe. "Sortir du monde, réflexions sur la situation et le développement des établissements monastiques des Kellia." *Revue de théologie et de philosophie* 26.2 (1976): 111–24.

Katos, Demetrios S. *Palladius of Helenopolis: The Origenist Advocate.* Oxford: Oxford University Press, 2011.

Kim, Young. *Epiphanius of Cyprus: Imagining an Orthodox World.* Ann Arbor: University of Michigan Press, 2015.

Kolbet, Paul R. "Athanasius, the Psalms, and the Reformation of the Self." *Harvard Theological Review* 99 (2006): 85–101.

Krueger, Derek. *Liturgical Subjects: Christian Ritual, Biblical Narrative, and the Formation of the Self in Byzantium.* Philadelphia: University of Pennsylvania Press, 2014.

———. "The Old Testament in Monasticism." In *The Old Testament in Byzantium*, ed. Paul Magdalino and Robert Nelson. Washington, D.C.: Dumbarton Oaks, 2010. Pp. 199–221.

Larsen, Lillian. "The Apophthegmata Patrum and the Classical Rhetorical Tradition." In *Studia Patristica vol. 39: Historica, Biblica, Ascetica et Hagiographica*, ed. Frances Young, Mark Edwards, and Paul Parvis. Leuven: Peeters, 2006. Pp. 409–15.

———. "Early Monasticism and the Rhetorical Tradition: Sayings and Stories as School Texts." In *Education and Religion in Late Antique Christianity: Reflections, Social Contexts, and Genres*, ed. Peter Gemeinhardt, Lieve Van Hoof, and Peter Van Nuffelen. New York: Routledge, 2016. Pp. 13–33.

———. "Monastic Paideia and Textual Fluidity in the Classroom." In *Snapshots of Evolving Traditions: Jewish and Christian Manuscript Culture, Textual Fluidity, and New Philology*, ed. Liv Ingebord Lied and Hugo Lundhaug. Berlin: De Gruyter, 2017. Pp. 146–77.

Maldonado Rivera, David. "The Letter Collection of Synesius of Cyrene." In *Late Antique Letter Collections: A Critical Introduction and Reference Guide*, ed. Cristiana Sogno, Brad K. Storin, and Edward J. Watts. Berkeley: University of California Press, 2017. Pp. 205–20.

Mathisen, Ralph, and Danuta Shanzer, eds. *Romans, Barbarians, and the Transformation of the Roman World: Cultural Interaction and the Creation of Identity in Late Antiquity*. Burlington, Vt.: Ashgate, 2011.

Mattingly, David J. "The Laguatan: A Libyan Tribal Confederation in the Late Roman Empire." *Libyan Studies* 14 (1983): 96–108.

McGuckin, John. "Aliens and Citizens of Elsewhere: *Xeniteia* in East Christian Monastic Literature." In *Strangers to Themselves: The Byzantine Outsider: Papers from the Thirty-Second Spring Symposium of Byzantine Studies, University of Sussex*, ed. Dion C. Smythe. London: Routledge, 2016. Pp. 23–38.

McKenzie, Judith S., Sheila Gibson, and A. T. Reyes. "Reconstructing the Serapeum in Alexandria from the Archaeological Evidence." *Journal of Roman Studies* 94 (2004): 73–121.

Mena, Peter. *Place and Identity in the Lives of Antony, Paul, and Mary of Egypt: Desert as Borderland*. London: Palgrave Macmillan, 2019.

Mena, Peter, and An Yountae. "Anzaldúa's Animal Abyss: *Mestizaje* and the Late Ancient Imagination." In *Divinanimality: Animal Theory, Creaturely Theology*, ed. Stephen D. Moore. New York: Fordham University Press, 2014. Pp. 161–81.

Miller, Patricia Cox. "Jerome's Centaur: A Hyper-Icon of the Desert." *Journal of Early Christian Studies* 4 (1996): 209–33.

Modéran, Yves. *Les Maures et l'Afrique romaine (IVe–VIIe siècle)*. Bibliothèque des Écoles françaises d'Athènes et de Rome 314. Rome: École française de Rome, 2003.

Muehlberger, Ellen. *Angels in Late Ancient Christianity*. New York: Oxford University Press, 2013.

Nuffelen, Peter Van. "Palladius and the Johannite Schism." *Journal of Ecclesiastical History* 64.1 (Jan. 2013): 1–19.

———. "Theophilus Against John Chrysostom: The Fragments of a Lost *liber* and the Reasons for John's Deposition." *Adamantius* 19 (2013): 139–55.

Osawa, Koji. "Jannes and Jambres: The Role and Meaning of Their Traditions in Judaism." *Sonderdruck Frankfurter Judaistische Beiträge* 37 (2011–12): 55–73.

Papadopoulos, Ioannis. "The Enemy Within: The Rise and Influence of Conspiracy Theories in Rome Before the Gothic Sack (410 AD)." *Leeds International Medieval Congress*, 2017.

Pekáry, Thomas. *Das römische Kaiserbildnis in Staat, Kult, und Gesellschaft: Dargestellt anhand der Schriftquellen*. Berlin: Gebr. Mann-Verlag, 1985.

Petersen, Lauren Hackworth. "The Presence of 'Damnatio Memoriae' in Roman Art." *Source: Notes in the History of Art* 30.2 (Winter 2011): 1–8.

Pietersma, Albert, ed. *The Apocryphon of Jannes and Jambres the Magicians: P. Chester Beatty XVI (with New Editions of Papyrus Vindobonensis Greek inv. 29456 + 29828 and British Library Cotton Tiberius B. v f. 87*. Leiden: Brill, 1994.

Plested, Marcus. *The Macarian Legacy: The Place of Macarius-Symeon in the Eastern Christian Tradition*. Oxford: Oxford University Press, 2004.

Pyke, Gillian, and Darlene Brooks Hedstrom. "The Afterlife of Sherds: Architectural Re-Use Strategies at the Monastery of John the Little, Wadi Natrun." In *Functional Aspects of Egyptian Ceramics in their Archaeological Context*, ed. Bettina Bader and Mary F. Ownby. Orientalia Lovaniensia Analecta 217. Leuven: Peeters, 2013. Pp. 307–25.

Rapp, Claudia. *Holy Bishops in Late Antiquity: The Nature of Christian Leadership in an Age of Transition*. Transformation of the Classical Heritage 37. Berkeley: University of California Press, 2005.

———. "The *Vita* of Epiphanius of Salamis: An Historical and Literary Study." 2 vols. Oxford: D.Phil. thesis, Oxford University, 1991.

Rassart-Debergh, Marguerite. "Les décors." In *Kellia: L'Ermitage copte QR 195* II, ed. Pascale Ballet, Nathalie Bosson, and Marguerite Rassart-Debergh. Cairo: FIFAO, 2003. Pp. 331–489.

———. "L'ermitage QIz 19/20: Choix de peintures." In *EK 8184 III: Explorations aux Quoçoûr el-Izeila lors des campagnes 1981, 1982, 1984, 1985, 1986, 1989 et 1990*, ed. Philippe Bridel, Nathalie Bosson, and Daniel Sierro. Leuven: Mission suisse d'archéologie copte de l'Université de Genève, 1999. Pp. 122–51.

———. "Les Peintures." In *Les Kellia, ermitages coptes en Basse-Égypte*, ed. Yvette Mottier and Nathalie Bosson. Geneva: Éditions du Tricorne, 1989. Pp. 57–80.

———. "Peintures Kelliotes, 1999." In *Coptic Studies on the Threshold of a New Millennium* II, ed. Mat Immerzeel and Jacques van der Vliet. Leuven: Peeters, 2004. Pp. 1471–77.

———. "Quelques croix kelliotes." In *Nubia et Oriens Christianus*, eds. Piotr O. Scholz and Reinhard Stempel (Cologne: J. Dinter, 1988). Pp. 373–85.

———. "Le Thème de la croix sur les peintures murals des Kellia, entre l'Égypte et la Nubie chrétiennes." In *Nubische Studien: Tagungsakten der 5. Internationalen Konferenz der International Society for Nubian Studies*, ed. Martin Krause. Mainz am Rhein: Philip von Zabern, 1986. Pp. 363–66.

Reed, Annette Yoshiko. *Fallen Angels and the History of Judaism and Christianity*. Cambridge: Cambridge University Press, 2005.

Regnault, Lucien. "Les Apophtegmes en Palestine aux Ve–Vie siècles." *Irénikon* 54 (1981): 320–30.

Rompay, Lucas Van. "Coptic Christianity, Syriac contacts with." In *The Gorgias Encyclopedic Dictionary on the Syriac Heritage (GEDSH)*, ed. Sebastian Brock, Aaron Butts, George Kiraz, and Lucas Van Rompay. Piscataway, N.J.: Gorgias Press, 2011. Pp. 103–6.

Roques, Denis. *Synésios de Cyrène et la Cyrénaïque du Bas-Empire*. CNRS, Paris, 1987.

Rubenson, Samuel. *The Letters of St. Antony: Monasticism and the Making of a Saint*. Minneapolis: Fortress Press, 1995.

———. "Textual Fluidity in Early Monasticism: Sayings, Sermons and Stories." In *Snapshots of Evolving Traditions: Jewish and Christian Manuscript Culture, Textual Fluidity, and New Philology*, ed. Liv Ingeborg Lied and Hugo Lundhaug. Berlin: De Gruyter, 2017. Pp. 178–200.

Russell, Norman. *Theophilus of Alexandria*. ECF. New York: Routledge, 2007.

———. "Theophilus of Alexandria as a Forensic Practitioner." *Studia Patristica* 50 (2011): 235–43.

Salzmann, Michelle R. *The Making of a Christian Aristocracy: Social and Religious Change in the Western Roman Empire*. Cambridge, Mass.: Harvard University, 2004.

Sauneron, Serge, and Jean Jacquet. *Les Ermitages chrétiens du desert d'Esna,* 2 vols. Cairo: Institut français d'archéologie orientale du Caire, 1972.

Schroeder, Caroline T. "Queer Eye for the Ascetic Guy? Homoeroticism, Children, and the Making of Monks in Late Antique Egypt." *Journal of the American Academy of Religion* 77.2 (June 2009): 333–47.

Shaw, Brent D. *Sacred Violence: African Christians and Sectarian Hatred in the Age of Augustine.* Cambridge: Cambridge University Press, 2011.

Shepardson, Christine. *Controlling Contested Places: Late Antique Antioch and the Spatial Politics of Religious Controversy.* Berkeley: University of California Press, 2014.

Sizgorich, Thomas. *Violence and Belief in Late Antiquity: Militant Devotion in Christianity and Islam.* Philadelphia: University of Pennsylvania Press, 2009.

Stefaniw, Blossom. "The School of Didymus the Blind in Light of the Tura Find." In *Monastic Education in Late Antiquity: The Transformation of Classical Paideia*, ed. Lillian I. Larsen and Samuel Rubenson. Cambridge: Cambridge University Press, 2018. Pp. 153–80.

Stewart, Columba. *Cassian the Monk.* Oxford: Oxford University Press, 1998.

———. "Imageless Prayer and the Theological Vision of Evagrius Ponticus." In *A History of Prayer: The First to the Fifteenth Century*, ed. Roy Hammerling. Leiden: Brill, 2008. Pp. 137–66.

Stewart, Peter. "The Destruction of Statues in Late Antiquity." In *Constructing Identities in Late Antiquity*, ed. Richard Miles. Repr. New York: Routledge, 2014. Pp. 159–89.

Taft, Robert F. *The Liturgy of the Hours in East and West: The Origins of the Divine Office and Its Meaning for Today.* 2nd ed. Collegeville, Minn.: Liturgical Press, 1993.

Thirard, Catherine. "Des Kellia au Wadi Natrun ou les Facteurs de pérennisation d'une colonie ascétique." In *Actes du Huitième Congrès International d'Études Coptes, 28 juin–3 juillet 2004*, ed. Nathalie Bosson and Anne Bouvarel-Boud'hors. Leuven: Peeters, 2007. Pp. 369–80.

Toda, Satoshi. *Vie de S. Macaire L'egyptien: Edition et traduction des textes copte et syriaque.* Eastern Christian Studies Series. Piscataway, N.J.: Gorgias Press, 2012.

Valantasis, Richard. "Daemons and Perfecting of the Monk's Body: Monastic Anthropology, Daemonology, and Asceticism." *Semeia* 58.2 (1992): 47–79.

Vivian, Tim. "The Peaceable Kingdom: Animals as Parables in the *Virtues of Saint Macarius*." *Anglican Theological Review* 85.3 (2003): 477–91.

Vos, Nienke. "Seeing *Hesychia*: Appeals to the Imagination in the *Apophthegmata Patrum*." *Studia Patristica* 97 (2013): 33–45.

Voytenko, Anton. "Paradise Regained or Paradise Lost: The Coptic (Sahidic) Life of St. Onnophrius and Egyptian Monasticism at the End of the Fourth Century." In *Actes du Huitième Congrès international d'études coptes: Paris, 28 juin–3 juillet 2004*, ed. Nathalie Bosson and Anne Boud'hors. 2 vols. Orientalia Lovaniensia Analecta 163. Leuven: Peeters, 2007. Pp. 634–44.

Wagner, Guy. *Les oasis d'Égypte à l'époque grecque, romaine, et byzantine d'après les documents grecs: Recherches de papyrologie et d'épigraphie grecques.* Bibliothèque d'études 100. Cairo: Institut Français d'Archéologie Orientale, 1987.

Watts, Edward J. *Riot in Alexandria: Tradition and Group Dynamics in Late Antique Pagan and Christian Communities.* Berkeley: University of California Press, 2010.

Wessel, Susan. *Cyril of Alexandria and the Nestorian Controversy: The Making of a Saint and of a Heretic.* Oxford: Oxford University Press, 2004.

Wipszycka, Ewa. *Les ressources et les activités économiques des églises en Égypte du IVe au VIIIe siècle.* Papyrologica Bruxellensia 10. Brussels: Fondation Égyptologique Reine Élisabeth, 1972.

Index

Acknowledgments

This book began as a kernel of an idea that has grown immensely in the last decade. I am deeply grateful to Elizabeth Clark for her support; she encouraged me to refine and clarify my argument even as she reminded me that I had something to say. For the many colleagues and friends during that stage of my journey, especially Kristi, Kyle, Susannah, Bart, and Lori, I remain indebted. When it came time to write this book, though, I realized I needed vocabulary around theories of violence that were sorely lacking and crucial to the argument I make here. It was the support and comradery of the Violence and Representations of Violence unit of the Society of Biblical Literature (SBL) where I found a home as I explored how I wanted to think about and with violence. As now a cochair of that unit, I cannot emphasize enough how important the members of and the many scholars who have given papers in that unit have been to my thinking over the last seven years. Thank you.

I have had the immense pleasure of writing this book among my colleagues turned friends at Union Presbyterian Seminary. The support in all forms, not just fiscal, that you all have shown me during my seven years at Union have been crucial to the success of this book and to my growth as a scholar and teacher. Thank you, especially, to Paul and Josh for many afternoons in coffee shops at the beginning; to Karen-Marie and Carol for many patient hours of listening during lunches and phone calls; and to Katie, who pushed me to write what I really meant and whom I miss immensely. Thank you as well to my two deans, Stan Skreslet and Ken McFayden, to President Brian Blount, and to the Board of Trustees for the support throughout, but especially for the time and space of my sabbatical year in 2018–19. The beginning of that time was spent polishing and sending off the first version of this book that would result in a contract by that year's end. Without that time, this book would still be in process.

But this book certainly would not be what it is without the encouragement of Jerry Singerman, Virginia Burrus, and Derek Krueger to hone my argument and claim my scholarly voice. While all errors and infelicities are mine, everything that is beautiful and strong about this book comes from their pressing me to make it so. I will be forever grateful for Derek's initial encouragement to submit my book to the Press when I barely thought I had a book idea. He believed in my idea before I was even sure I fully did. I am deeply grateful to everyone at the Press for all the work put into my book, in particular, for the editing suggestions of Noreen O'Connor-Abel and Kathleen McQueen. I also would like to express my gratitude to the two anonymous reviewers whose thoughtful words made this a better book and helped me keep refining on the hard days.

As is always the case with anything worth doing, this book was created in community. It was only possible because of the love, patience, and support of friends and family. Candida, Kristi, Jenny, Carrie, and Becky, thank you for your friendship, scholarly curiosity, desire for social justice, and unfailing support across so many years. I could not have a better community of amazing humans around me. You all continue to amaze and inspire me. Thank you to the friends who have supported us since we landed in Richmond, especially Sarah Fox, who has jumped in and rescued me in more than one kid-related situation. I'm glad our kids found each other.

And the deepest expressed gratitude is reserved for my family. To my parents, Lisa and Denzil, and my in-laws, Paul and Nancy, thank you for all the countless hours you played with your grandkids so that I might have space to write and attend conferences. Thanks especially to my mother for coming to our rescue on more than one occasion when we were all quite sick and a deadline was pressing, lovingly feeding and caring for us in her warm way. Thank you to Sarah, Gregg, and Michelle for shared laughter at crucial moments. Thank you, especially, to my sister, Robin, without whom my life would be deeply diminished in so many ways. She is always there, ready to support, cajole, laugh, and cry with me. She has been among my biggest supporters in the process of writing. Thank you to Elias and Asher for keeping me grounded and reminding me what matters. The shared excitement you had on the day the book contract arrived reminded me why mommy's doing all that work was worth it. But my biggest gratitude I must save for Tim, to whom I've dedicated this book. He has heard or read every imaginable version of this book, has held our life together when I needed to hide away and write, has built the beautiful life with me in which this book is possible. Thank you, my love.